A History of Russian Economic Thought

The collapse of the Soviet Union at the end of the 1980s was perceived as a victory for capitalist democracy, yet the significance of socialist economic theory remains contentious. As a consequence, Vincent Barnett provides the first comprehensive account of the historical development of Russian and Soviet economic thought across the nineteenth and twentieth centuries and considers the future for Russian economics in the twenty-first century.

Utilising an extensive range of historical materials and sources, this book examines the many different strands of economic thought that have been present in Russia, including classical, neoclassical, historical, socialist, liberal and Marxian schools. Barnett traces the influence that the different schools of thought exerted domestically and overseas, and the impact that their ideas had on shaping government policies both before and after 1917. This book contains a detailed time line of the most significant works published by Russian economists, and analyses the effects that historical discontinuities have had on the institutional structure of Russian economics as a discipline.

This book will prove essential reading to all those interested in international economic history and the evolution of Russian economic thought.

Vincent Barnett is the author of many books and journal articles exploring the intellectual history of Russia.

Routledge history of economic thought
Edited by Mark Blaug
Co-Director, Erasmus Center for History in Management and Economics, Erasmus University, the Netherlands

A History of Japanese Economic Thought
Tessa Morris Suzuki

A History of Australian Economic Thought
Peter Groenewegen

A History of Canadian Economic Thought
Robin Neill

A History of Swedish Economic Thought
Bo Sandelin

A History of Portuguese Economic Thought
Jose Luis Cardoso and Antonio Almodovar

A History of Latin American Economic Thought
Oreste Popescu

A History of Norwegian Economic Thought
Olov Bjerkholt and Pal Lykkja

A History of Russian Economic Thought
Vincent Barnett

A History of Russian Economic Thought

Vincent Barnett

Routledge
Taylor & Francis Group
LONDON AND NEW YORK

First published 2005
by Routledge
2 Park Square, Milton Park, Abingdon, Oxon OX14 4RN

Simultaneously published in the USA and Canada
by Routledge
270 Madison Ave, New York, NY 10016

Routledge is an imprint of the Taylor & Francis Group

Typeset in Times New Roman by Wearset Ltd, Boldon, Tyne and Wear
Printed and bound in Great Britain by MPG Books Ltd, Bodmin

British Library Cataloguing in Publication Data
A catalogue record for this book is available from the British Library

Library of Congress Cataloging in Publication Data
A catalog record for this book has been requested

ISBN 0–415–35264–9

Contents

Preface

Memory is a cornerstone of human experience. Wittgenstein remarked that memory experiences were the accompaniments of remembering, but such experiences are purposeful acts that require a definite impetus, be it conscious, preconscious or subconscious. Consequently, how all the memories of the past are recorded, transmitted, ignored, distorted, destroyed, hidden, resurrected and enshrined could be seen as a gauge of the nature of the societies in which people live. In many countries today, popular interest in reconnecting with experiences of the past has perhaps never been greater. Whether such reconnections are inevitably tinged with the flavour of the period in which they actually occur, rather than the periods about which they purport to tell, is an impossible question to finally answer. But this does not prevent the attempt to make such reconnections as authentic as possible.

This book attempts to resurrect some of the memories, thoughts and experiences of long-neglected Russian economists of both the nineteenth and twentieth centuries.[1] It does not in any way claim to be a definitive and complete account of this expansive topic. Rather, it aims first of all to rekindle and extend interest in the West about the history of Russian economic ideas divorced from predominantly Marxian or planning-related concerns, to present some of the most important elements of these ideas in a clear and unbiased fashion, and to reconstruct some feeling of the context in which they arose. The author has been studying specific aspects of this topic off and on for the last 15 years, and this volume presents a distilled essence of some of these studies, together with the addition of much new material, for interested readers.

The book is organised so as to provide a multitude of concentrated thematic bursts or 'tasters' of the most important elements of the work of as many different Russian economists as is possible in its relevant historical context, in order to whet the reader's appetite to pursue the subject further. An exhaustive and comprehensive account of all aspects of the work of all economists of the period under review would require ten large volumes; as only one modest volume was currently feasible, the approach has been adapted to this structure so as to indicate the range of economic thought that was present in Russia. Consequently, some sacrifice of narrative continuity has inevitably been made in order to include as much theoretical 'meat' as is possible under such constraints. But in truth, history itself does not always provide a smooth narrative flow; it is historians who sometimes fabricate it in their writings.

What's the point?

The approach adopted in this work has raised some eyebrows amongst various different professional academic groups (in its most naked form, 'what's the point?').[2] Some (but certainly not all) Russian studies scholars have criticised such work for lacking empirical rigour: the answer to such criticism is that it is not meant to be so, as its primary focus is ideas and its primary goal is the stimulation of further consideration of such ideas. A few (but certainly not many) contemporary economists have poured scorn on the work of Russian economists of the period, implying that, as even Western economics of the period under review is now only a historical curiosity, what gain can be had from examining its inferior Russian counterpart? One answer is that this is begging the question. Without a detailed examination, how can it be known whether Russian economics was indeed 'inferior'? And even some historians (but certainly not all) have questioned the purpose of focusing mainly on 'ideas'. History should be about facts, events, social movements, wars and the like. The answer to this is that many events are driven by ideas at least in part. Ideas are often the flipside of events, and whilst events rarely turn out as the propagating ideas first intended, considering the content and influence of ideas of the past is just as much a legitimate part of resurrecting historical memories as studying the empirical unfolding of a particular war certainly is.

Thus, if the study of history ever really needs a justification outside of itself, surely it is so that we do not forget both the mistakes and the successes of the past, and the ideas of the past are just as much a part of the fabric of history as good old-fashioned events. And if events rarely repeat themselves, except perhaps as tragedy and farce, then ideas more frequently re-appear, albeit in mutated or adapted form, as the various spirals of historical development unfold. Economic thought is certainly a specialised area within the field of intellectual history in general, but the relevance of such ideas often transcends the narrow confines of such speciality, especially in the particular context under review in this book. So with this supporting rationale, the attempted resurrection of Russian economic memory for an English-speaking audience can reasonably begin.

Acknowledgements

I acknowledge a significant debt to the work of all past and present historians of economic thought in Russia itself, the valuable and sometimes brave efforts of whom have done much to ensure the long-term survival of the ideas of many leading Russian economists. I have consulted and utilised their ongoing efforts over a number of years of research, and so it is only fair that I dedicate this book to them.

Timeline

Key developments in Russian economics and statistics

Year	*The Russian State and Russian Ministers of Finance*	*Key Developments in Russian Economics and Statistics*
1802	Russian Ministry of Finance first established	
1815		Mordvinov's *Some Considerations on Manufactures in Russia* and Storch's *Course of Political Economy*
1818		Turgenev's *Essay on the Theory of Taxation*
1823	Minister of Finance Kankrin	
1825	Tsar Nicholas I	
1847		Milyutin's *The Proletariat and Pauperism*
1852	Minister of Finance Brok	
1855	Tsar Alexander II	
1858	Minister of Finance Kniazhevich	Vernadsky's *Studies in the History of Political Economy*
1860		Chernyshevsky's *Notes on the Principles of Political Economy by J.S. Mill*
1862	Minister of Finance Reutern	
1867		Mendeleev's *On the Contemporary Development of the Chemical Industry*
1869		Bervi–Flerovsky's *Condition of the Working Class in Russia*
1870		Bunge's *Foundations of Political Economy*
1871		Sieber's *Ricardo's Theory of Value and Capital*
1872		Babst's *Exposition of Principles*
1875		Chuprov's *Railway Economy*
1877		Mendeleev's *Petroleum Affairs in Pennsylvania and the Caucasus*
1881	Tsar Alexander III and Minister of Finance Bunge	Plekhanov's *New Directions in the Field of Political Economy*

Year	*The Russian State and Russian Ministers of Finance*	*Key Developments in Russian Economics and Statistics*
1882		Vorontsov's *Fate of Capitalism in Russia*
1884		Witte's *Principles of Railway Tariffs*
1886	Minister of Finance Vyshnegradsky	
1890		Tugan-Baranovsky's *Marginal Utility of Economic Goods*
1891		Mendeleev's *Explaining the Tariff* and Kovalevsky's *Modern Customs*
1892	Minister of Finance Witte	Chuprov's *History of Political Economy*
1893		Danielson's *Studies in Our Post-Reform Social Economy*
1894	Tsar Nicholas II	Tugan-Baranovsky's *Industrial Crises in Contemporary England* and Struve's *Critical Notes on the Question of Russian Economic Development*
1897		Bulgakov's *Markets in Capitalist Production*, Mendeleev's *Foundations of Manufacturing Industry* and Chuprov's *Influence of the Harvest*
1898		Tugan-Baranovsky's *Russian Factory in 19th* Century, Kovalevsky's *Economic Growth of Europe* and Ozerov's *Income Tax in England*
1899		Lenin's *Development of Capitalism in Russia* and Migulin's *Russian State Credit*
1900		Frank's *Theory of Value* and Bulgakov's *Capitalism and Agriculture*
1904	Minister of Finance Kokovtsov	Dmitriev's *Economic Essays* and Kropotkin's *Mutual Aid*
1906		Woytinsky's *Market and Prices*
1909		Chuprov's *Studies in the Theory of Statistics*
1910		Ozerov's *Foundations of Financial Science*
1912		Bogdanov's *Tektology*, Bulgakov's *Philosophy of Economy* and Slutsky's *Theory of Correlation*
1913		Struve's *Economy and Price*, Slutsky's *Essence of Cooperation* and Svyatlovsky's *History of Economic Views in the West and in Russia*
1914	Minister of Finance Bark	Bukharin's *Economic Theory of the Leisure Class*
1915		Slutsky's *Theory of the Budget of the Consumer*, Shaposhnikov's *Protectionism and Free Trade* and

Year	*The Russian State and Russian Ministers of Finance*	*Key Developments in Russian Economics and Statistics*
		Bukharin's *World Economy and Imperialism*
1916		Lenin's *Imperialism, the Highest Stage of Capitalism* and Tugan-Baranovsky's *Social Foundations of Cooperation*
1917	Minister of Finance Shingarev then Bernatsky; V.I. Lenin takes control of the Russian state	Tugan-Baranovsky's idea of 'marginal planning' and Bogdanov's notion of 'war communism' are proposed
1918		Litoshenko's *Socialisation of the Land*
1919		Bukharin's *Economics of the Transition Period*, Yurovsky's *Studies in Price Theory* and Chelintsev's *Organisation of Peasant Economy*
1921		Preobrazhensky's *Finance in the Epoch of the Proletarian Dictatorship* and Lenin's *Tax in Kind*
1922	I.V. Stalin becomes the General Secretary of the Communist Party	Lenin's *On Cooperation*, Kondratiev's *World Economy and its Conjuncture* and Kondratiev's *Grain Market in War and Revolution*
1923	People's Commissariat of Finance first established under Commissar of Finance Sokol'nikov	Slutsky's *Calculating State Income from Emission*, Slutsky's *Notes on Currency Emission* and Litoshenko's *Evolution and Progress of Peasant Farms*
1924	Death of Lenin	Chayanov's *On the Theory of Non-Capitalist Economic Systems*
1925		Chayanov's *The Organisation of Peasant Farms*, Groman's *On Some Empirical Regularities*, Pervushin's *Economic Conjuncture* and Kondratiev's *Long Cycles of Conjuncture*
1926	Commissar of Finance Bryukhanov	Bazarov's *Curve of Development*, Popov's *Balance of the National Economy*, and Preobrazhensky's *New Economics*
1927		Slutsky's *The Summation of Random Causes as the Source of Cyclic Processes* and Makarov's *Organisation of Agriculture*
1928		Fel'dman's *Towards a Theory of National Income Growth*, Yurovsky's *Monetary Policy of Soviet Power* and Kondratiev's *Industry and Agriculture*
1929		Slutsky's *Propositions on the Stochastic Limit* and Vainshtein's *Problems of Economic Prognosis*

Year	*The Russian State and Russian Ministers of Finance*	*Key Developments in Russian Economics and Statistics*
1930	Commissar of Finance Grin'ko	Preobrazhensky's *Theory of Depreciating Currency* and Strumilin's *First Experiences of Perspective Planning*
1932		Kondratiev's *Basic Problems of Economic Statics and Dynamics*
1934		Varga's *Great Crisis and its Consequences*
1935		Brutzkus's *Economic Planning in Soviet Russia*
1936		Trotsky's *The Revolution Betrayed*
1938	Commissar of Finance Zverev	
1939		Kantorovich's *Mathematical Methods*
1941		Leontief's *Structure of American Economy*

1 Introduction – analysing the Russian economic mind

The Union of Soviet Socialist Republics – the USSR – was the first ever nation-wide experiment conducted in purposely creating a completely new economic system apparently based on non-capitalist principles of operational control. This was a system that a significant number of Russian economists played an important role in first actively campaigning for (or against), and then actually designing (or criticising). The dramatic collapse of the system thus generated at the very end of the 1980s, and the various attempts at capitalist restoration in the 1990s, has set the political backdrop for the beginning of the twenty-first century in a unique and spectacular fashion. Many politicians have triumphantly pronounced the end of history and the final victory of liberal representative democracy, and it appears that the upstart competitor to capitalistic individualism has been vanquished by its more powerful Western neighbour. An era of bi-polar international authority and a high-temperature Cold War has been replaced by an era of multi-polarity and ongoing low-level regional and politico-religious conflicts.

However, amongst all the triumphant celebrations, it is easy to forget that the Soviet economic system was not created on a completely blank canvas, but was actually fashioned in a particular and very unique country – or combination of countries – and these countries had long histories and intellectual traditions that went back many centuries before 1917. Moreover, the people who created the economic system of the USSR were themselves the products of specific cultures in particular times and places, and the actual components of the Soviet economy were sometimes more the result of these particular national and cultural features, rather than of the abstract socialistic principles that the revolutionaries claimed to be implementing. Consequently this book attempts to explain some elements of these national features by focusing on documenting the history of economic thinking in Russia and in some closely proximate states both before and after 1917.

The general approach adopted

Ideologically, the book attempts to be politically neutral, i.e. to be neither pro- nor anti-socialist and neither pro- nor anti-capitalist, but rather simply to present the history of the particular topic as it happened to be found. Of course, in selecting the particular economists and topics that are discussed, some choices have inevitably been made. But the criterion for such selection was always to try to include the best quality, the most original and the most influential economic thought that was encountered, rather than the ideas that supported any single philosophical or political point of view. Moreover all the various different perspectives on economics should be presented with equal force, no single point of view dominating the narrative. Hopefully, if this defiant deadpan neutrality has been successfully maintained throughout the book, then both fervent socialists and rabid anti-socialists should be dissatisfied with the outcome, as their particular predispositions will not have been confirmed. Reality in all its multi-layered richness rarely conforms to any particular one-sided political philosophy; neither should the history that claims to document such reality.

Methodological questions

Various different methodological approaches to studying the history of economics have been articulated in the past, such as the Whig approach – how today's finally correct views were developed and all past errors were exposed – or the Marxist view – how economics (as part of the ideological superstructure of society) simply reflected the economic base at any given time. Both these approaches tend to result in biased history, biased either from the point of view of the eventual victor, or in terms of reducing all ideas simply to expressions of materialistic interest.

In contrast to both of these extremes, the approach adopted in the book will be to combine the history of ideas, the history of economic thought, the analysis of economic/financial policy and economic/financial history, and also the role of specific individuals ('great thinkers'), to fashion a historical reconstruction of some of the beliefs, behaviour and legacy of economists and policy-makers of the period under review. Maintaining a sceptical attitude to the question of whether any particular theory is true in an ultimate sense, relativism is generally preferred, but with due sensitivity to the absolute consequences of the paradox of relativism. If adopting a bias cannot be avoided, then the bias of approach of those people being studied and of the period under review is generally best adopted, in order to better recreate the 'feel' of the period in question.[1]

Moreover, the book analyses the work of 'economic theorists' rather than 'economists', or what can be called 'economic thinking' in a general sense rather than what today is often narrowly defined as 'economics'.

This is because in much of the period under review, 'economic thought' in Russia was a much broader activity than what it is perceived as 'mainstream economics' today. It was something closer to what was called 'political economy' in the West, but wider than this even, including elements of other disciplines such as philosophy, law, statistics and sociology. Put another way, these disciplines had not yet fully separated from each other, or multiple discipline demarcation was an essential part of the story. This notion will be explored further later on in the introduction.

Regarding the absolute/relative methodological distinction in writing the history of economics, Mark Blaug wrote that:

> No assumptions about economic behavior are absolutely true and no theoretical conclusions are valid for all times and places, but would anyone seriously deny that in the matter of techniques and analytical constructs there has been progress in economics?[2]

This apparently sensible middle path is however open to further dispute, as it all depends on exactly what is meant by 'progress'. If by this word is meant only change, development, greater sophistication and uncovering of more obvious errors, then 'progress' (in a weaker sense) is indeed made in economics. If however by 'progress' is meant an inevitable progression towards an ultimate and permanent truth that explains everything about the economy (a stronger sense of the word), then this is less clearly the case. In a thousand years time, will scholars be able to say for certain that Milton Friedman came closer to 'the truth' than Irving Fisher? Or that Kondratiev was a definite improvement over Tugan-Baranovsky?

In the case of the Russian national history examined in this book, progress will be documented only in the weaker sense of the word, i.e. in terms of documenting change and development. The progression from Tsarist to Soviet economics is not nowadays usually seen as 'progress' in an analytical sense, in fact it could easily be seen as a regressive development for the health of economics both in Russia and also in the West. On the other hand, if oppositional currents within early Soviet economics are considered, then some impressive socialist-inspired developments could certainly be documented. Moreover, the benefits of the progression from Soviet to post-Soviet economics in the 1990s, while discussed only briefly in this book, are also questioned by some, whilst being praised by many others. Hence, it all depends on what perspective is being adopted as to whether progress in the stronger sense is seen as being made between two specific points in time, and this book will deliberately refrain from making an ultimate choice of one 'true' perspective from which to judge all past developments. The discovery of such an Archimedean point will be left to others more qualified for this difficult and as-of-yet unaccomplished task.

Russia and its economists

To begin with, a key question: is there a nation-specific and clearly identifiable 'Russian tradition' in the history of economic thought? The answer is very likely no, there is not only one single Russian tradition but many, just as there are many American or French traditions in the history of economic thought; and the various Russian traditions have periodically intertwined with those of other nations, most notably Germany and the UK in the nineteenth century and the USA after 1989. This book is in part the rich life story of some of these cross-fertilisations in the period 1870 to 1940, with particular emphasis on the individual economists involved and the connections to related areas such as policy-making initiatives and important political events. Eschewing the idea that a purely national current in economics could ever be completely isolated (wasn't the founder of English classical economics Scottish, and a key member of the English historical school Irish?) reoccurring themes and ideas in Russian economics will be discussed in their institutional and historical context, and in comparison with the economic ideas that were developed in other nations.

Russia has usually been seen as being a separate and ring-fenced national case for study by many historians, with unique features and special dispensations that make it unsuitable to compare directly with other countries in either Western Europe or North America. While this is true in many respects for empirical or events history, it will be suggested that this is less accurate when intellectual history is considered, or at least that it might fruitfully be considered as being so. Hence in this book a concerted effort will be made to 'bring Russia in from the cold'; that is, to reintegrate the history of Russian ideas with other European and even some international currents of economic thinking, in order that Russia's true contributions might better be gauged, and Russia's significant place in the world culture of ideas be forcefully reaffirmed.

In qualitative terms, Russian economists – even the best of them – have sometimes been considered as only playing for the second eleven, i.e. as not being of first rank status, lacking in the magnitude of policy influence effected by someone like J.M. Keynes, or the conceptual originality of an Irving Fisher. Measuring the impact of Russian economists in the period 1940 to the present day, this evaluation is undoubtedly true, but the situation was less clear-cut when the period before 1940 is considered. In fact it will be suggested here that between 1870 and 1940, Russian economic theorists did occasionally reach the level of the first eleven, albeit inconsistently so, and for only relatively short periods of time. Frequently substituted and spending long periods on the reserves bench, when in play they did sometimes score spectacular goals.

It was not inevitable that their influence and originality would have to decline after 1940; rather this was due to a number of contextual factors that could have been different, if the actual historical path that was chosen after 1940 had been modified. The responsibility for the decline in Russian economics after 1940 cannot really be laid at the feet of the economists themselves, either in an intellectual or an organisational sense. Much more powerful forces outside the control of small groups of intellectual specialists were in operation, social and political forces that swept purely theoretical expressions aside like so many peacock feathers in a violent tornado. This maelstrom was not a purely Soviet creation, but was also conditioned by the Western response to the challenge of the appearance of an apparently new economic system, a response that was at least in part fuelled by fear and lack of understanding.

Special features of Russian economics

One unusual feature of the history of Russian economic thought, at least in its Soviet manifestation in much of the twentieth century, was what might be called the extremity of doctrinal orthodoxy, extreme at least in relation to the dominant political currents that existed in the West at this time. Perhaps more than any other nation state in living memory, Russia between 1929 and 1985 promoted a highly politicised doctrine that was government-sponsored and glaringly fanatical about its own validity. Defining all non-Soviet economics as an intellectual excrescence fashioned by the ideologues of capitalism, Russia after 1917 developed a coldly imprisoning variety of Marxist economics that served as doctrinal justification for the Soviet variety of planned economy. The story of the progress of some of the early stages of the tragicomically named 'Marxist-Leninist-Stalinist' economics is documented here, at least up until the outbreak of the Second World War, with an epilogue bringing the story up to date.

J.K. Galbraith called the Cold War a 'grim and angry cleavage', and it set the iron tone and overall framework for global international relations in the second half of the twentieth century.[3] However, before 1945 the ideological chasm between East and West was certainly less pronounced than it was after this date, making for a more fluid bi-directional movement of economic ideas between Russia and the rest of the world. This applied both to the period before 1913 and to a lesser extent in the interwar period.

Less overtly dramatic than the onset of the Cold War, but equally worthy of study, was the story of Russian economics in the second half of the nineteenth century, where English, German, French and even American influences can readily be detected, together with the development of indigenous Russian concepts and links to domestic policy-related questions. Another feature of nineteenth century Russian economics was the emergence of various important and enduring thematic currents, such as the progress of business cycles, the role of foreign capital and the creation of indigenous economic formations, many of which were connected to the problem of the relation of Russia to the West and to the particular type of capitalism that was developing in Russia. It will be seen from what follows that many such enduring themes survived across the political discontinuities of Russian history, notably those that occurred in 1861, 1917, 1929 (and even 1991), or at least went into a period of hibernation, to re-emerge only sometime later in a modified form.

The few well known Russian economists easily remembered today – people such as Tugan-Baranovsky and Dmitriev at the end of the nineteenth century and Kondratiev and Slutsky at the start of the twentieth – were really only the tip of an iceberg of quality in terms of the contributions made by Russian thinkers to economic issues broadly conceived. Whilst not always original and sometimes plainly derivative, exactly how the work of foreign economists was employed by theorists within Russian boundaries is frequently an enlivening topic in itself, and the many lesser Russian figures were often skilled in adapting Western ideas to the native context.

Given the nominally red turn that history took in Russia after 1917, the importance of considering the reception of Marxist ideas in nineteenth-century Russia is unquestionable, although Marxist economics itself was certainly not the dominant current in Russia before 1917. In fact, a number of separate currents flourished – historical political economy, classical notions of free trade, socialist teachings and so on – and these currents even intermingled with each other to some extent. In terms of influence on governmental policy-making, some currents were undoubtedly more successful than others, although different social groups often supported particular economic doctrines against the overarching will of the state.

It is certainly true that the species of Marxism that came into existence in the USSR after 1929 bore no striking resemblance to that which had existed in Russia prior to 1917. Pre-revolutionary Marxian economics was sometimes quite a sensitive animal, with due attention being paid to historical context and the contributions of various non-Marxist thinkers; after 1929 a hideously distorted and caricatured doctrine was created, the style of which was sometimes as ominous as the content. This reversal did not take place overnight, but rather in a stage-by-stage transformation that was the result of various social, political and other factors that warrant detailed examination.

The changing borders of 'Russia'

Over a very long period of time, spatial entities such as Muscovite Russia, the Russian Empire, Soviet Russia, the USSR and the Commonwealth of Independent States (CIS) encompassed a number of significant geographical modifications and transformations that had important consequences for defining the nature of what could be labelled as 'Russian' or 'Soviet' economic theory. Some of these changes and their variant impacts are briefly sketched in what follows as a prolegomena to discussing the ideas themselves.

Russia itself underwent significant territorial expansion between the sixteenth and nineteenth centuries, for example in Siberia, Central Asia and in the Caucasus. Peter the Great took control of much of the Baltic coastline at the beginning of the eighteenth century, and sometime later areas such as the Ukraine, Belorussia and Finland were added to the territories of the Russian Empire. In 1867, Alaska was sold to the USA and at the end of the nineteenth century, attempts were made to expand the Russian Empire in the Far East. From a history of ideas perspective, the acquisition of the Ukraine and the Baltic states was particularly significant, as the latter provided a geographical bridge to Germany, and the former would add its own unique sub-territory for contributions to 'Russian' economics widely interpreted.

After 1917 a new set of geographical transformations occurred in relation to the large-scale political upheavals that were occurring, for example a short-lived independent Ukraine came into existence. Control of the Baltic States was transferred to Germany, before independence was declared by both Latvia and Estonia. Finland and the Polish provinces were lost, and the Bolshevik government eventually renounced all claim to Poland, Ukraine, Finland and the Baltic States. During the ensuing civil war period, Soviet-style republics were created in parts of Ukraine, Belorussia and Transcaucasia that quickly entered into cordial relations with the Russian Socialist Federative Soviet Republic, before the USSR itself was created in 1922. Many territorial changes to the USSR occurred thereafter. For example after the Second World War the three Baltic republics were reincorporated into the USSR, some territory was taken from Poland, and in the Far East some lands were re-taken from Japan.

To give an indication of the full complexity of the national mix comprising the USSR, the 1926 census recognised the existence of 169 nationalities categorised under 25 main headings. The dominant ethnic group was the Slavs, comprising Great Russians, Ukrainians, White Russians, the Western Slavs and the Southern Slavs. Turkic groups included Tartars, Kazakhs, Uzbeks and Siberian Turks. Slavonic-Baltic groups, Caucasian groups, Mongols and Jewish traditions also existed in significant numbers within Soviet borders. Hence the national current connoted as 'Russian' economics included contributions from many of the ethnic groups listed above, at least in terms of overall territorial expanse, if not always in direct exertion of ethnic influence.

The question of the balance of intellectual impact of the various different nationalities is a complex one, but some preliminary observations can be made. The idea of a pan-Russian culture was occasionally mooted, in opposition to the notion of the cultural autonomy of the constituent groups.[4] Another ethnic-related current, pan-Slavism, was explicitly directed against the apparently individualistic culture of Western Europe. In terms of the smaller regions, some have suggested that the major cities of the Ukraine eventually became 'Russianised', although others might reasonably have disputed this claim. The nationalities question often arose across various debates and issues, suggesting that in fact Russification was never an entirely accomplished goal. According to J.F. Normano:

> Russians, Jews, Poles, Armenians, Georgians … all nations of the Russian Empire participated in the heated discussions … which colored a large part of the 19th century and the beginning of the 20th.[5]

This multi-ethnic mixture was not so different to (for example) the UK in abstract terms, where Scottish, English, Welsh and Irish influence could be found, but was distinct in terms of the number of national groups that were involved. Sometimes quantitative differences do change into qualitative ones.

The two most dominant urban centres for Russian economic discourse were of course Moscow and St Petersburg. As a general rule of thumb the latter city was more theoretically constituted and Western orientated; the former favoured a more empirical approach and was domestically focused. For example in terms of philosophy, the Slavophiles were Moscow-based, whereas the Westernisers favoured St Petersburg. Other important urban centres were Kiev in the Ukraine, and to a lesser extent Rostov-on-Don and Minsk, as well as various regions surrounding Moscow such as Yaroslavl and Saratov. Commercial Institutes played an important role in fostering economics as a discipline before 1917, although government ministries were also important. After 1917 the role of government bodies increased significantly, with new management organs being created specifically for the study of (and direct control over) the national economy.

In terms of the influence of such territorial changes on the intellectual milieu of Russian economics, an acknowledgement that Russia was not the focal point for all of world culture was perhaps easier for Russian theorists than (for example) for British economists, where imperialistic pretensions sometimes led to universal relevance being assumed for all nationally-sponsored ideas. On the other hand, Russia's self-perception as being on the periphery of Europe sometimes led to the wholesale rejection of mainstream Western doctrines, when careful adaptation might have been more appropriate. In general, the frequently changing borders of Russia meant that a core of permanent grounding elements were usually supplemented with an outer circle of continually fluctuating additions and modifications.

The relation between Russia and the Ukraine

A special place should be allotted to the Ukraine in understanding Russian economics widely interpreted, especially in the period 1870 to

1930. Figures such as Tugan-Baranovsky, Slutsky, M. Yasnopol'sky and P. Chompa deserve significant attention in terms of both their individual contributions to the subject and their dual national importance. Tugan-Baranovsky and Slutsky both began their contributions to economics from the Ukraine, but then moved to Russia, although Tugan-Baranovsky did this at a comparably earlier stage in his career than Slutsky. Tugan-Baranovsky eventually returned to his Ukrainian homeland shortly before his death, and his political sympathies also returned to the land of his birth after 1917.

The question naturally follows of whether some unique and identifiable 'Ukraine-ness' can be found in the work of these economists, which is clearly distinguishable from the work of wholly Russian-born thinkers. Some have identified a definite humanistic focus in Ukrainian thought, influenced for example by the Italian renaissance, although this was more evident in the period when political economy had not yet been formed as a distinct social science discipline, i.e. before 1800.[6] In truth, the work of noted Ukrainian economists such as Slutsky and Tugan-Baranovsky was sufficiently diverse to indicate no common thematic element, apart from the exceptional quality and originality of the work produced.

Perhaps the continuing ambiguous political status of the Ukraine itself vis-à-vis its Russian neighbour provided an extra impetus for Ukrainian thinkers to distinguish themselves internationally, so that more attention could be focused on the Ukraine and its plight from non-Russian directions. A similar motivation has been noted for the work of the Irish mathematician W.R. Hamilton, inventor of quaternions, whose national pride was central to his intellectual efforts. Certainly without question the Ukraine provided the most important sub-national current within the Slavic grouping, except of course for Russia itself.

Economics and other academic disciplines in Russia

As noted previously, in the nineteenth century the boundaries between academic disciplines were in many respects much less rigid than they became after the Second World War. In Russia in the nineteenth century, political economy had close links with social theory, philosophy, political ideas, geography and law, and some individuals who wrote on political economy also published extensively in some of these related areas.

In Russian sociology for example, a subjectivist school, a historico-genetic school, anarchistic, revolutionary and Marxian currents have been identified. The subjectivists stressed the role of intellectuals in initiating social progress and the relative nature of historical evolution. The historico-genetic school, as represented by Maxim Kovalevsky, emphasised the study of social institutions, a historical-comparative method and the psychological relations that constituted the social fabric. The anarchic sociology of Peter Kropotkin analysed the forces generating the moving equilibrium of social harmony, such as a sense of oneness with others and the principle of federation. Russian Marxism, as represented by Georgy Plekhanov, emphasised a materialistic interpretation of Marx, with environment reacting upon consciousness and the economic base of society determining the social and political superstructure.[7]

All the above-mentioned individuals – Kovalevsky, Kropotkin and Plekhanov – wrote works that straddled the borderlines between social theory, politics and political economy, and such an interdisciplinary focus was seen at the time as an essential practice. For example Tugan-Baranovsky wrote a book entitled *The Theoretical Foundations of Marxism* first published in 1905, which was partly sociological and partly economic in approach. This work included an account of the materialist interpretation of history, a chapter on the relation between economy (*khozyaistvo*) and social life, and a quasi-sociological analysis of social classes and the struggle between them. A long section was also devoted to the Marxian concepts of value and surplus value, and bringing all these disparate components together in a single volume was not seen as at all unusual.

Regarding the relation between political economy and philosophy, the methodological foundations of economics were still closely allied to philosophical currents in Russia throughout the nineteenth century and well into the twentieth. V.I. Lenin for example claimed to be a materialist, the meaning of which he described thus:

> To be a materialist is to acknowledge objective truth, which is revealed to us by our sense-organs. To acknowledge objective truth, i.e. truth not dependent upon man and mankind, is … to recognise absolute truth.[8]

This naïve realism had important ramifications for areas outside of philosophy, in that Lenin in his economic work was presumably searching for 'absolute truth' independent of human cognition, which when discovered could not ever be questioned due to its exalted epistemological status. Indeed Lenin's book *Materialism and Empirio-Criticism* was a sustained attack on philosophical relativism, which was gaining some ground in Russia at the beginning of the twentieth century due to the original and impressive work of thinkers like A.A. Bogdanov and V.A Bazarov, even though they were far from being sceptics in the technical sense of the term.

Another important philosophical current in pre-revolutionary Russia was neo-Kantianism, which attracted support from thinkers such as Tugan-Baranovsky. Advocating a return to universal ethical concerns over class-based materialistic ones, Russian neo-Kantianism was still socialistic in overall sympathy, despite being critical of economistic interpretations of Marx. Placing ethical issues centre-stage had important consequences for the methodology of socialist economics, in that exclusively working class interests and issues would no longer be paramount.

However, the triumph of the Bolshevik current of Social Democracy led to neo-Kantianism being lost as an indigenous philosophical current in Russia after 1917.

Economics and statistics

A very important overlapping thread could be observed in relation to economics and statistics, with both the theory of statistics and empirical statistical description having relevance to developments in Russian political economy. Within late nineteenth century Russian statistical theory, two competing currents have usually been identified. A St Petersburg school of statisticians, including P.L. Chebyshev, A.A. Markov and A.M. Lyapunov, and a Moscow school headed by P.A. Nekrasov. Both worked on similar topics, the law of large numbers and the central limit theorem for example, but adopted rather different approaches to the subject and sometimes came into direct conflict.

In general terms Russian statistical theory has been identified as laying emphasis on observation as a process relating to a sequence of random events, the phenomenon under study being subject to the action of a large number of independent stochastic actions, each exerting a small influence.[9] This was in contrast to the English and German schools, which have been characterised as originating in the science of facts relating to the state (or social measurement), then developing with a more abstract concern for numerical aggregates. Slutsky employed new developments in statistical theory in his work on modelling business cycles, and he also produced original work in various fields of pure mathematics, and through Slutsky's work the connection between economics and statistical theory reached new heights in the Russian context.

In terms of empirical statistics, *zemstvo* (local government) statisticians pioneered the gathering of detailed data observations in Russia, for example on peasant economy and agricultural land use. This also had relevance to economic ideas with regards to the consequences of statistical description for gauging the accuracy of economic theory. In addition to statistical theory, geographical concerns also played a role in helping to stimulate the development of economic statistics in Russia. For example, the Russian Geographical Society organised topographical expeditions that laid the ground for the preparation of statistical surveys of the population and economy of various regions within Russia. Before this time M.V. Lomonosov had proposed the general idea of economic geography and the notion of a lexicon of Russian commodities.[10] In general, the connection between economics and statistics in Russia before 1917 was strong, and this link continued to develop after 1917, although in a modified form.

Issues in the history of Russian economic thought

A number of important issues relating to the development of Russian economic thought that have been articulated previously need to be raised at the outset of this book. Firstly, Normano has been accused of attempting to minimise the originality of Russian economic thought, and of thus being the spokesman of 'bourgeois cosmopolitanism', by suggesting that in the nineteenth century, Russian thinkers merely adapted the economic doctrines of the West.[11] In similar vein, I.G. Blyumin has suggested that economic thought in Russia in the first half of the nineteenth century was (in the main) simply imported from the West. The extent to which Russian economics was a direct copy of its Western neighbours, and the degree to which genuinely new ideas came forth from Russian soil, is a contentious question with many component parts. At first glance it might appear to be the case that true originality in Russian economics reached its peak at the end of the nineteenth century and the beginning of the twentieth, when most of the famous names in Russian economics still known today were at the height of their powers. Whether this perception is entirely accurate will be re-evaluated at the end of the book, when the detailed material presented in it has been fully considered.

Another general issue is the notion of competing currents in economic theory; classical, neoclassical, Marxist, institutionalist and so on. Did such labels have the same meaning in Russia in the nineteenth century as they have today in the West? Certainly, Marxists such as Lenin clearly identified themselves as fierce opponents of the established intellectual order. However, since one component source of Marxism was classical economics, Marxist economics was doctrinally related to its orthodox forebear in an important manner. If from today's perspective, Marxist and mainstream economics are seen as being diametrically opposed, then in late nineteenth-century Russia, the distinction was a little less clear-cut, given that classical rather than neoclassical conceptions defined the mainstream itself.

Soviet historians of economic thought have divided the Russian economists of the pre-revolutionary era into various groups based on political and class criteria. For example, the following categories have been identified: the reactionary nobility (A.S. Suvorin), the liberal nobility (V.P. Bezobrazov), bourgeois liberals (A.I. Chuprov), revolutionary peasant democrats, liberal *narodniki*, and Legal Marxists.[12] There is an element of truth is this type of classification schema, but it is less useful in identifying the sources of the more technical elements of the work of these pre-revolutionary economists, and hence it accurately captures only some aspects of their work.

Moreover, Russian historians have, since the advent of *perestroika*, put a great deal of effort into research and promotion with respect to the famous names in Russian economics; efforts which are very welcome and which have produced much of genuine interest. For example in terms of new interpretations, a notable effort was made by G.N. Sovina to identify an original Russian school of political economy said to be in existence at the beginning of the twentieth century. The characteristic features of this school were given as: the preservation and development of the principles of the classical school of political economy; the inclusion of social analysis in economic theory; a synthesis of the labour theory of value with the marginal utility approach; an emphasis on political economy as a science of national economy; the pioneering elaboration of the principles of macroeconomics and economic dynamics; and finally a stress on the practical relevance of theoretical inventions.[13] In Sovina's view the Russian school had an underlying predilection for the classical approach.

Whether all these various components naturally fitted together to form a genuine school, which was said to include people as diverse as Dmitriev, Tugan-Baranovsky and Kondratiev, and whether the classical approach actually dominated, are matters for further investigation, but many of the features identified by Sovina were certainly important to Russian economics in general both before and after 1900.

Social structure, organised groups and economic ideas

The question of the relation between social structure and economic ideas needs to be addressed for application to the Russian context. According to Joseph Schumpeter, social location was a powerful factor shaping human minds, but was certainly not the only influence, and hence ideology was not always false, or simply the expression of ruling class interests.[14] In this respect, Schumpeter distinguished between the notion of social classes – farmers, artisans, merchants, aristocrats – and what he called economic types – capitalists, entrepreneurs, workers and so on. The latter were economic categories for use in theoretical analysis, the former were social groups that were observed empirically.[15] It was social class that was more likely to exert an influence over the development of ideas, as economic types were only (at least in Schumpeter's view) a theoretical abstraction.

Perspectives other than that of Schumpeter might also be employed in this respect. According to Marxist doctrine, the ruling class owned the means of production, the middle class were self-employed through the possession of independent skills, and the working class sold only its labour power. In Weberian analysis class was defined differently, through the availability of life chances and opportunities, which were conditioned by family and other social ties. The Russian historian of Western economics I.I. Rubin noted a tripartite division of proprietors, cultivators and industrial workers that had been expounded by Francois Quesnay.[16]

In the Russian context, both social classes and economic types need to be considered in relation to economic ideas. The class structure of nineteenth-century Russia differed somewhat to that in Western Europe, with the peasantry being a much larger social group in Russia than it was in some other parts of Europe. Whether the economic types found in classical economic theory were directly applicable to Russia needs to be considered, as does whether economists created any new abstract types from Russian experience.

Various authorities have dissected the Russian class structure as follows. For Mackenzie Wallace, the hereditary nobility, personal nobility, clerical classes, town classes, rural classes and military classes could be found, of which the rural classes were the vast majority.[17] In another classification scheme, the peasantry, industrial and artisan workers, the intelligentsia, the nobility, the clergy and the merchants were detected. One measure of the Imperial Russian social structure was taken from the 1897 census. In this calculation peasants were by far the largest social grouping, accounting for approximately 83.5 per cent of the total population at this time, with merchants making up only 0.25 per cent of the total, and workers, artisans and shopkeepers 11.5 per cent. The hereditary nobility, while only 1 per cent of the total, wielded much more power than their size might indicate.[18]

Another related aim of this book is to trace groups and networks of Russian economists, statisticians and policy-advisers, and to demonstrate some of the common ideas and practices that bound them together. For example, ideologically constituted groups such as Legal Marxists, Social Democrats (in the Marxian sense), historical economists, liberal thinkers and conservatives, or geographically-based groupings such as networks centred in Moscow or St Petersburg could be identified. With respect to policy-advisers, specific spheres of influence need to be highlighted, such as banking and finance (P.P. Migulin and I.Kh. Ozerov), tariff policy (D.I. Mendeleev), agriculture (P.A. Stolypin and A.I. Chuprov) and industrialisation in general (S. Yu. Witte and M.I. Tugan-Baranovsky). Moreover, links between academic institutions and government bodies were sometimes strong, for example Tugan-Baranovsky's work in the Ministry of Trade and in St Petersburg University, and connections between business groups and economists also need to be considered. Closely-knit officially designated units should be clearly distinguished from broad currents in political economy, both in terms of membership and general influence.

In terms of the institutional framework of economic discourse in Russia and then the USSR, one commentator has outlined the following changes brought about by 1917:

> Prior to the 1917 revolution economic education in Russia was imparted in commercial colleges in Moscow, Kharkov, Kiev and a few other towns. In addition, economic subjects were taught at St Petersburg Polytechnical Institute, where professors of world celebrity lectured. After 1917, economics faculties were instituted at Moscow, Leningrad, Kiev, Kharkov, Odessa, Tomsk, Kazan and at other universities.[19]

This was followed by the opening up of a number of planning colleges, as part of the system of higher educational establishments of Gosplan, and also the creation of various financial colleges, forming part of the educational system of the People's Commissariat of Finance. However, while the 1917 revolution brought a substantial growth in economics-related research and teaching activities in Soviet Russia, this should not be interpreted as denigrating the pre-revolutionary system, which served to foster cooperation between academic and governmental activities and also facilitated the coexistence of a plurality of currents in economic doctrine.

The legal foundations of Russian capitalism

In the evolutionary view, the progress of legal institutions was of crucial significance in explaining economic change. For example, John Commons considered that exchange of personal services and/or physical products was a defining feature of feudal relations, as opposed to the monetary exchange relations that were dominant under capitalism.[20] Put another way, bargains in terms of use-values were prevalent, as opposed to bargains in terms of exchange relations. In the Russian context, the transition from feudalism to capitalism was a protracted and complex process that had not been fully consummated even by 1913, either in law or in reality.

At the beginning of the nineteenth century, possessional factories – with a bound labour force, wages and working time regulated by government decree – were common. The specific position of an individual factory depended on the terms of the original contract declared by the state, which usually stipulated that the factory and its ascribed peasants must be maintained as indivisible.[21] However, as the nineteenth century unfolded and technological improvements became possible, the relation of bonded labour to the factory changed as defined by government decrees, and the development of proto-capitalist factories began to occur. Peasants that had been ascribed to possessional factories were allowed to become members of other classes such as merchants or small householders, and free artisans with a newly acquired trade came into existence as a consequence of the decline of the possessional form of bondage.

A very significant reform of direct relevance to understanding developments in Russian economy after 1870 was the abolition of serfdom, which occurred by official proclamation in 1861. Serfs had offered both personal duties and physical products in service of their lord. The emancipation of the serfs was of some importance in liberating labour from fixed agricultural employment, and it increased labour mobility to some degree. However, the 1861 legislation was designed to keep peasants within land estate control for a significant period by making them contribute redemption payments to land owners for the plot of land that they were allotted. Hence peasants were forced to find additional sources of income in agriculture or in industry, which contributed to some degree to increased economic activity after 1861.

One section of the emancipation legislation itself entitled 'On Laws of Property' declared that 'every peasant can acquire their own moveable and fixed property' and asserted that the rural commune could also do the same.[22] Moveable property included household and agricultural tools and equipment, fixed property consisted of land and dwellings. Thus an effort had been made to encourage the development of private property amongst peasants at this time, although in practice some obstacles to this (such as the redemption payments) remained.

Sometime later, between 1906 and 1911, a series of agricultural reforms were introduced by Peter Stolypin that attempted to encourage peasants to move away from communal forms of agriculture to privately-owned farms. The timescale envisaged by Stolypin for this programme to be carried out was in the order of twenty years, and hence it is perhaps not a great surprise to document that by 1913, only limited success in the outlined aims had been achieved. One of the goals of the Stolypin reforms was to inculcate into peasants the very notion of private property itself, as social conceptions of land ownership had been widely prevalent in the rural commune. As will be seen throughout this book, differing economic ideas in Russia were often clustered around such legislative reforms, which were frequently the subject of heated debate by economists, politicians and many other interested parties.

'Russia' in the eyes of Western economists

It is worth briefly sketching at least a few examples of how some Western economic thinkers viewed Russia as a nation and (more importantly) as an economy in the nineteenth century. In general, Russia was regarded by many as being outside of the pattern of economic progress exhibited in Western Europe. The potential for future development was not denied, but some substantial hindrances were noted. For example T.R. Malthus explained that:

> Russia has great natural resources. Its produce is, in its present state, above its consumption; and it wants nothing but greater freedom of industrious exertion, and an adequate vent for its commodities in the interior parts of the country, to occasion an increase of population astonishingly rapid. The principle obstacle to this is the vassalage or rather slavery of the peasants, and the ignorance and indolence which almost necessarily accompany such a state... The consequence is that the lands in the country are left half cultivated and the genuine spring of population impaired in its source.[23]

This suggested that Malthus would have enthusiastically supported the emancipation of the serfs after 1861. The economic situation in Russia did not appear radically different to some other Western onlookers in the twentieth century, as it had done to Malthus before this date.

For example, in his study of business organisation from 1919, *Industry and Trade*, Alfred Marshall wrote that:

> Great futures may also await Russia and China. Each is large, continuous and self-contained: each has enormous resources, which could not be developed so long as good access to ocean highways was a necessary condition for great achievement. Their populations differ in temperament; the persistence of the Chinese being complementary to the quick sensibility of the Russian: each has inherited great powers of endurance.[24]

Marshall also provided an appendix on cooperative and collective organisation of industry in which he distinguished the attitudes of Anglo-Saxon workers to cooperatives from those in Germany, in that the latter were said to care much less about individual freedoms.[25] Vilfredo Pareto on the other hand was concerned about the duplicitous nature of some Russian politicians. He wrote prophetically following the revolutionary events in 1905 that:

> Some years ago the followers of agricultural collectivism, like Laveleye, emphasised the beneficial effect of the Russian *mir*. . . . How opinions have changed. Why? It seems to me that the new elite praises and support collectivism as the means to the end of taking over power. . . . The Russian government tends more and more to become a socialist bureaucracy.[26]

Pareto characterised the Tsarist system as one in which the level of despotism was fierce and immoral, yet he still believed that the economic foundations of socialist theory were mistaken.[27] Many other Western economists thought the same at this time. Pareto also suggested that as socialist leaders came into management positions, the Marxian sentiment equating value with crystallised labour tended to lose its impetus.

Conclusion

The introduction has provided a prologue to some of the themes and topics to be explored in more detail throughout the book, and has outlined the underlying approach that will be adopted. It has also surveyed aspects of Russian history of direct relevance to understanding the development of intellectual currents in the period concerned, so that readers who lack any specialist knowledge of Russian history can follow the contextual references being made throughout the book. The next chapter begins to focus on Russian economic thought in detail by providing a short sketch of the development of economic ideas in Russia before 1870, as a prelude to the more expansive account of such ideas after this date.

2 Prelude – the Russian economic mind before 1870

Throughout the nineteenth century, the social and political tensions exerting influence on Russian life were extremely varied and enduring. Some of these tensions related to opposing forces such as agrarian interests against industrial, town against country, nobility against industrialists, government bureaucracy against reformers, and democratic forces against conservatives. Set against such social tensions, it has been suggested by some that the propagation of Western economic doctrines in Russia through the nineteenth century occurred in various waves of rising and then falling influence, for example in relation to closely allied themes such as free trade against protectionism and classical economics against the historical school.

There is an element of truth in this idea with respect to the governmental employment of economic ideas, but (as will be seen) the work of individual economic thinkers cannot so easily be pinned down to strict cycles of bi-polar esteem. More accurately, an ongoing flow of multiple influences should be expected, especially regarding the impact of Western economic ideas in Russia, in both the pre-classical and the classical periods of advancement. The formation of indigenous Russian currents of political economy began to occur well before 1870, but these were often an eclectic mix of a number of different elements. Consequently the impact and development of both Western and native Russian traditions will be examined in this chapter.

Western economic theory in Russia

Two important pre-classical currents in Western economics that made a mark upon Russia well before 1870 were the physiocrats and the mercantilists. For E.F. Heckscher the mercantilists did not want simply state activity in economic affairs, but rather private initiative stimulated by government measures.[1] In this interpretation, mercantilism should have been a very important current in Russian economics, but how far was this actually the case? Some have interpreted the efforts of Peter the Great (1672–1725) in terms of promoting Russian industrial development as being of mercantilist inspiration. If mercantilism meant equating only precious metals and an export surplus with wealth, then Peter the Great did not identify national wealth only with money. He was, however, concerned with the flow of specie in relation to the conduct of war, and he did prohibit the export of money from the country.[2] Mercantilists supported strong central government and detailed business regulations, the first of which was certainly relevant to Russia. Peter the Great was not, however, an economist, and this highlighted the distinction between the governmental employment of economic ideas and their adoption by native thinkers.

Another Western current that found a limited expression in Russia was physiocracy. The physiocrats were represented in Russia through the work of D.A. Golitsyn (1734–1803), who in 1796 published a book entitled *On the Spirit of Economists*, which in part attempted to exonerate economists of any responsibility for the French revolution.[3] Golitsyn was the only Russian thinker directly inspired by physiocracy, although for a limited time in the reign of Catherine II, the physiocrats had become quite popular. Given that physiocracy opposed nearly all governmental restrictions, then its lack of lasting popularity in Russia was understandable, even if an emphasis on the productive nature of agriculture might be thought relevant to an understanding of the plight of the Russian peasantry. Golitsyn had emphasised the centrality of the productivity of agricultural labour to economic development, increases in which required full individual freedom; he thus supported the abolition of serfdom. After various peasant uprisings at the very end of the eighteenth century the ideas of the physiocrats were declared to be dangerous by the Russian government, and strict censorship then followed.[4]

The dissemination of classical economics

If both mercantilism and physiocracy were of only moderate influence in Russia before 1870, then of much greater impact were the various classical economists starting with Adam Smith. Classical economics is conventionally defined as being prevalent from the time of publication of Smith's *The Wealth of Nations* to the advent of the marginal revolution in economic theory, approximately 1776 to 1870, and as being of predominantly, but not exclusively, British inspiration. Throughout the nineteenth century up until 1870, the classical economists dominated Western European analytical thinking about business activity, although this domination was certainly not complete. Consequently, one significant question is, to what extent was this domination paralleled in Russia in the same period?

J.F. Normano divided the overseas influences on economics in nineteenth century Russia into English, French and German components. The English influence was said to consist mainly of Smith and Jeremy Bentham and be concerned with free trade and liberalism, but was only an isolated early episode. The French influence occurred via the physiocrats and the utopian socialists, the latter being particularly favoured with respect to the propagation of anti-capitalist sentiment. The German influence was said to be the strongest and most enduring of the three, and occurred via geographical proximity, trade relations and personal contacts. Such an account is oversimplified, but it suggests that the idea that classical economics might have dominated Russian economics was not in any way accurate. The real story is of course more complex than this.

The works of Smith, John Stuart Mill, Thomas Malthus and Bentham, whilst certainly not having decisive influence in Russia in the nineteenth century, were reasonably well known in intellectual circles.[5] For example I.G. Blyumin declared that the influence of Smith on Russian economic literature in the first two decades of the nineteenth century was very strong indeed.[6] This influence was accompanied by (or perhaps achieved in part by means of) the production of various Russian editions of Smith's works. The first complete Russian translation of Smith's *The Wealth of Nations* was published in St Petersburg in four parts between 1802 and 1806. The Emperor Alexander I, who according to Normano was for a time 'completely under the influence' of Smith and Bentham, ordered the translation, which was undertaken by N.R. Politkovsky.[7] As one source explained:

> Though it was not remarkable for exactness, especially in the definition of the terms employed, it had a great influence on Russian students, who very quickly accepted the economic ideas of the great Scotchman.[8]

Russian was sequentially the eighth language into which *The Wealth of Nations* was translated, German being the very first.[9] Currents in nineteenth century Russian thought affected by Smith included the Decembrists, a liberal movement named after an ill-fated uprising that was active in the 1820s and 1830s. For example the Decembrist P.I. Pestel argued in favour of large-scale capitalist ownership of the land, such arguments being heavily influenced by Smith.[10]

Smith's teachings were also expounded in the official Russian government publication *The St Petersburg Journal* in the first decade of the nineteenth century, where it was suggested that the obligations of the government with respect to manufacture were limited to 'protecting the natural freedom of industry'.[11] Smith's ideas were apparently so popular in government circles that in 1803 the Russian Minister of Internal Affairs had spoken of the tasks of government in purely Smithian language, for example referring to the need for 'removing all constraints' from industry and trade.[12] In the second decade of the nineteenth century the Russian free trade weekly *Spirit of Journals* combined sympathy for Smith with support for serfdom by opposing government intervention in the existing agrarian system.[13] Another edition of Smith's *The Wealth of Nations* was published in three volumes in St Petersburg in 1866.[14]

Smith was not the only classical economist to find Russian expression. An edition of Thomas Malthus's *Essay on the Principle of Population* was published in St Petersburg in 1868. A Russian edition of Bentham's selected works was issued in St Petersburg in 1867, and J.R. McCulloch's *On the Principles, Successes, Special Object and Importance of Political Economy* was issued in Moscow in 1834. As well as English classical economics, the ideas of some French economists were also disseminated in Russia at this time. For example, a Russian translation of Say's *Catechisms on Political Economy* was published in St Petersburg in 1833. Within the classical group David Ricardo was a special case, as his impact in Russia did not begin to be felt until after 1870, and hence he is more appropriately discussed in the next chapter.

Regarding the content of classical economics, the core of classical theory is still disputed today, but key themes within it included a concern for the labour theory of value, the three factors of production (land, labour and capital), the rationale for international trade and the economic concept of rent. The idea of a natural, self-adjusting mechanism – an invisible hand – that coordinated economic activity in market control systems of business affairs was crucial, as was the notion that individual self-interest was the fundamental motivating drive of human behaviour. In Russia's more communitarian-based tradition however, the idea of self-interest motivation was more controversial, and hence the economic theory that was constructed on this foundation was sometimes regarded with a little more suspicion.

In general, a significant part of the Russian commentary on the content of classical economics was critical in nature, not only in the sense of disagreeing with specific aspects of classical doctrine, but also of using classical ideas as a general springboard for further thoughts on the topics in question. Even so, Russian economists of this period did not develop anything resembling a complete system that could compete with the classical canon as an entirely separate set of analytical principles; instead, many of the assumptions of classical thinking were either adopted in themselves or were subject to challenge, but most Russian thinkers accepted that classical economics was a powerful intellectual system that was a useful starting-point for further analysis. Some examples of such a springboard effect are discussed in the next section, which turns the spotlight on a number of native Russian thinkers active in the period before 1870.

Indigenous economic thought

Despite the significant influence of Western ideas on Russian economics, native thinkers developed their own contributions to political economy widely considered that were not always simply copies of Western ideas.[15] In this regard, important economic thinkers in Russia before 1870 included H.F. Storch, N.G. Chernyshevsky, N.S. Mordvinov, N.I. Turgenev, V.A. Milyutin, V.P. Bezobrazov, V.V. Bervi-Flerovsky and I.V. Vernadsky. A short account of some of the ideas of these individuals follows directly, with the caveat that these sketches are of only a very preliminary nature, of use in setting some of the background to the more detailed examination of indigenous thinkers that will begin in the next chapter.

H.F. Storch (1766–1835)

Storch straddled the German-Russian divide, but his work also had an effect in France. He was born in Riga, studied at Jena and Heidelberg and then returned to Russia in 1788. He entered the Russian government service in 1789 and embarked on a large historical and statistical account of the Russian Empire that was published in nine volumes between 1797 and 1803. As a tutor to the future Tsar, Storch's major work of economic theory was his *Course of Political Economy* of 1815, which was first published in French; because of its liberal nature, a Russian translation was at the time forbidden. J.K. Ingram evaluated it as 'a work of a very high order of merit', and noted its theoretical importance in relation to the doctrine of immaterial goods (such as health and talent), the distinction between productive and unproductive labour and the differences between individual and national revenue.[16] Mark Blaug, on the other hand, characterised it as a series of not particularly distinguished glosses on *The Wealth of Nations*. In terms of the empirical aspects of Storch's work, the account of the effects of serfdom in Russia was particularly noteworthy.

Whilst in general terms Storch was a critical follower of Smith and Say, supporting the upholding of individual freedoms and the security of private ownership as the keys to economic success, he also believed in the impossibility of economic theorems of general validity and the necessity of studying economic phenomena in relation to concrete historical development.[17] Hence some elements of the approach of the German historical school were also present in Storch's work, together with many of those of the classical school. He also discussed the problem of measuring national income in some detail. Sometime after Storch's death, Karl Marx described something that he called Storch's law, which was that the rent of the most fertile land determined the rent of the last land to yield any rent at all.[18] Storch had written that:

> The rent of the most fertile land determines the rate of rent on all other lands competing with the most fertile lands. So long as the produce of the most fertile land is sufficient to satisfy demand, the less fertile lands … cannot yield rent. But as soon as demand exceeds the amount of produce that the best land can supply … it is then possible to cultivate the less fertile soil and to draw a rent from it.[19]

Marx reported that Storch's law contradicted Ricardo's view on this question, Ricardo believing instead that it was goods produced under the least favourable conditions that determined market prices.[20]

Marx also discussed Storch's criticisms of J.B. Say. For example regarding Say's notion that for an entire nation in any given year there was no net product, only a gross product, i.e. the total value of all products made was equal to their cost of production, Storch wrote in criticism:

> imagine a family which through its own labour is self-sufficing in all its needs, such as there are so many examples of in Russia … is the revenue of such family equal to the gross product coming from its land, its capital and its industry? Can it live in its barns or its stables, eat its seed and forage, clothe itself with its labouring cattle, amuse itself with its agricultural implements? According to Mr Say's thesis, all these questions would have to be answered in the affirmative.[21]

Against this conception, Storch suggested that the net revenue of a nation was not the excess of values produced over all values consumed, but only the excess of values produced over the values consumed in order to produce. A part of the values produced each year actually went towards maintaining the means of production; if this was not the case, if all values were actually consumed, then the capital stock would be eroded and eventually cease to exist. In debating this type of question in this way Storch showed himself to be a direct follower of the classical tradition.

Storch was important in the Russian context as a significant example of an economic thinker who had one foot within Russia and one foot outside the country, in his case this other foot being divided between France and Germany. Storch's concern with Say's economic theory was not of crucial concern to a general Russian audience, and as a more cosmopolitan type of thinker, Storch can be contrasted with someone whose economic work had a much more immediate relevance in Russia such as Chernyshevsky.

N.G. Chernyshevsky (1828–1889)

Chernyshevsky is perhaps best known in the West for his novel *What Is To Be Done?* of 1863, which through its leading characters advocated both collective ways of working and personal equality between men and women, but he was also an important economic thinker with a wide range of intellectual interests. He eventually spent around 25 years in various states of imprisonment and exile as a consequence of his membership of revolutionary groups, and his most famous philosophical work was entitled *The Nature of Human Knowledge*. In this realm Chernyshevsky articulated what he called 'the anthropological principle', which was that humankind must be regarded as a single being with only one nature, with the entire organism participating in every aspect of individual behaviour.

One of Chernyshevsky's most important economic articles was his 'Critique of Philosophical Prejudices Against Communal Ownership' of 1858. In this work he questioned the idea that communal ownership of the land would necessarily be replaced by private ownership, and disputed the notion advanced by many Western economists that private property was a more advanced form of ownership than collective control. In fact for Chernyshevsky it would be the presence of the commune in Russia that would enable the transition to full communism to occur with particular ease. In this respect he outlined a 'stages' view of economic development in which the highest stage of socialism would be a return to the first stage (primitive communism), and the intermediate stage (individualism) would necessarily be replaced by its opposite.

Chernyshevsky also provided access for Russian readers to Mill's economic ideas through his own Russian translation of part of Mill's *Principles of Political Economy* that was published in 1860. The motivation for this translation was to enable Russian readers to make up for deficiencies in their knowledge of existing tracts in political economy, and also to save them from distorted versions propagated by French economists. Chernyshevsky was thus concerned about the effect such deficiencies were having on intellectual progress in Russia. In the preface to his translation, Chernyshevsky explained that Mill's book was recognised by economists as the best, most accurate and profound exposition of the theories created by Adam Smith. Hence, translating it might clear up any misunderstandings that existed in Russia about the true nature of classical economics.[22]

Added to the translation of Mill were Chernyshevsky's own notes, together with a short account of the sections of Mill that had been excluded from the translation. Here Chernyshevsky stressed that whilst Mill adhered to the individualist point of view in constructing his system of political economy, in fact the perspective of humanity as a whole (or all of society) should better be adopted. Chernyshevsky was one of the most significant radical intellectuals in Russia in the 1860s, and the economic aspect of his work was a crucial part of his legacy.

Other notable indigenous economists

N.S. Mordvinov (1754–1845) was the President of the Free Economic Society between 1823 and 1840 and an Admiral in the Ministry for Maritime Affairs. He became a Count (*graf*) in 1834, and his basic viewpoint has been characterised as one of the liberal nobility. His most significant book in economics was *Some Considerations on Manufactures in Russia and of the Tariff* of 1815, which argued for the necessity of industrial protection as a means of encouraging Russian manufacturing. Mordvinov also supported the need for agricultural reforms in order to improve labour productivity. He authored various other works on topics such as monetary circulation, the state budget and the banking system, in which he suggested that both monetary wealth and general prosperity depended on private enrichment, and argued that taxes should be levied only on net income, not on capital.

N.I. Turgenev (1789–1871), the son of a Freemason, served in the Russian Ministry of Finance and was the author of *An Essay on the Theory of Taxation* of 1818. As a moderate Decembrist, one of his major intellectual efforts was to argue for an end to serfdom, but with the preservation of the landholding by the original landowners and the subsequent use of free hired labour. He thus supported the freeing of peasants without allotting them land grants; as a reformer he was cautious of the power of the gentry and the dangers of aristocratic oligarchy, this leading him to a moderate position on land reform. In his *Essay* he came out against protectionism as the final error of mercantilism, and believed that free trade ideas were fully suitable for application to the Russian situation. He opposed the peasant commune as an obstacle to further agricultural development.

V.A. Milyutin (1826–1855) was a socialist who was critical of the 'apologetic' nature of some classical economists such as Say and Malthus, viewing their work as an expression of class interests and the notion of freedom that they promulgated as fictitious. For example, he wrote a work examining Malthus and his various critics in some detail, yet he was also critical of Western utopian socialism. Milyutin made a detailed study of the history of Russian law and property rights, and he published *An Essay on National Wealth and the Principles of Political Economy* in which he viewed the economic laws of capitalism as imaginary, and the real task of political economy as medicinal. In his book *The Proletariat and Pauperism in England and in France* of 1847, Milyutin was critical of the function of landlords in Western capitalism, and he also advocated significant reform of the serf system in Russia. A member of the Petrashevtsy circle – an underground discussion group of radical intellectuals – Milyutin's philosophy was close to that of the positivists.

V.P. Bezobrazov (1828–1889) was a specialist in money and finance who wrote a number of significant works such as *Land Credit and its Contemporary Organisation in Europe* of 1860 and *On Monetary Circulation in Russia in Connection with Industry, Trade and Credit* of 1863. He also made notable contributions to analysing the sources and classification of state income, and his general approach to economic theory has been described as that of a Manchester liberal. In the 1840s he worked in the Ministry of Finance and sometime later on the Politico-Economic Committee of the Russian Geographical Society. One of his first publications was a book on *Stock Exchange Operations* in 1856, whilst his later works focused on financial law and the Russian national economy as a whole.

V.V. Bervi-Flerovsky (1829–1919) studied at Kazan University and served for a while in the Ministry of Justice, but in 1862 he was arrested for participating in political protests. Bervi-Flerovsky's most significant work was his *Condition of the Working Class in Russia* of 1869, which was a *narodnik*-inspired critique of the development of capitalism in Russia that owed a clear intellectual debt to Friedrich Engels. According to one source it provided a vivid and shocking description of Russian working class life in the 1860s.[23] It also showed the increasing destitution of the peasantry as a consequence of the development of Russian capitalism, and it was subsequently evaluated highly by Marx, who studied the particularities of the Russian situation in detail whilst working on *Capital*. In addition, Bervi-Flerovsky wrote a more general work entitled *An ABC of the Social Sciences* published in 1871, and a *Critique of the Fundamental Ideas of Natural Science* of 1904.

I.V. Vernadsky (1821–1884) was a Professor of Political Economy at Kiev, Moscow and then St Petersburg, authoring *Studies in the Theory of Consumption* in 1857 and *Studies in the History of Political Economy* in 1858. He supported the application of free trade ideas to the Russian situation as a means of combating feudal monopoly, and was a strong critic of socialist ideas in general and Chernyshevsky's support of the commune in particular. He believed that the task of political economy was the uncovering of the natural laws of production, and defined such economy as the science of value, not of wealth.[24]

Considering all of the above indigenous thinkers together, the rich diversity of Russian economics even in this relatively early period is apparent. Moreover, the names mentioned in this section were by no means all the individuals who worked on economics-related topics before 1870, and hence the true picture was even more expansive than this brief outline might suggest. Regarding the categorisation of indigenous thinkers, a few did fit within conventionally accepted labels – Bervi-Flerovsky was a *narodnik* and Bezobrazov an economic liberal – but many straddled the borders of Western-style classification both in terms of the scope and the content of their work. In terms of their native originality, none ranked alongside Smith or Ricardo in terms of influence or insight, but some of their interest and appeal derived from exactly how they adapted Western themes for Russian use.

Russian economy for Western readers

As a country often seen by those in the West as being of exotic distinction, Russian economy before 1870 was the subject of study by some important non-Russian commentators. One significant and well-publicised source for Western readers on the Russian economy in the mid-nineteenth century was M.L. Tegoborski's substantial *Commentaries on the Productive Forces of Russia*, which was published in London in 1855. In this work Tegoborski surveyed many aspects of the Russian economy in detail, including the geography, the government, the population, the commerce and the industry of the Russian Empire.

Regarding the various provincial governments in Russia, he outlined how there were large disproportions between them in terms of territorial extent, soil composition, forms of administration, regional wealth and financial management. With these elements in mind Tegoborski reasoned that:

> the extent and the geographical position of Russia is sufficient to make us perceive the great importance of those undertakings which have for their object to multiply our means of communication, and to complete by canals, roads, and railroads, the facilities offered by our lakes and watercourses.[25]

Tegoborski also highlighted the importance of uniquely Russian forms of economy such as the various large-scale commercial fairs, held for example annually for four weeks in Nizhni Novgorod at a time of favourable transport capacity. Such forms of commerce were conditioned by the particular geography of Russia, with vast scales of communication, the concentration of manufactures in a small range of districts and the scarcity of commercial towns in which trade could easily take place.[26] Tegoborski also emphasised various physical characteristics of Russia as follows:

> excessive variety in the distribution of the soil, which is not found in the same degree in any other country, must necessarily exercise a great influence not only on … the progress of rural economy, but also on … the whole economical and social conditions of the different provinces of the Empire.[27]

Due to its English-language form, Tegoborski's account was widely available in the West, and although it presented a primarily empirical approach to the topic, it was still influential in moulding Western thinking about Russia at this time. It even reached a Russian audience when Milyutin commented on it in a Russian journal.

Another important source for Western readers was Baron August von Haxthausen's *Studies on the Interior of Russia*, which was first published in German in 1847. Haxthausen wrote of a uniquely Russian institution:

> The expanded family is the Russian commune. The land belongs to the family or the commune with the individual enjoying only the right to use it. Because everyone in the community has exactly the same rights, the land is equally divided among all the living for temporary use. Consequently, the right of the children to inherit their father's allotment cannot exist.[28]

Other features of the peasant commune highlighted by Haxthausen included rule by a respected elder, family unity, a specific principle of land allotment (which varied by commune), and fields divided into square plots that were then sub-divided into long strips. The precise nature and internal resilience of the commune would turn out to be a very controversial topic amongst Russian economists in the last quarter of the nineteenth century, but Western economists would sometimes view such an institution as an unfamiliar creation without a direct parallel outside of the Russian context.

Conclusion

In the period before 1870, there was a varied mixture of foreign influences plus the development of numerous indigenous currents in political economy, which made Russian economic thinking somewhat more diverse than its Western counterpart at this time, at least at the academic level. Before 1870 social, political and economic thinking in Russia was often part of the same general overall system, and hence the strict subject distinctions prevalent today had not yet been fully formed.

In terms of genuine innovation, greater originality was perhaps found in the documenting of native empirical features of the Russian economy, rather than in the invention of pure theory or the creation of new analytical concepts. In the next chapter attention is turned to economic theory in Russia from 1870 onwards, when the momentum of originality displayed by Russian thinkers began to gather pace. This acceleration was conditioned in part by the emancipation of the serfs in 1861, but also by intellectual developments such as the importation of Marx's ideas into Russia in the 1870s and 1880s and new developments in Western economics such as the marginal revolution.

3 The Russian economic mind under Tsarism, 1870–1890

The 1870s witnessed two events of notable significance for the development of Russian economic thought in the last three decades of the nineteenth century: the marginal revolution in Western economics beginning around 1870, accomplished through the works of W.S. Jevons, Leon Walras and Carl Menger; and the publication of the first Russian translation of volume of Karl Marx's *Capital* in 1872. The marginal revolution shifted at least some of the focus of economic investigation away from classical concerns such as the distribution of wealth, the determination of relative prices, and the constituents of economic growth, towards neoclassical concerns such as production efficiency and the subjective evaluation of consumer utility. As characterised by Mark Blaug, classical economics was concerned with the effects of changes in quantity and quality of labour and capital on the rate of growth of output, whereas neoclassical economics was concerned with the optimal allocation of productive services.[1] This shift in emphasis had some relevance for economics outside of Western Europe, even though marginalism was not always transmitted outside of European boundaries in a pure or unadulterated form.

The first publication of Marx's *Capital* in German in 1867 had been a major step in the creation of an alternative socialist economic theory that was built on classical foundations such as the labour theory of value and the falling rate of profit, but arrived at much more radical political conclusions through the concept of surplus value, and hence its widespread availability to a Russian audience was eagerly anticipated by some. However, the exact significance of both the marginal revolution and the Russian translation of *Capital* were controversial for a number of reasons.

With respect to the marginal revolution, its status as a genuine temporally specific fundamental shift in approach has been questioned by some historians, given that some marginalist ideas had appeared in economics well before 1870. A socialist critic of the spread of marginalism after 1870 might suggest that in fact, the idea that free markets achieved an optimal allocation of resources by means of taking economic activity to marginal limits, came noticeably to the fore only after volume one of *Capital* had been published in 1867, even though the margin concept itself was born well before this date. Thus the large-scale dissemination of marginalism occurred only after socialist economics had begun to make some headway into the appeal of classical economics, the latter perhaps lending itself more easily to socialistic reinterpretation than the more narrow and subjective neoclassical approach.

Regarding the impact of the marginal revolution in Russia specifically, this was certainly far less than its impact in many other regions of Western Europe, and delayed for some period of time. Its influence was not fully apparent until the 1890s and 1900s, when people like V.K. Dmitriev and M.I. Tugan-Baranovsky attempted to introduce some elements of marginalism to a Russian audience. Indeed in the 1870s it was Marx who received more attention in Russia than the margin. However the precise influence of Marx in Russia is again controversial, with a number of different interpretations of his importance being encountered. Marx himself was ambiguous about the future socialistic possibilities of the Russian situation, and hence competing currents claiming his guiding authority soon arose within Russian borders.

An 'economistic' interpretation of Marx's concept of the materialist conception of history, with Russia having to pass through strictly defined stages of evolution before capitalism was finally overcome, competed with a more 'voluntaristic' view of Marx's account of historical development, which allowed that Russia might jump across or skip parts of the journey to the communistic future. It was the voluntaristic view that the Bolsheviks would make use of after 1917, although before this date the Social Democratic position was less clear-cut. Some Russian socialists were very critical of the entire Marxist historical schema, and non-Marxian socialists were a significant if less vociferous element of the intellectual milieu in Tsarist Russia in the 1870s and 1880s.

Moreover it is wise to distinguish between Marx's economic theory of capitalist production – the law of the tendency of the rate of profit to fall, the concept of surplus value, reproduction schemes and so on – and Marx's theory of historical evolution – conflict between the forces and the relations of production, the various stages of societal development: feudalism, capitalism and then socialism. It was possible for a person to adhere to one of these strands in Marx without necessarily believing in the other, and the precise relation between the two was again the topic of some controversy. If capitalism itself was not yet fully developed within Russian borders, then the concepts designed by Marx to describe capitalist production would presumably not be fully applicable. What then were the appropriate theoretical concepts to describe the reality of the Russian economy at this time? Russian economic thinkers answered this question in various ways as partly outlined in what follows.

Classical economics in Russia

The propagation of some aspects of classical economics in Russia before 1870 was discussed in the previous chapter, but its diffusion continued to occur after this date. For example, in 1895, four years before V.I. Lenin's *The Development of Capitalism in Russia* was first published, a Russian edition of Adam Smith's *Theory of Moral Sentiments* was published in St Petersburg. This work opened with an acknowledgement of human motivations higher than self-interest, something that Marxist critics of Smith were sometimes reluctant to acknowledge. Following this, in his entry on Smith in the Russian *Encyclopedic Dictionary*, Tugan-Baranovsky pointed out that in *The Wealth of Nations* and *The Theory of Moral Sentiments* Smith had proceeded from feelings both of sympathy and egoism.[2] Regarding the ideological significance of Smith's work, Tugan-Baranovsky's evaluation was that:

> Smith was completely free from a conscious defence of the interests of the upper classes, the bourgeoisie or land owners, which characterised the social position of his pupils of recent times. On the contrary, in all cases when the interests of the workers and the capitalists come into conflict Smith energetically comes down on the side of the workers. Nevertheless the ideas of Smith were put to use in service of the bourgeoisie. In the irony of history is written the transitional character of Smith's epoch.[3]

This interpretation contrasted with other less positive appraisals of Smith's motivations by more deterministic Marxists like Lenin.

Russian government officials did not always receive Smith's works positively after 1870. On 5 January 1884 both *The Wealth of Nations* and *The Theory of Moral Sentiments* could be seen in a list of books that were to be banned from all reading rooms and public libraries in Russia.[4] This ban was probably short-lived and less than vigorously enforced, but it suggests that some uneasiness about Smith's ideas existed in Russia even before 1917. Smith was also the subject of various Russian biographical portraits, such as V.I. Yakovenko's *Adam Smith: His Life and Scientific Activity* published in St Petersburg in 1894. In general, *The Wealth of Nations* was reasonably well disseminated in Russia throughout the nineteenth century – a final one-volume edition being issued in 1895 – although opinion about its ultimate validity was split along predictable political lines.

As noted in the previous chapter, the dissemination and influence of David Ricardo's works in Russia was a special case within the classical group, as it did not begin to occur until the last quarter of the nineteenth century. N.I. Sieber undertook the first Russian translation of Ricardo's selected works that was published in Kiev in 1875, although a part of this edition had appeared previously in a periodical in 1873. The first separate

Russian translation of Ricardo's *Principles of Political Economy and Taxation* was published in Moscow in 1895. This was part of a series of books called 'The Libraries of the Economists', which also included translations of Malthus, J.S. Mill and Bentham.[5] The 1895 edition of Ricardo included a short introduction and a longer account of his life and works. Volume one of Ricardo's collected works, which contained the *Principles of Political Economy*, was published again in St Petersburg in 1908 under the editorship of D. Ryazanov.[6] A Russian edition of both Malthus and Ricardo's writings on rent was issued separately in 1908.

Russian dissemination of some of Mill's works was discussed previously, but continued to occur after 1870. For example, a Russian translation of Mill's account of *Utilitarianism* was printed at least three times in the period up to 1900, and his *Autobiography* was published in St Petersburg in 1874. Mill's works were popular as they presented to Russian readers a synthesis of classical ideas in codified form, as had been noted by Chernyshevsky. As explained previously, it was sometimes the case that classical economics was treated with more scepticism in Russia than it was in the West at this time. By this is meant that the political underpinnings of classical economics were more openly accepted as being so, and its philosophical foundations were treated with a little less reverence. This is perhaps due to the existence of various currents of socialist thinking in Russia at this time, but was also sometimes the case within government-related circles. Classical economics was certainly not dismissed as unimportant, but nor was it placed on an intellectual pedestal.

It is unquestionably true that, from within British classical economics, Smith had more influence in nineteenth century Russia than Ricardo. However, the suggestion that Ricardo's influence was negligible is not fully accurate if the mediated effect of Ricardo via Marx is considered.[7] Smith had a significant head start on Ricardo in that Smith's major works were published approximately four decades prior to those of Ricardo, and hence in one sense Smith's greater influence is hardly surprising. Also of interest were the particular elements of Smith and Ricardo that were taken up in the Russian context. Marxian thinkers focused on the labour theory of value in both Smith and Ricardo, whilst liberals adopted the free trade ideas of Smith alone. Ricardo's notion of comparative advantage was less frequently discussed, perhaps due in part to its rather analytical nature and also to the influence of historical school ideas in Russia. In general, classical economics found a critically appreciative audience in Russia who were often concerned with the issues being raised, but did not always agree with the conclusions that were usually drawn.

Historical political economy in Russia

Something that was perhaps more naturally at home within Russian borders than classical economics was historical political economy widely interpreted, as was prevalent in Germany at this time, and also developed by some Irish-born economists such as T.E. Cliffe-Leslie. Some key themes of the work of the German historical school have been identified as the importance of understanding historical specificity; an emphasis on socio-economic phenomena at the level of the national economy; and the use of a metaphor of a biological organism to explain economic life.[8] The idea of sequential stages of economic development was also very popular, as was an evolutionary conception of social change and an emphasis on descriptive empiricism.

The work of the German historical school was certainly well known amongst Russian economists and political theorists at the end of the nineteenth century. For example, a Russian translation of a Wilhelm Roscher work entitled *Principles of National Economy* was published in Moscow in 1860–62, and Russian versions of two separate Gustav Schmoller works on national economy and statistics were issued in 1873 and 1902 respectively. Moreover, as noted in the introduction, the links between Germany and Russia were strong in relation to personal connections and spatial proximity, the Baltic States serving as a geographical bridge through which both ideas and personnel could flow. There were also many similarities between the actual circumstances of the German and Russian economies, which were seen as being 'backward' and disorganised in comparison with the UK. Hence it might be thought natural that historical political economy could develop a strong presence within Russian borders, and Russian thinkers who have been identified as belonging to this category included I.K. Babst and A.I. Chuprov.[9]

I.K. Babst (1823–1881)

Ivan Kondratevich Babst was Professor of Political Economy first at Kazan University between 1851 and 1857 and then for a long period at Moscow University between 1857 and 1874. His theoretical works have been identified as attempting to combine the ideas of the classical political economists with those of the historical school.[10] According to Babst's most famous student he played a leading role in introducing the work of the historical school into Russia, even giving it the definite right of citizenship there.[11] Indeed in 1869 Chuprov took various examinations in political economy that had been set by Babst, one of which was concerned exclusively with the historical school and its main representatives.[12] Following Babst's death in 1881, Chuprov wrote of him:

> At Moscow University Babst expressed a new direction in political economy that had, owing to the works of Roscher, began to force for itself a place in Germany at this time. As a historian by education and a man with great knowledge of Russian life, Babst delivered the tasks of the historical school with particular sympathy – to explain the

> observed changes in general economics laws which occurred over place and time – and was equipped with all the means necessary for its fulfilment.[13]

Babst was thus attempting to follow Roscher's injunction that the purpose of history was to establish the laws of historical evolution.[14] Babst believed that the main cause of the economic backwardness of Russia was insufficient capital together with insufficient skills to utilise the existing capital in production. The reason for this capital insufficiency was partly that Russia lacked the security of labour and property given by a well-functioning administrative structure, Babst thus emphasising implicitly the importance of the institutional framework to promoting economic development.

In 1872 Babst published his *Exposition of the Principles of National Economy*, which demonstrated at least some influence of historical school principles. For example, expositing on the relation between specific and general interests, Babst wrote:

> Personal interest must be subordinate to the general good, but in what degree and what measure the egoism of individual people or economy is restrained and curbed by the carrier of the general good, i.e. the state, depends on particular historical conditions and relations.[15]

Babst also highlighted the importance of machine production to recent economic developments and emphasised the difference between the use of machinery and the use of artisan equipment, the former requiring the existence of significant quantities of capital.[16] This implied that the use of machines produced a very different economic structure than that which was naturally formed without them. It is apparent that Babst was at least very interested in the work of the German historical school and was influenced by them in an important way.

A.I. Chuprov (1842–1908)

Babst's most famous pupil, Alexandr Ivanovich Chuprov, was a very eminent Russian economist, lecturing on political economy at Moscow University and eventually becoming president of the Statistical Department of the Moscow Juridical Society. Chuprov had been sent to Germany as part of his education programme, returning to Russia in 1874, and thus he had first-hand experience of the home state of historical economics. In three 'Letters from South Germany' sent to the journal *The Russian Register* in 1873, Chuprov noted various similarities between living conditions in Bavaria and those in some regions of Russia, and suggested that it would be very difficult to identify another part of Western Europe where the conditions of economic life approximated so closely to those in Russia.

For example the climate, the percentage of the population occupied in agricultural activities and the extent of development of large-scale factory types of industry were all very similar in Bavaria to the way they were in the central regions of Russia.[17] Such a concern for regional particularities was a major concern of the historical approach, and in some of his first lectures Chuprov had characterised the historical school as being a middle way between the extremes of purely abstract economic analysis and the socialistic approach that placed politics centre stage.[18] In various other areas, Chuprov's analysis also echoed that of the historical school. For example in his early works Chuprov highlighted the importance of technical change to an understanding of economic phenomena. In 'On the Contemporary Significance and Tasks of Political Economy' of 1874, Chuprov suggested that in the previous decade the national economy had entered a new phase of development. He wrote:

> Thanks to the success of natural science. . . . Beginning from the end of the last century there has continuously occurred a series of inventions that have gradually replaced manual labour by machines, leaving for humans only the role of leader of the mechanism. The introduction of machines brings essential changes in the existing economic order.[19]

This process resulted in the further development of the division of labour and hence produced significant increases in labour productivity.

One element of Chuprov's thinking with evolutionary overtones was his views on legal institutions. Chuprov acknowledged that for Marx legal institutions were the direct consequence of economic relations, being part of the superstructure of society that was determined by its economic base. For Chuprov however, the economic life of humanity was by contrast the result of legal institutions, and hence he directly contradicted the Marxist conception of the relation between base and superstructure.[20] In his textbook *History of Political Economy* Chuprov noted that the idea of a close connection between economics and law was a central tenet of the historical approach. Here Chuprov also stressed the importance of Auguste Comte's holistic view of society as a complex organism, all components of which were in constant interrelation, to the creation of historical economics in the second quarter of the nineteenth century. The idea that an economy could only be truly understood in terms of its dependence on all other aspects of national life was thus of central importance, as were the ideas of constant change and the relativity of economic systems.[21]

Another element of Chuprov's thinking with historical school connotations was his enthusiasm for the development of statistics in Russia. He defined the task of statistics as being to compose the large mass of facts describing phenomena observed in society in systematic quantitative expression and with the help of a special method, in order to elucidate the laws that underlay them and to determine the causes of their provocation.[22] He outlined that the successes achieved by economic statistics in

Russia in the previous quarter of a century were huge, for example the formation of a Central Statistical Committee in 1863, which competed with government departments in providing statistical data. Chuprov believed that statistics was particularly important because a careful acquaintance with the facts of economic life was a necessary condition for the elaboration of expedient norms for civil rights.[23]

One component of Chuprov's work with an institutional affinity was his emphasis on the importance of knowledge to economic development. For Chuprov, European history demonstrated the fundamental importance of intellect to the structure of human life. In an article of 1892 investigating 'Knowledge and National Wealth' Chuprov wrote:

> The closest application for the production of wealth is so-called technical knowledge ... with the help of which occurs reforming items of the external world for human aims. The composition of industry at every given moment is determined by the existing level of technical knowledge in society; humans exploit nature in direct proportion to their knowledge of it.[24]

Chuprov suggested that progress in technical knowledge was observed in two main directions. Firstly in the gradual opening up of new ways to influence the forces of nature, and secondly by inventing new tools and improving the existing tools that were used in the production process. Chuprov listed some examples of economically important new inventions such as the telegraph, the telephone, galvanisation, electrical illumination and the chemical extraction of paint, and stressed the importance of theoretical work in enabling them to occur. Moreover in true institutional style he pointed out the role of tradition in propagating economically useful knowledge over many centuries.[25]

The crucial function of education in the economy was analysed in detail by Chuprov. For example the expenditure of many Western European governments on technical schools was noted, with such special schools being used in Sweden to assist in developing dairy farms and in South Germany to encourage small artisan production. In Russia, schools specialising in dairy affairs had been constructed in the district of Tver'. He concluded that the single best method for struggling with poverty was increasing labour productivity, which in turn could best be achieved through improved knowledge and education.[26]

In a more philosophical vein in 1900 Chuprov published an account of 'The Role of the Individual in Society' that ruminated on the role of individual initiative in the progression of social movements. He suggested that the conditions of place and time established boundaries for the actions of individuals and set the tasks that individuals were required to provide solutions for. In many cases the range of possible answers were extensive and hence individual initiative was required in selecting the right solution, for example in the case of the various options for the requisite transformation of small-scale farming in Russia.[27] With respect to the linking of scholarly research with policy proposals it has been suggested that Chuprov attempted to emulate the work of the German *Verein fur Sozialpolitik*, this connection being designed to improve the living conditions of the Russian people.[28]

Other elements of Chuprov's work are also worth considering. For example, he wrote on small credit institutions in Russia such as the association (*tovarishchestvo*), emphasising that the most important condition for the success of such bodies was the correct coordination of their connectivity. Success was most likely when credit associations acted within a limited regional locality, as in such conditions the creditworthiness of loan seekers could be more accurately estimated. Some difficulties could also be overcome by cooperating with larger institutions that had already pooled their resources. Chuprov suggested that there were up to 700 credit and savings associations and around 500 rural banks in Russia, but invariably such institutions were isolated and suffered from capital deficiency. Non-coordination of activity was thus a serious hindrance to success.[29]

From this presentation of a number of elements of Chuprov's work it is possible to conclude that historical political economy was a major component of his work, perhaps even that he could be classified as a historical political economist, the leading representative of the Russian historical school in Moscow. The influence of German economics in Russia in the period 1870 to 1890 was thus extensive. It was perhaps the most sustained impact of the three Western European traditions in the second half of the nineteenth century – that of Britain, France and Germany – conditioned in part by the fact that the Russian economy itself was most comparable to that of Germany in terms of its empirical historical situation.

Marxist economics in Russia

It is necessary to first undertake some terminological clarifications with respect to the import of Marxist economics into Russia. Marx had made a distinction between what he called 'scientific' political economy (e.g. Smith and Ricardo) and 'vulgar' political economy (e.g. Say and McCulloch). In the former, objective concerns with the truth were said to be paramount, but these concerns were distorted by non-conscious elements such as social position; whereas in the latter, political economy was seen solely as the naked ideological expression of the interests of the ruling class. This distinction was applied mainly in a chronological sense, with the early representatives of classical economics being characterised as 'scientific', the later representatives as 'vulgar'. I.I. Rubin dated the disintegration of the classical school at the middle of the nineteenth century, when class contradictions became much more intense.[30]

To give the early representatives of economics some credence was vitally necessary for Marx, as he had tried to connect his account of value theory directly with that of Ricardo in particular. Dismissing all classical economics as simply the uncovered ideological expression of class interests would have thus been problematic. Another term sometimes used by Marxists was 'bourgeois' economics, meant to refer to political economy written from the perspective of capitalists, either classical or (sometime later) neoclassical and Keynesian. Hence 'bourgeois' economics could be either 'scientific' or 'vulgar'. Of course, these distinctions do not always hold the same meaning today and are useful as a textual guide to understanding the historical context in which they were created and utilised.

G.V. Plekhanov (1856–1918)

G.V. Plekhanov, often cited as the 'father' of Russian Marxism, made a significant contribution to establishing the type of socialist political economy that was prevalent in Russia in the 1880s. His own term for his political position was Social Democrat, which was a term for Marxian socialists prevalent at this time. Plekhanov had written an introduction to a Russian edition of *The Communist Manifesto* in 1882, which he also translated, where he argued that the tasks of Russian socialists differed essentially from the tasks of those in the West. The first task was actually to accomplish the 'bourgeois' revolution, which would be followed only after a significant period of time by the socialist revolution, an idea that some had characterised as 'economistic', i.e. as making political goals subordinate to economic development considerations.

In 1881 Plekhanov published an article on 'New Directions in the Field of Political Economy', which was a detailed survey of recent developments written from a socialist perspective. For example whilst characterising Ricardo's works as the point of culmination of classical political economy, Plekhanov was keen to demonstrate the indifferent attitude of the classical economists to the plight of the working class. Ricardo had set the natural price of labour at that level which was necessary for the supply to workers of means of subsistence for them and their family without growth or diminution, and Richard Cantillon had limited the number of supported offspring to two.[31] The implication was that this was a rather inhuman attitude to take with respect to living beings.

Plekhanov also discussed the work of Friedrich List and the German historical school in detail. He paid particular attention to List's idea of the stages of industrial development that every country had apparently to go through, this being particularly relevant in the Russian context. Beginning with the predominance of agriculture in the country under consideration, manufactured goods were first imported from overseas in exchange for the export of agricultural produce. From such imports the country in question first obtained the means for independent industrial activity. Local industry then began to make products for satisfying domestic markets, and foreign imports were then unnecessary in this respect. Finally, the export of industrial goods started, in association with the import of raw material products, and the country under review had made the transition from the first to the last stage of industrial development.

Moreover, according to Plekhanov, a series of changes to trade policy went along with the various stages of development as follows: unhindered free trade was at first a suitable policy, enabling the exchange of domestic agricultural goods with wealthy industrial states; then the government of the country in question would gradually introduce protective tariffs, in order to give growing national industry a boost on world markets. As domestic industry became firmly established, a return to non-intervention was the required policy.[32] Thus for List trade policy was dependent on the stage of economic development that had been reached in any given country, something that was again especially relevant to Russia, but which went against the classical teachings on this question.

Plekhanov was keen to point out that at the basis of what he called the Smith–Ricardo school of political economy was the idea that every individual pursuing their own enrichment improved the welfare of all members of the nation, what was called the egoistic principle. Plekhanov accepted that this was partially correct, but in addition he specified other principles that also played a part in human conduct, namely the social spirit, which was expressed in the family, the commune and the state.[33] Hence the notion that only egoistic aims were pursued was inaccurate. Plekhanov also argued that:

> [the workers'] share of production is only that amount absolutely necessary to maintain their lives and the reproduction of their race. But the capitalists are continuously and inevitably striving to reduce even these indispensable expenditures, which constitutes the workers' wages.[34]

This 'minimum survival level' conception of the determination of workers' wages was part of the Social Democratic canon in economic theory at this time, although it was not accepted uncritically by all socialists.

In 1884 Plekhanov published a much longer and more influential work entitled *Our Differences*, which gave a detailed analysis of the economic structure of Russia from a Marxian perspective. Plekhanov's basic position was that capitalism was successfully developing in Russia at this time, and that appeals to romanticised conceptions of rural life were not helpful in promoting socialist political goals. In the chapter on 'capitalism in Russia', Plekhanov documented how capitalism was ousting independent producers and creating an army of workers, with large-scale private production continuously increasing and a growing import of foreign capital. In particular, the growth of credit institutions and the expansion of the railways were enabling capitalist development in Russia, with an expansion of the domestic market occurring in association with the opening up of some overseas markets.[35] Hence the *narodnik* notion that capitalism was fundamentally alien to Russian culture was simply inaccurate.

In terms of the position of the village community in the Russian countryside, Plekhanov outlined that it was being undermined both by the development of commodity production and through the influence of the state. Economic inequality within the village community was rife, with those at both ends of the village divide desiring the replacement of the commune by a family and inheritance system. Such inequality tended to lengthen the period of allotment (i.e. to delay the re-allotment of land), which in turn caused further inequality. Moreover the introduction of improved methods of agriculture would further accelerate the disintegration of the commune.[36] Plekhanov concluded that the true tasks of Russian socialists was to build a party of the working class, as communism could not grow out of peasant socialism.

Plekhanov's analysis of ongoing trends in the Russian economy had an underlying political motivation, in that it was directed primarily against the views of his *narodnik* opponents. Plekhanov's account could be questioned for downplaying the stability of the village community and exaggerating the success of capitalist development, points that were presented extensively by his adversaries and which are discussed in more detail in section IV of this chapter. Plekhanov's analysis might also be contrasted with the late Marx's positive view of Russian communal potential.

N.I. Sieber (Ziber) (1844–1888)

One of the most significant interpreters of Marx's economic ideas in Russia was N.I. Sieber. His most important works were *David Ricardo's Theory of Value and Capital in Connection with the Latest Contributions and Interpretations* of 1871, later revised as *David Ricardo and Karl Marx and their Social-Economic Investigations* of 1885, and *Studies in Primitive Economic Culture* of 1881. The aim of the latter was to conduct a comparative review of the known material on the structure of economic organisation, and also to investigate the institutional laws of various primitive peoples (so-called). Sieber also wrote a number of economics-related articles, for example on J.S. Mill, on factory laws in Russia and on the history of the peasant commune, as well as defending Marx's economics against some of its Russian critics.

In terms of Sieber's pure economic theory, he claimed that the value of a commodity was nothing other than the labour materialised within it, and hence he advocated a version of the labour theory of value. The unit of measurement of labour was said to be simple average labour, which itself varied by country and cultural epoch, but that in a given society was fixed.[37] Marx's distinction between labour and labour power was expounded by Sieber, but he claimed that Marx's method was actually that of the English school, i.e. a deductive approach. Sieber located the historical origin of the exchange of commodities at the geographical boundaries between different tribal communities, where the bartering of products first facilitated inter-community contact.[38] Marx himself was somewhat favourably disposed to Sieber's account of the Marxian schema, describing it as an 'excellent work' at least with respect to the theoretical standpoint, but other Russian Marxists such as Plekhanov and (sometime later) Lenin showed little concern for Sieber's faithful exposition. Russian Marxists did not readily acknowledge the late Marx's communal sympathies.

Narodnik economics in Russia

Much of Plekhanov's economic efforts were devoted to a critical evaluation of his major opponents in this area, the *narodniki*, sometimes translated as 'populists', but the term also had a nationalistic overtone. In general terms the *narodniki* were in part inspired by French socialists such as Henri Saint–Simon, although the economic component of their work had a more uniquely Russian character. The two most significant *narodniki* in the economic field were V.P. Vorontsov (1847–1918), who wrote under the pen name of 'V.V.', and N.F. Danielson (1844–1918), who wrote under the pen name of 'Nikolai-on'. In general terms the *narodniki* argued that the development of capitalism in Russia would be impossible to fully accomplish due to the underconsumptionist bias of capital, a feature that could only be overcome through external sources of demand. In the case of Russia, foreign markets were already saturated from the exports of more developed states, and hence Russia could not generate enough domestic demand to create a 'mature' form of capitalism within its own borders.[39]

Such arguments were in part based on empirical scholarship, but were also in part politically inspired, as the *narodniki* desperately wanted Russia to retain its traditional communal forms of agriculture, against the individualistic forms they believed were promoted by capitalism. Hence, Vorontsov supported the peasant commune and the *artel* as superior types of economic organisation, whilst in part conceding that they might in some instances be less efficient that their capitalist counterparts. Vorontsov's alternative to capitalist development in Russia involved the nationalisation of large-scale industry and the state subsidy of *arteli*, cooperatives and communes, and the introduction of new technology through cooperatives and small-scale industry.[40] For Marxists like Plekhanov and Lenin, such notions were romanticised fantasies based on a rose-tinted evaluation of indigenous Russian traditions, and an inaccurate evaluation of the unstoppable force of capitalist progression.

Other important *narodniki* of indirect relevance to economic affairs included P.L. Lavrov (1823–1900), P.N. Tkachev (1844–1885) and N.K. Mikhailovsky (1842–1904). Two of these three individuals have been charged with authoring two of the three founding documents of the *narodnik* movement, Lavrov's *Historical Letters*, which contained a conscience-stricken assault on 'progress', and Mikhailovsky's article 'What is Progress?', which distinguished between social progress and individual improvement, the two being seen as diametrically opposed.[41] Bervi–Flerovsky's *Condition of the Working Class in Russia*, discussed in the previous chapter, was given as the third such originating work.

Mikhailovsky was primarily a sociologist and philosopher, but his work had much significance for economic thinking widely considered, as he defined the task of sociology as being to relate objective wealth to subjective happiness in consumption. He attached particular importance to the effect of the division of labour, considering its physiological, social and economic aspects, and he believed that the latter two types of division could produce the atrophy of human characteristics. The task of devising forms of economic cooperation that safeguarded the integrity of the individual was thus of great importance to Mikhailovsky's approach.

Lavrov was born into a family of wealthy landowners, but became a radical intellectual who wrote on philosophical, sociological and economic concerns together. For example he defined sociology as being concerned with individual solidarity and cooperation, and set out three types of solidarity as follows: unconscious solidarity related to custom and necessity; emotional solidarity based on impulses; and conscious solidarity related to rational goals.[42] In general, the work of the *narodniki* demonstrated an underlying concern for a holistic view of political, social and economic development in which strictly economic concerns were seen as being inextricably linked to those of many other realms of human activity. In one sense they were reactionary, deploring the effect of economic progress on human welfare, but they did have a positive programme for future improvements, even if it was based on a longing for a return to an idealised past.

Ministers of Finance

A number of different Russian Ministers of Finance held office in the period from 1870 to 1890. The following section will examine N.Kh. Bunge's tenure in more detail, but before Bunge assumed the position in 1881, M.K. Reuturn had been Minister, and after Bunge left office in 1886, I.A. Vyshnegradsky occupied the post. Both Bunge and Vyshnegradsky were scholars as well as statesmen, providing an important bridge between academic economics and governmental affairs in Russia at this time.

Reuturn's period in office was characterised by his efforts to promote the development of private credit institutions and to stabilise the ruble, and also to develop a single state budget. His approach to foreign trade policy was to reduce export duties and to develop a free trade agenda, but the Russo-Turkish war of 1877–78 seriously affected his efforts to promote currency stability and marked the end of his period in office. Vyshnegradsky's tenure as Minister was noted for an attempt to restrain public expenditure, and for the partial relaxation of employment laws (under some pressure from manufacturing interests) that had first been implemented by Bunge. Vyshnegradsky was a director of a railway company with significant engineering knowledge, and he also endeavoured to accumulate a substantial state gold reserve aided by some favourable harvests.

Overall the various Russian Ministers of Finance in this period were often impressive figures with wide-ranging interests and a detailed knowledge of economic and management questions, the efforts of whom were sometimes affected by circumstances outside of their immediate control. Although Ministers of Finance were rarely sympathetic to the socialist cause, they were not always totally blind to issues of concern such as employment conditions, as was apparent from Bunge's efforts in this area.

N.Kh. Bunge (1823–1895)

Nicholai Khristianovich Bunge was Minister of Finance from 1881 to 1886. Prior to this he had been an academic, teaching economics in Kiev and obtaining a doctorate for work on credit theory. In 1870 Bunge published an account of *The Foundations of Political Economy* that contained a detailed discussion of the concept of property. Bunge explained that philosophers, political thinkers and economists had all striven to understand the notion of property, and consequently there were various different conceptions of its origins and nature. For example, juridical scholars explained property by means of law, Kant saw state ownership as the origin of all other types of property, for Hegel ownership involved people expressing their personalities through inanimate objects, for Hobbes property originated in the power of the state, for many socialists ownership was a form of illicit monopoly, and for Bastiat property was the result of human labour.

Out of these various conceptions, Bunge synthesised three basic approaches: property as seizure; as a declaration of law or social power; and as the rewards of labour. The relevance of all this was that, according to Bunge, the right of free individuals to own property in Russia was breached, or at least was dependent on social power or class structure to an unacceptable degree.[43] Hence the implication was that this situation required a remedy, and some of Bunge's economic policies as Minister were devoted to achieving this aim. Moreover Bunge was a conditional interventionist, believing that in assisting private business activity the government should base its policies on the following three principles:

1 Aid should be given to private concerns only when state interests required it.
2 Consumer-oriented businesses such as communications and harbours should be state controlled.

3 Private individuals should be granted a share in public economy when greater efficiency was the result.[44]

After his period in office was over, Bunge composed a memorandum discussing the problems that Russia had faced between 1881 and 1894, which throws some light onto the financial policies that he had pursued as Minister. Bunge divided measures designed to improve public well being that he had supported into two categories: those relating to public economy and those relating to finance. In the former category were the creation of a Peasant Bank and laws relating to factory work, in the latter category were the abolition of the poll tax and the extension of taxes to income not previously targeted. The goal of the creation of a Peasant Bank was to promote private property amongst the peasantry; the aim of factory legislation was to help protect the health of workers.

Regarding taxation, the correct system was said by Bunge to be one based on a combination of direct and indirect taxes that distributed the tax burden feasibly in relation to private income, and served to satisfy both personal and public needs. Additional measures deemed necessary in relation to direct taxation were:

1 Strengthening Russian colonisation in Siberia and Central Asia.
2 Introducing uniformity in land taxes.
3 Expanding the urban property tax.
4 Introducing a tax on urban dwellings.
5 Developing a property transfer tax.
6 Lowering peasant taxes.
7 Creating an insurance tax.
8 Improving patent dues.
9 Establishing a general income tax.

In general, Bunge called for a complete reform of financial administration in the future so that tax collection powers could be further strengthened.[45]

With respect to monetary policy, Bunge was set the task in a decree of 1st January 1881 of reducing the amount of credit notes (*kreditnykh biletov*) in circulation. In order to do this he recognised the necessity of restoring the circulation of metallic coins and allowing the rate of exchange between notes and coins to be freely determined. Over Bunge's period in office the amount of credit notes in circulation did indeed decline, from 1,133.5 million rubles in 1881 to 1,046.4 million in 1886, suggesting that his methods were at least partially successful in this respect.[46]

Various evaluations of Bunge's efforts as Minister have subsequently been made. In one account the Peasant Bank was deemed not particularly successful, since in its 11-year existence it had increased peasant land ownership by only 1.5 per cent. Bunge's efforts to reduce the burden of taxation on the peasantry were however deemed more successful, the overall burden falling by one quarter across his period in office. Much credit was also due to Bunge for involving the Ministry of Finance in improving Russia's railway system and in the passing of various factory laws limiting child labour.[47] In another evaluation Bunge was praised for taking steps to abolish the chronic budget deficit, which he did by both increasing revenue (through raising tariffs for example) and reducing the expenditure of certain ministries (war, maritime and ways of communication).[48]

Bunge himself rarely exhibited any left-leaning sympathies, indeed he wrote an account of the struggle with socialist ideas in which he suggested that socialism only arose whenever social discipline had lapsed and the wealth of others had become a heightened target for hateful desires. In this account Bunge also wrote of the positive effects of capital:

> There is not doubt that without monetary capital, humans could never have got out from a primitive state, and all that makes us proud of contemporary civilisation: knowledge, science, art, the use of the forces of nature – would then have been inaccessible.[49]

Bunge was thus an economic liberal in terms of supporting the development of an economy based on both property rights and private capital.

Conclusion

Russian economic discourse in the period 1870–1890 was certainly not as original analytically as the best economic thinking in the West at this time, but it still presented an impressive array of varied contributions, especially given the 'backward' nature of the Russian economic and political system at this time. There was a strong influence of historical school ideas applied in adapted form, the two historical economists presented in detail in this chapter – Babst and Chuprov – being by no means the only representatives of this current in Russia before 1890. Other theorists such as I.Kh. Ozerov and D.I. Mendeleev, discussed in detail further on in this book, also had strong sympathies with the historical approach.

In addition, the development of historical economics in this period occurred together with the further critical propagation of classical economics, the birth of Russian Marxism and the development of *narodnik* ideas. Some of these elements were combined in various eclectic forms, mediated by either the Russian social and political context or the admixture of indigenous intellectual traditions. Academic economics also affected some aspects of government policy through the efforts of Ministers of Finance like Bunge. In fact the two decades before 1890 laid much of the groundwork for the impressive flowering of Russian economics that occurred after this date, to which attention is now turned in detail.

4 Socialism and development in late Tsarism, 1890–1913

Some general developments in economic theory need to be highlighted for the period 1890–1913, before attention is focused mainly on Russia. The third volume of *Capital* finally appeared in 1894, containing Marx's solution to the transformation problem, or of the problem of how to get (in accounting terms) from values to prices. Many were disappointed with Marx's solution, which was that prices deviated from values so as to equalise the rate of profit across industrial branches. To some, this solution seemed to be just too convenient to be factually real, and criticisms came from many different directions. The 1890s also witnessed the further strengthening of the marginalist approach to economics that had been pioneered in Western Europe during the 1870s, which further eroded the classical foundations on which Marx had tried to build his oppositional system of political economy. Specifically, the labour theory of value was resolutely discarded in favour of a subjective utility approach.

Perhaps the single most immediately significant event in Western economics during this period was the publication of Alfred Marshall's *Principles of Economics* in 1890, which became the standard textbook account favoured for some time after. Other notable works from the 1890s were Irving Fisher's *Mathematical Investigations* of 1892, Knut Wicksell's *Interest and Prices* of 1898, J.B. Clark's *Distribution of Wealth* of 1899, and Thorstein Veblen's *Theory of the Leisure Class* of 1899. In the 1900s, Fisher's *Capital and Income* of 1906 and *Rate of Interest* of 1907 were very significant, whilst Rudolf Hilferding's *Finance Capital* of 1910 and J.M. Keynes's *Indian Currency and Finance* of 1913 were important mid-level landmarks. In some ways, this was a period dominated by lone intellectual giants who made important contributions to the foundations of economic theory separately, new ideas that would only be developed and integrated fully at a later date, and this phenomenon applied in some respects to Russia itself, as well as to Western Europe and America.

In direct opposition to the Marxist current headed by G.V. Plekhanov, a Russian edition of Eugene von Bohm-Bawerk's *Karl Marx and the Close of His System* appeared in 1897. In this work Bohm-Bawerk, a significant opponent of socialist ideas, argued that the most important flaw in the

Marxian system was that Marx had not deduced the fundamental principles of his system from factual investigation, but instead had used a formal dialectical method to create its underlying structure.[1] In the Russian context this criticism might be thought especially apt, as a key question turned out to be: how applicable was the Marxian schema to the semi-feudal economy of Russia? This question could only be finally resolved empirically, and works by various authors such as V.I. Lenin, P.B. Struve and M.I. Tugan-Baranovsky focused in part on answering it. The specific answers provided by various Russian economists during the period 1890–1913 will be examined in what follows, together with an account of their most significant contributions to economics generally.

The 1890s were a decade when revisionist Marxism made some definite headway in Russia, i.e. when some socialist thinkers began to question important parts of the Marxian theoretical schema, and also when concerns about national economic development achieved a new level of importance. Russian revisionists have been divided into two distinct currents. These were the Kantian revisionists, including Struve, S.N. Bulgakov and Tugan-Baranovsky, and the Nietzschean/Machist revisionists, including A.A. Bogdanov, V.A. Bazarov and A.V. Lunacharsky.[2] Both of these strands rejected the anti-individualism of Social-Democratic Marxism, but from rather different points of view. The Kantians promoted a return to the ethical foundations of socialism, whilst the Machians were more concerned with epistemological questions vis-à-vis the exalted status of class. In relation to economic theory, the Kantian revisionists made much more of a direct contribution before 1917, although Bazarov would become an important economic thinker in the 1920s. One significant expression of revisionist ideas in Russia of direct relevance to economics was Legal Marxism.

Legal Marxism

Legal Marxism is sometimes defined as being Marxist writings printed in legal publications, but it also referred to a distinction between those who pursued legal political activities as against those who lived 'underground', i.e. under the threat of arrest for illegal political acts. Over a period of time the term also acquired an ideological meaning in opposition to hard-line Social Democrats such as Lenin and Plekhanov. Philosophically, Legal Marxism can be seen as a broad church that encompassed various nuances of Marxian socialism including neo-Kantianism, Bernstein-inspired reformist elements and purely academic concerns.

In terms of its economic content, theorists such as Tugan-Baranovsky, Struve and Bulgakov are usually identified as central representatives of Legal Marxism, although the range of interests pursued by these people was not limited to solely economic concerns. Other important members of the group can be given as N.A. Berdyaev and S.L. Frank. In fact, even the range of strictly economics-related topics investigated by these individuals was significant – including business cycles, the theory of value and epochs of societal development – and hence the term 'Legal Marxism' lacked exact precision in relation to the categorisation of purely economic theories.

In terms of the abstract foundations of economic theory, one very significant theme pursued by some Legal Marxists was a synthesis of the labour theory of value with the new marginal utility approach that had become popular in the West. Both Tugan-Baranovsky and Frank pursued this goal at length, with Tugan-Baranovsky's 1890 article being one of the very first papers published on marginalist economics in Russia. Frank attempted the combination by proposing the notion of a labour theory of real or absolute value, as against exchange value; absolute value originated from the organisation of the economy or from its technical-psychological element. Labour value was thus social subjective value, which although playing no role in actual production or distribution, still had real psychological meaning.[3] In terms of explaining actual exchange relations Frank wrote that:

> the exchange value of the product … is determined by the capacity of producers to seize a greater or lesser part of the social income for their own use, in other words, by the relative *power* possessed by individual members of society in the struggle for distribution.[4]

This quasi-institutionalist conception of exchange relations in capitalism was obviously a significant departure from Marx's labour theory of value, which in Frank's schema became only a philosophical ideal to be accomplished by socialist politicians. Frank was however only a relatively minor figure compared to Tugan-Baranovsky, who should be regarded as Russia's leading pre-revolutionary economist.

M.I. Tugan-Baranovsky (1865–1919)

Tugan-Baranovsky was born on 8th January 1865 in the village of Solenoe, near Kharkov in the Ukraine. He attended high school in Kiev and Kharkov and enrolled at the age of 19 in Kharkov University. In 1889 he married Lydia Karlova Davydova, the daughter of the director of the St Petersburg Conservatoire. Through this marriage, Tugan-Baranovsky came into contact with intellectual circles in St Petersburg. After obtaining a Master's degree from Moscow University in 1894 he began his academic career by being appointed as *privat-dotsent* at St Petersburg University in 1895. He also had a civil service career that lasted for almost five years. At the start of 1893 he was employed in the Department of Trade and Manufacture in the Ministry of Finance, this appointment lasting until his resignation in October 1897.

When his first wife died in 1900 this had a great effect on Tugan-Baranovsky's life, triggering a crisis of confidence in orthodox Marxist theory. In 1902 he married his second wife Olha Fedorivna Rusinova, the daughter of aristocratic friends from Poltava province in the Ukraine. Tugan-Baranovsky accepted the post of Minister of Finance in the Ukrainian central Rada in August 1917, but vacated this post soon after in December 1917. During 1918 he helped to establish the Ukrainian Academy of Science in Kiev. He died of a heart attack in January 1919 while on a train on his way to the Paris Peace Conference.

Tugan-Baranovsky and business cycle analysis

In terms of mainstream economic theory, Tugan-Baranovsky's most significant contribution was made to the further development of business cycle analysis.[5] His most important work in this field was entitled *Industrial Crises in Contemporary England, Their Causes and Immediate Influence on National Life*.[6] This book was first published in 1894 in Russian, and while a German edition was issued in 1901 and a French edition in 1913, a complete English edition has yet to appear. A substantially revised second Russian edition was published in 1900 with the title *Industrial Crises: Studies in the Social History of England*, and a final revised edition was published in 1914 with the title *Periodic Industrial Crises: A History of English Crises and a General Theory of Crises*. This book was important not only within Russia, contributing significantly to the debate over the precise form of the development of capitalism, but it also influenced Western macroeconomic theorists such as Keynes, Dennis Robertson and Michael Kalecki.

One of the key features of the empirical aspect of *Industrial Crises* was Tugan-Baranovsky's concern to demonstrate that (in modern terminology) policy regimes created the framework for particular forms of cyclical patterns to occur. He divided the economic history of England into various sub-periods that set the environment for the manner in which cyclical tendencies were manifested. Tugan-Baranovsky's periodisation for the nineteenth century was as follows: before 1820; 1820–50; 1850–70; and 1870–98: these sub-periods corresponded to definite epochs in the history of cycle typology. For example while crises had occurred in the nineteenth century before 1823 – in 1811, 1815 and 1818 – this type of crisis belonged to those of the eighteenth century, which had exogenous causes of a political character. Crises after 1823 had mainly endogenous causes.[7]

Some examples of this approach to specifying policy frameworks can be given as follows. According to Tugan-Baranovsky, the history of trade policy in England between 1820 and 1850 represented an uninterrupted series of concessions to the principle of free trade, which culminated in the repeal of the Corn Laws in 1846. The subsequent period of 1851–70 was an epoch of free trade, with a large increase in English foreign trade. The second half of the 1870s saw the beginnings of the relative decline of English industry, which led to an absence of large-scale volatility in the level of economic activity between 1871 and 1898. The first decade of the twentieth century was characterised by an easing of the amplitude of industrial crises.[8] With respect to monetary policy regimes, Tugan-Baranovsky highlighted changes made in 1844 to the reserve requirements of the Bank of England – Robert Peel's Bank Act – and the effect this had on efforts to control financial crises.

Another crucial element of *Industrial Crises* was Tugan-Baranovsky's in-depth analysis of the sequence of events pertaining to specific crises that had affected the English economy in the nineteenth century. Such analyses were provided in relation to the 1825, 1836, 1847, 1857, 1864 and 1866 crises. Of key significance for explaining industrial crises according to Tugan-Baranovsky were movements in the level of gold bullion in the Bank of England. His account of the 1825 crisis in this respect was as follows. At the start of the 1820s English trade was in stagnation and the loan market was overcrowded with capital. The level of bullion in the Bank of England had grown from £3.6 million in 1819 to £12.7 million in 1823, causing a continuous decline in the interest rate. The jolt that led to revival was the opening up of new markets in America: in 1824 and 1825 many new cotton factories had been constructed in Manchester which exported cotton fabric to Central and South America.[9]

In addition to his empirical description of the development of cycles, Tugan-Baranovsky provided an analysis of various types of economic crisis in an entry to a multi-volume *Encyclopedic Dictionary*. He divided them into three main types: monetary, credit and trade-industrial crises, with a special sub-category for agricultural crises (this division being based on the particular field of circulation that was affected). Monetary crises were characterised by an insufficient supply of cash in relation to the requirements of circulation. Credit crises were characterised by a rapid decline in the availability of credit, while industrial crises were characterised by a general disruption (*rasstroistvo*) of industry and trade in consequence of an excess of the supply of goods over demand. In general, Tugan-Baranovsky's analysis of the empirical progression of business cycles was a pioneering contribution that pushed the boundaries of the topic in a number of important areas.

Tugan-Baranovsky's theoretical explanation of crises

A number of separate themes reoccurred in Tugan-Baranovsky's theoretical explanation of crises that were not always fully integrated. The first theme was disproportion between various branches of the economy, most notably means of consumption and capital goods. As the driving force behind capitalism was the reproduction of capital on an ever-expanding scale, pressure was constantly applied to increase productive capacity.

However in order that production be realised in sales, proportionate distribution of production between branches of the economy must be obtained. But as capitalism lacked any mechanism for harmonising total production with consumption, it created a continuous tendency towards overproduction, which expressed itself in a difficulty in finding markets for goods.[10] In certain instances this difficulty became acute and an industrial crisis would result. It was this aspect of Tugan-Baranovsky's explanation that has led to the label 'disproportionality' being attached to his approach and which the often-encountered reproduction schemes were intended to portray.

Another crucial aspect of Tugan-Baranovsky's explanation of crises, what might be called the second theme, was the concept of 'free loanable capital' or 'free monetary capital' (*svobodnyi denezhnyi kapital*). Tugan-Baranovsky wrote that free money capital or latent purchasing power was 'that which is lying in the bank in the form of a deposit and is not spent by the bank for discounting notes'.[11] Wilhelm Ropke interpreted Tugan-Baranovsky in this sense, noting that 'a storing up of money capital can take place by way of savings being accumulated as bank deposits instead of being invested in securities'.[12] Tugan-Baranovsky suggested that the accumulation of free capital could be visualised as steam in the cylinder of a steam engine: when the pressure of the steam attained a certain level, the resistance of the piston was overcome and it was set in motion, before returning again to its original position when the steam was exhausted.[13] This mechanistic analogy for the use of free capital was taken up by Tugan-Baranovsky's continental successors such as Spiethoff and Gottfried Haberler.[14] Wesley Mitchell suggested that Tugan-Baranovsky's scarcity of capital approach was 'most in favor among business men'.[15]

An additional clue to Tugan-Baranovsky's conception of free loanable capital was found in an article that he published in 1916 entitled 'The Significance of Exchanges in the Contemporary Economic Order'. Here he argued that the stock exchange was the essential institution of capitalist economy. This was because capitalism created a huge quantity of free capital that could not be used in those units in which it had arisen. Banks were one type of institution where such capital was stored, in the form of short-term deposits. However, an institution for the distribution of free capital was required which mediated the supply and demand for it from organisations and individuals: this was the stock exchange. As banks were reservoirs in which capital requiring temporary investment was accumulated, the stock exchange was a reservoir in which capital requiring permanent investment was concentrated. Thanks to the stock exchange it became possible to merge many small amounts of capital into the large mass required in capitalism.[16]

A third theme in Tugan-Baranovsky's explanation of cycles was maldistribution of income, or the lack of sufficient purchasing power among certain classes of the population. While he believed that crises were provoked by changes in the formation and consumption of capital, the underlying cause was the poverty of people, or the low level of consumption of the working classes. Proportional distribution of production was a problem only because production was driven solely by profit, not by genuine need. Since profit accrued only to capitalists, this allowed the link between production and consumption to be severed, out of which the possibility of crises arose.[17] It was the first and third aspects of Tugan-Baranovsky's approach to cycles – disproportion and maldistribution – that were highlighted by later Marxists, in particular in relation to Tugan-Baranovsky's development of Marx's reproduction schemes. For example Rosa Luxemburg mocked the implication that if social production was proportionally organised then there would be no limit to the expansion of the market, or 'production thus creates its own demand'.[18] That this was only a partial view of Tugan-Baranovsky's overall contribution to trade cycle analysis is apparent.

Evaluating the account thus far, in one sense there is a contradiction between Tugan-Baranovsky's empirical account of the progress of crises and his theoretical explanation(s) of them. The latter involved quasi-Marxist notions such as 'disproportionality' and 'maldistribution' that were not fully integrated into the empirical description of actual crises, but which did however employ the concept of 'free loanable capital'. This contradiction arose in part because of Tugan-Baranovsky's attempt to synthesize existing elements of cycle analysis from disparate sources such as British classical economics and Russian Marxism. Writing on the question of Tugan-Baranovsky's account of cycle periodicity, S.A. Pervushin noted:

> Here the author sharply breaks with the abstract-deductive and social-organic method, which he used to explain the basic cause of crises, and transfers to a purely statistical and individualistic method to analyse the factual history of crises.[19]

The implication was that this shift was unwarranted, or at least unsubstantiated.

The immediate influence of Tugan-Baranovsky's work on business cycles was in all likelihood felt more outside of Russia than within, at least in terms of the lasting significance of such influence. The French and German editions of *Industrial Crises* ensured that it was soon accessible across Western Europe and beyond, being quoted by economists as diverse as Keynes, Veblen, Robertson and Hayek. In the West it was Robertson, who had reviewed Tugan-Baranovsky's book in the *Economic Journal*, who used it most of all, although not without some criticism: Keynes followed on from Robertson's account. In Russia it laid the general groundwork for some later cycle analyses provided by Kondratiev and Pervushin. However, no specific economist followed Tugan-Baranovsky's overall approach in any detail; rather only selective use was made of his eclectic combination of elements. Within Russia it was certainly the subject of much heated debate, but this discussion was somewhat more insular in nature, focusing on its relevance to Russia in particular rather than to explaining trade cycles in general. After all, the book was on the face of it at least about cyclical movements in England, not Russia.

Tugan-Baranovsky and economic methodology

Tugan-Baranovsky is best known today for his work on business cycles (and the history of the Russian factory), but he also wrote on many other topics.[20] For example in 1908 he published an article entitled 'The Methodology of Political Economy' in the journal *Education*, in which he discussed the basic aims of economic science, something of relevance to establishing his underlying approach.[21] He began by distinguishing between two fundamental tasks of political economy – description (the first stage) and explanation (the second stage). Description (*opisanie*) involved cognition of the factual particulars of the phenomena under investigation; explanation (*ob"yasnenie*) involved uncovering causal laws. Tugan-Baranovsky wrote of the first stage:

> The scientific description of the world of phenomena must, from this point of view, give as it were a cast (*slepok*) of the external, objective world. The more exactly this cast reproduces all the complexity of the world, the better this scientific description is, the ideal of which is achieved when we fix in our understanding all the empirical richness of the world.[22]

However Tugan-Baranovsky admitted that science could never achieve this goal because nature was infinitely diverse, and consequently the attempt to understand nature by reflecting it fully in human consciousness was impossible. The method used to overcome this problem was to ignore the large number of individual phenomena and construct a logical system of classes and sub-classes, or a system of generic types of phenomena.[23]

The possibility of finding a universal point of reference for economics was clear, given that an approach which cancelled out competing social interests was indeed available: that of ethics. For Tugan-Baranovsky ethical philosophy recognised the morality of good and evil independent of particular group interests and hence offered the chance of achieving results of general significance. Moral consciousness could not be reduced to class interests in that moral approval consisted of recognising good for its own sake, independent of the material outcome for the person involved. Hence ethics gave the possibility of finding a foundation for a responsible economic science: Immanuel Kant's idea of the supreme value of the human individual.

Implicit in Tugan-Baranovsky's analysis was the idea that capitalism erred by treating workers simply as a way to produce commodities, rather than also being concerned with them as fully developed human beings. His favoured slogan for contemporary socialists was 'forward to the creation of a new theory of socialism', where both Kant and Marx were valuable but surpassed stages of thought.[24] Thus Tugan-Baranovsky rejected the class-based methodology of orthodox Marxism and turned instead to ethics to ground his socialist beliefs. How divergent this was from the Marxism of the time is apparent from the following passage written by Tugan-Baranovsky in a separate account of his philosophical views:

> Marxism and Kantianism are exceedingly ordered and complete logical systems ... recognising an extra-class moral is incompatible with the materialist conception of history and the with class point of view – since, if ethics are the same for all social classes ... this means that class interests do not play such a predominant role in social life.[25]

Consequently, the question arises of how best to categorise Tugan-Baranovsky's general approach to economic explanation. Was he only a Legal Marxist? In fact it might be more accurate to also place Tugan-Baranovsky within the historical current of political economy, given that his work contained historical, sociological, evolutionary, statistical and institutional elements, although they were not always unified in a harmonious fashion. From this characterisation Tugan-Baranovsky's work can more easily be situated alongside fellow contributors like A.I. Chuprov and I.Kh. Ozerov, although this does not mean that Tugan-Baranovsky should be excluded from the Legal Marxist family. In reality he straddled both camps, something that was not seen as unusual at least for Russian economic thinkers of the time.

P.B. Struve (1870–1944)

Subsequent to Tugan-Baranovsky, Struve was the next most significant economist in the Legal Marxist category. His work covered a number of different eras in Russian history, from Tsarism to post-1917 exile, and his later work as an émigré is discussed in Chapter 8. In terms of his political views, Struve was in the 1890s and 1900s a Legal Marxist revisionist who, like Tugan-Baranovsky, was sympathetic to the neo-Kantian philosophy of the day. After the revolutionary events of 1905, he moved rightwards and in 1920 he emigrated from the USSR, becoming a staunch critic of Soviet economic policies.

Struve's most significant work in economic theory was undoubtedly 'Economy and Price', the first publication of an incomplete version of which occurred in 1913. Part one of this work gave an account of economic and social structures and their various connections. Struve suggested that the economic relations of society could be organised in a number of different ways, highlighting three basic organisational types or economic structures. The first such structure was an aggregate of stationary economy, which was defined by the absence of significant contact between the constituent elements involved. The second was a system of interacting economy, in which all the individual elements were connected but still separate. The third was a system of social economy, where a subjective teleological unity united all elements into a single collective unit. In the first type of economic structure, autarky was at its highest level, whereas in the third type, the autonomy of economic subjects was at its least. An example of the first type was a natural economy, in which what little interaction that did occur was based on dominance and submission, whilst an example of the third type would (presumably) be communism.[26]

In addition to the three types of economic structure just outlined, an exceedingly diverse range of social structures could be identified. Struve believed that it was logically possible for various combinations of economic and social structures to occur, and that socialism as a social system was compatible with more than one economic structure. Distinction between social structures could be made according to the degree of prevalence of the principle of equality that was observed, i.e. the social structure was characterised by the relations of dominance and subordination between individual people. Various examples of collectivism such as peasant democracy and the feudal commune were given.[27]

Comparing Struve's work to that of some of his colleagues, it might reasonably be argued that Tugan-Baranovsky's work was more original and influential in terms of its theoretical content, especially in relation to its impact on mainstream economics in the West, but that Struve's influence was greater as an individual, with respect to the organisation and development of economic and political ideas in Russia in general. The other leading member of the Legal Marxist group was S.N. Bulgakov, who was less of an economist than either Struve or Tugan-Baranovsky, but was still an important figure of the day.

S.N. Bulgakov (1871–1944)

Bulgakov was the son of a priest, graduating from Moscow University in 1894 and becoming Professor of Political Economy in 1917. Between 1898 and 1900 he travelled extensively throughout Western Europe, gathering materials on the development of agriculture. Always critical of orthodox Marxism, Bulgakov abandoned it completely in the first years of the twentieth century, moving instead towards religious idealism. Central to Bulgakov's later philosophy was the idea that the world was an organic whole, and that mediating between the physical world and God was 'Sophia', or divine wisdom.

Even though he was perhaps better known as a philosopher and religious thinker, Bulgakov also made important contributions to political economy, most notably with respect to the philosophy of economics and Russian agriculture. For example, whilst Bulgakov was sympathetic to aspects of socialist doctrine, he was concerned to maintain a holistic view of social development. In *The History of Social Teachings in the Nineteenth Century* of 1913, he wrote:

> Socialism and individualism are not contradictory … socialism is only one aspect of the solution of the question of individualism. Socialism is in this sense a means for the realisation of individualism, but also limits individualism, because where individual rights end, the rights of society begin.[28]

The crucially important question of the relation of the part to the whole, or of the individual to society, was for Bulgakov common to all types of social theory and to all historical epochs.

In another work published in 1913, *Studies in the History of Economic Teachings*, Bulgakov ruminated in detail on the philosophy of economics or on what he called general economic worldviews (*mirovozrenii*). In particular, Bulgakov discussed the consequences of specialisation for people's life paths, given that the onus to select a life-long speciality was placed on individuals as early as in high school. While freely admitting that the dangers of dilettantism could only be avoided by having a definite and limited task in life, Bulgakov warned that the necessity of specialisation brought with it a very sensitive spiritual danger. This danger was of constricting spiritual horizons and of splitting the integrity of the human person into fragments. Bulgakov wrote:

> Between the Scylla of specialisation and the Charybdis of dilettantism stands a path that could unite the fullest specialised knowledge with a conscious relation to life and the special tasks of life. … Here is why … it is necessary to inquire not only about specific techniques of knowledge, but also about their higher meaning and the higher value. … Therefore together with the technical disciplines, school education must be provided in general and social-philosophical disciplines.[29]

According to Bulgakov, people invariably held a known philosophy of economy, i.e. a system of evaluation of the ideals and norms that were applied to economic life, and hence education in this area was very important. He contrasted very different systems of evaluation such as the contemporary Western European worldview and Eastern Buddhism.

In a work examining the basic concepts of political economy published in 1898, Bulgakov interpreted the topic from the point of view of the philosophy of economics. Like Marx, Bulgakov viewed capital as a social relation between producers arising from the ground of the social labour process. Capitalistic social relations were expressed in the particular structure of tools and materials of production, with capital itself encompassing the capacity to obtain profit.[30] Bulgakov also interpreted *Capital* itself as being primarily devoted to understanding social relations, the first volume investigating the social relations between capitalist and worker, the third volume investigating the social relations amongst various capitalists.

Bulgakov's major work on matters of rural economy was entitled *Capitalism and Agriculture*, and it was issued in two longish volumes. The conclusions provided in this work were that capitalist production was nowhere a purely national economy, but was already on the first steps to having an international character. Capitalism was world economy and could be fully comprehended only as such, the development of agriculture standing in exclusive dependence on international markets.

Bulgakov outlined that both capitalist and non-capitalist countries were connected by several important links. The first such link was international trade in a proprietary sense, the result of the international division of labour that was the natural consequence of growth. The particularity of this division was that all exchange was based on relations of equality between states.[31] The second link was that between one specific country and international exchange. According to Bulgakov, capitalist development involved a self-satisfying market, the ability to expand automatically alongside the continuing development of the division of labour. The necessity of a market external to the country in question meant that (in part) this automatic augmentation occurred overseas. Bulgakov wrote:

> It is easy to see why foreign markets play such a role in the early stages of capitalist development. Capitalist production is only instigated in countries with the dominance of natural economy; complex and multi-faceted capitalist production, itself composed from markets, would not yet be in prospect to create. The first branches of capitalist production (cotton, wool) in older states are necessarily exported.[32]

The third link related to the law of diminishing fertility of the soil, constituting a connection between a country's export of agricultural products and their imports. The dependence of a country on goods imported from other states related directly to the phenomena of the development of international capitalism.

In *Capitalism and Agriculture*, Bulgakov also passed some judgements on Marx's prognoses of the future. Marx had stated at one point that the natural concentration of production occurring within capitalism would lead inevitably to the transfer of the means of production from private to social control. Bulgakov explained that in fact the concentration of production was only one among many economic tendencies, including a decentralising tendency. In agriculture not only had no significant concentration been occurring, in fact the decentralising tendency was acting with strong force. Bulgakov wrote:

> Marx's mistake … is explained by his general social-philosophical worldview. … He considered it possible to measure and predetermine the future from the past and the present, whilst in reality every epoch supplies new facts and new forces of historical development. … Therefore, all prognoses of the future based on current data are inevitably false.[33]

Hence it is clear that Bulgakov did not share Marx's vision of post-capitalist development.

One of Bulgakov's most important works was *Philosophy of Economy: The World as Household*. Here Bulgakov outlined his general attitude to economic matters broadly conceived, with production and consumption being defined as the essential economic functions. Each economic age was for Bulgakov marked by its own defining spirit and specific type of person.[34] Moreover, the idea of wealth was itself an essentially contested concept, being defined arbitrarily and pragmatically, depending on the particular orientation adopted. Wealth might be defined as money, agricultural produce, the material products of all labour, or even everything that gave joy or was useful, with any one of these definitions being equally valid and equally arbitrary.[35] Human life encompassed the strive for economic freedom, or power over wealth and nature, with the individual urge to acquire wealth resulting in competition among individuals, groups, classes and nations, at least in the capitalist epoch.

Bulgakov suggested that, as conceived in the science of political economy, the individual existed only as an average specimen of a social type or class – capitalist or worker for example – and was only viewed as such in a set of social relations projected onto reality by collectives. In individual terms, no 'capitalists' or 'workers' actually existed as stylised types, only concrete subjects with unique personal histories and specific individual characters could actually be found. Bulgakov implied that the neglect by political economy of the individual personality and the consequent deterministic denial of freedom was a very significant error, as it was precisely the single individual that was the creative factor in economy broadly conceived.[36]

The outcome of the debate

The above account of aspects of the work of the Legal Marxists should be seen in counterpoint with the economic views of the *narodniki* and the Social Democratic Marxists discussed in the previous chapter. Rosa Luxemburg believed that the Legal Marxists had achieved a victory over the *narodniki* in terms of demonstrating the possibilities of Russian capitalist development, and also that the Marxist revisionists successfully demonstrated that the foundations of socialist theory had previously been frail and poorly constructed.[37] In reality, both of these apparent victories turned out to be Pyrrhic, in that the Social Democrats simply glossed over the superior arguments of the Legal Marxists with authoritarian assurance, and the *narodniki* still kept faith with their rather backward-looking utopia, despite any evidence that was mustered against them. As is sometimes the case, superior arguments were defeated by non-intellectual means, as they failed to chime with the self-interest of the most powerful political groups of the time.

National development

Since the time of Peter the Great, the development of the national economy was a goal of crucial significance for most leaders of the Russian state. This goal had a political and an economic motive, both in terms of maintaining Russia's status on the international stage, and also for improving the material conditions of the Russian population. The debate about how best to accomplish this general goal had taken many twists and turns in the nineteenth century in relation to poles of economic thinking such as free trade against protection, national isolation against integration and manufacturing against trade and commerce. Economic analysis of such issues was not lacking in the Russian context, which produced a rich tradition of consideration of the best means for encouraging national development.

D.I. Mendeleev (1834–1907)

Mendeleev is perhaps Russia's most famous natural scientist, and he came to the study of economic affairs through this scientific work. Born in Tobolsk, Siberia, Mendeleev's mother established a successful glass works after his father went blind, and at 16 years of age Mendeleev himself was sent to study chemistry in St Petersburg. After much careful work on topics such as the specific volumes of liquids and the determination of physical constants of compounds, he eventually became Professor of Chemistry at the St Petersburg Technological Institute in 1863.

It has recently been suggested that Mendeleev proposed an evolutionary economic model that was fundamentally opposed to emergent Marxist doctrine, a model instead based on the notion of the constant circulation of vital economic coordinators such as labour, statisticians, meter-sticks and capital throughout the Russian Empire. The aim of this model was to modernise the Empire gradually along a universal evolutionary path, eschewing the Marxian notion of conflict, using analogies between scientific concepts (for example the movements of gas molecules) and social and political structures such as scientific societies and agricultural unions.[38] As opposed to this general account, the various details of Mendeleev's industrial policies are examined in what follows.

Mendeleev's general analysis of industry

As early as 1863 Mendeleev had began the study of various aspects of the industrial development of Russia.[39] Initially his interest focused on specific branches of industry such as chemicals, petroleum, coal and metallurgy, these being branches where his natural scientific knowledge was obviously relevant. Out of this early interest, Mendeleev published works such as 'On the Contemporary Development of the Chemical Industry Applied to Russia' (1867) and 'Petroleum Affairs in Pennsylvania and the Caucasus' (1877). From the beginning of the 1880s Mendeleev's interests broadened and he began working on the more general topic of the origins of industry and on the economic development path best suited to Russia. As a result he published works such as 'On the Conditions of the Development of Factories in Russia' (1882) and 'Foundations of Manufacturing Industry' (1897).

Mendeleev came to believe profoundly in the strategic significance of heavy industry. He argued that a few basic types of industry were connected to a multitude of other industries and that without securing these basic types within the country, the development of other secondary branches would be unthinkable. These strategic types of industry were specified as being coal, iron, steel, metallic tools and machinery.[40] A summary of Mendeleev's general conception of industrial development can be found in 'Foundations of Manufacturing Industry' of 1897. Here he initially distinguished between various types of economic activity such as agriculture and hunting and various types of industry such as artisan industry (*remeslennaya*), mining industry (*gornaya promyshlennost*) and manufacturing industry (*fabrichno-zavodskaya promyshlennost*).[41] Analysing manufacturing industry in particular he concluded that:

1 Factories were the natural result of the development of industrial activity, being determined both by complex heterogeneous needs and the growth of scientific understanding.
2 The basic goal of manufacturing industry was to substitute animal products by vegetable, and vegetable products by mineral. This path for industry facilitated the liberation of people from the naturally existing inequalities that were created by various differences in the climate, soil and access to air, water and the oceans.
3 The contemporary significance of manufacturing industry was that it increased national income and enlightened the nation-state generally.
4 Manufacturing industry should capture ever wider fields of human activity.
5 In order to strengthen manufacturing industry and for the influence of

science on nature to prevail, all countries and peoples must aspire to participate in the progress of humanity.[42]

These five points marked out the position of manufacturing industry against all other types of industrial activity and suggested why for Mendeleev such industry needed to be vigorously fostered in Russia.

Overall, Mendeleev strongly supported the necessity of the capitalistic industrialisation of Russia based on machine production, and he continually emphasised the benefits of this process in terms of the increased welfare of the general population and the growth of education and culture that would result.[43] In order to assist this process Mendeleev advocated the establishment of special banks that could offer financial capital to industrialists at low rates of interest.[44] He believed that history taught that industrialisation had begun in the UK and the USA through state assistance, and in turn this general approach led Mendeleev to the idea of industrial protection.

Mendeleev and protectionism

The idea that protectionist policies were beneficial to Russian economic development permeated Mendeleev's voluminous writings on economic affairs, indeed it might be seen as the doctrinal bedrock on which they were based. Mendeleev simply did not countenance the notion that Russia at the end of the nineteenth century might have benefited from unfettered free trade, and the allegedly positive effects of protection were highlighted repeatedly in his works. A good general example of Mendeleev's doctrinal justification of protection, taken from a work entitled 'Explaining the Tariff' published in 1891, went as follows:

> Since in the majority of cases Russian requirements for foreign goods can be compensated for by products of Russian production, customs duties on foreign goods increases the possibility of the domestic production of the taxed good, and all increases in productivity inside the country provide wages and increase the weight of internal free circulation within our borders.[45]

Mendeleev clearly believed that indigenous Russian producers could and should match foreign producers in many cases.

Another example of Mendeleev's justification of protection was from a work published in 1893:

> The great increase in the home production of cotton goods, cast iron, coal, sugar, the products obtained from the treatment of petroleum ... coinciding with the temporary introduction of protective duties, clearly demonstrates the expediency of the application of the principles of protection with the object of rousing the people to strengthen

> those forms of industry to which the natural resources and forces of the country correspond.[46]

Note that, in this passage, Mendeleev saw protection as being conducted in harmony with natural factor endowments rather than against them, or of being the spark that ignited a dormant existing potential. This might easily be interpreted as the infant industry argument for protection. Mendeleev also believed that protection should be intricately connected to the overall state management of industrial growth. In an article from 1897 entitled 'The Justification of Protectionism' he wrote:

> the state has a duty to stimulate, promote and protect the industry and trade of its country by all possible means. ... Protectionism encompasses not only customs tariffs but all the totality of state measures favouring industry and trade.[47]

A mercantalist overtone might be detected in this approach, although Mendeleev explicitly rejected the mercantile desire for a country to accumulate gold.[48]

Mendeleev's argument for protection was historically as well as theoretically grounded, relying partly on K. Lodyzhensky's *History of the Russian Customs Tariff* of 1886 for support. Regarding the history of tariff policy in Russia Mendeleev outlined:

> From 1822 right up to 1850 and especially in 1867 the general plan remained the same: protectionism was obvious but not extreme, now and then it was provocative; prohibition of some imports was repealed but permitted goods were taxed on a large scale; export duties were reduced and then abandoned; all industries that began production were protected.[49]

Mendeleev explained that the customs duties adopted from 1857 to 1877 protected those branches of industry that transformed raw materials into finished goods, the tariff itself applying only to finished goods in this period. Consequently Russian mills and manufactures of the time had the character of finishing works only, turning foreign cast iron into iron rails, having received raw materials and semi-manufactured goods from overseas. The 1891 tariff however further extended protection to all kinds of minerals, for example to sulphur and pyrites, all sorts of ores, stones and coal. Mendeleev explicated:

> The present industrial policy of Russia is directed precisely to the end that the productive forces of the country should be turned to the manufacture of the abundant supplies of agricultural and mineral raw materials in the Empire.[50]

Thus Mendeleev implied that since tariffs had succeeded before 1891, their application should certainly be expanded.

On other occasions, Mendeleev's justification for protection involved comparison with the industrial development of other countries. At a meeting of the Anglo-Russian Literary Society in June 1894, Mendeleev gave a speech in which the idea that protection would be in the interests of Russia was reasoned as follows:

> The Professor [i.e. Mendeleev] pointed to the lessons of history, which show how other countries have been enriched. He considered that the laws which gave a monopoly to the English merchant-fleet, and other exclusive measures, had contributed two-and-a-half centuries ago … to strengthen the industrial and commercial power of this country.[51]

Thus Britain had used first interventionist policies to achieve its developed status, and only then did it turn to promoting the ideology of free trade. This was a standard 'free trade benefits only the wealthy' argument for protection. Even though Mendeleev's efforts to develop the Russian economy spanned across the last quarter of the nineteenth century, the height of his policy influence was certainly the 1891 tariff, the effects of which are still controversial today, with some industry benefiting, but at a definite cost to the consumer. Mendeleev's emphasis on developing heavy industry found an echo sometime later in the Stalinist period.

S.Yu. Witte (1849–1915)

In the 1890s the efforts of the modernising Russian Minister of Finance were also focused on encouraging national economic development, by means of generating confidence for overseas investors through the creation of a stable gold-backed currency. Witte's tenure as Minister lasted from 1892 to 1903, and in this period he implemented a programme of industrialisation that included significant levels of new railway construction, government subsidies to private businesses, and the strengthening of state finances. Witte had been a railway manager before becoming Minister of Finance and his first book published in 1883 was on railway freight tariffs. Although this volume was mainly a technical account of transport issues it also contained an analysis of the application of economic theories to the Russian situation, in particular the ideas of the German historical school.

Even more significantly, Witte published a pamphlet entitled *Concerning Nationalism: National Economy and Friedrich List* in which Witte followed List in suggesting that customs tariffs would encourage industrial development, something that both Mendeleev and Witte's predecessor (I.A. Vyshnegradsky) had concurred with. Witte also published his *Lectures on National and State Economy* and an account of the laws of governmental life. In the former, a universally relevant 'stages' account of economic development was provided, and various obstacles to Russian progress such as a lack of indigenous entrepreneurial initiative were listed.[52] Witte's programme for development was certainly successful, with rates of industrial growth increasing noticeably, but agricultural reform proved a much more difficult task.

Non-Marxian socialism

Whilst after 1917 it sometimes appeared that Marxism had played a dominant role in the radical intellectual environment of late Tsarism, in reality it was only one amongst many different varieties of socialism that had flourished in this period. There were anarchistic socialists, agrarian socialists, ethical socialists and romantic socialists, each of which had imparted their own particular spin on non-capitalist economic theory. A few of such non-Marxian currents are examined below.

Anarchistic economics

Anarchism was a separate branch of radical dissent in Russia before 1917, which contained some original economic criticisms and ideas not found in its Marxian cousin. One prominent example of an anarchistic thinker was P.A. Kropotkin (1842–1921), who was born into a noble family but who rejected his privileged background. One of his most controversial economic ideas was that designers of a new social order must seek to combine brain work with manual labour, i.e. they should promote the integration of various types of work rather than encourage the further specialised division of labour. Kropotkin wrote that:

> the greatest sum total of well-being can be obtained when a variety of agricultural, industrial and intellectual pursuits are combined … man shows his best when he is in a position to apply his usually-varied capacities to several pursuits in the farm, the workshop, the factory, the study or the studio, instead of being riveted for life to one of these pursuits only.[53]

Marx had expressed a similar notion through the phrase 'hunter, fisherman, shepherd and critic', but Kropotkin gave it a more prominent place in his mature theoretical system than Marx. For Marx it was the distant end-state of full communism, but for Kropotkin it was an immediate goal and first priority.

One way in which this integration of labour could happen was through each nation becoming a manufacturing nation and producing within its own borders all types of goods for domestic use. Another way was to reform the education of children to be much broader in scope. Kropotkin disputed the idea that specialisation was more economically efficient than the holistic integration of labour tasks, in that he argued that the effect of the division of labour on human welfare in a general sense was negative. Others aspects of Kropotkin's economic work included an emphasis on the role of mutual aid in social evolution and on creating a federative structure for future socialist society, and on the positive role of science in human progress. Anarchistic socialism was really the absolute opposite of Social Democracy, at least in its Leninist form, and was as a consequence completely ignored by the Bolsheviks after 1917.

E.E. Slutsky (1880–1948)

Within the non-Marxian current in Russian socialist thought, the idea of cooperatives was a popular and reoccurring theme. Cooperatives should however be clearly distinguished from the peasant commune, which was a different institution altogether. While the commune was a wholly rural form of economy, cooperatives could be either agricultural or industrial in nature. Economists as diverse as E.E. Slutsky and Tugan-Baranovsky were sometime captivated by this topic, and provided varying accounts of aspects of the cooperative movement as follows.

Slutsky is the Russian economist most often discussed by mainstream economists today for his landmark contributions to the theory of consumer behaviour and business-cycle analysis. His early statistical work is discussed in the next chapter, his account of random cycles in Chapter 7, and his work after the closure of the Conjuncture Institute in Chapter 8. However, in 1913 he wrote an article entitled 'The Essence of Cooperation and its Forms' in which he gave an analysis of types of cooperatives, the motivating drive of cooperatives, and the history of cooperatives in Russia and the West.[54] Slutsky's basic attitude was extremely positive. He stressed that cooperatives were a child of their time, and placed the origins of cooperation in the growth of trades and cities that occurred as rural overpopulation forced peasants to seek employment off the land. Increasingly, the mass of workers became concentrated into factories, artisans were compelled to exist in impoverished conditions, and peasants were also placed in a difficult position as their land was broken up on transfer from father to son.[55] In response to this process, a new force came into being which could, according to Slutsky, stand up against the forces of capital and fight for better conditions for the masses: this force was solidarity (*solidarnost'*).

The essence of cooperation for Slutsky was association (*tovarishchestva*). If several people voluntarily agreed to combine to form a farm, if several people combined their capital to form a trading association, or if a number of craftsmen combined their forces, then a cooperative association was created. Slutsky stressed that such associations could be exceedingly diverse in nature. In one association, participation was through individual labour, in another it was by capital. One association was formed for production, another for trade, a third for purchasing, and a fourth for credit. One association would be composed only of capitalists, another from artisans, a third from peasants, and a fourth from consumers.[56] The cooperative spirit was defined by Slutsky as the conscious aspiration to create an economic union not only in the interest of those individuals currently participating, but also in the interests of a wide circle of society, which helped to link the society together.

Slutsky analysed cooperatives by first focusing on their structure, which was determined by the following basic principles of operation:

1 Cooperatives were built on the principle of full equality of rights of all participants.
2 Membership was unlimited.
3 The aim of monetary profit was not pursued.
4 Competition was not encouraged.
5 The interests of all, not just the members, were protected.
6 Skills training was provided.

For Slutsky, point three was crucial, since the pursuit of individual gain served to corrupt solidarity rather than engender it.[57] Slutsky outlined five main types of cooperative: consumer societies, producer associations, credit associations, purchasing cooperatives, and associations for specific goods. In Russia the consumer movement was developing strongly, 4,767 consumer societies with half a million members being in existence in January 1911. Very successful in Russia was the development of credit associations, with a total of 4.5 million members in January 1912. Purchasing associations, however, were only weakly developed in Russia. Finally, associations for specific goods such as grain, dairy products, wine and so on had recently begun to develop in Russia.[58] Slutsky concluded by stressing that cooperative business had only just started to develop, but that it had achieved significant results. He confidently predicted that cooperatives would have a huge future, as they were beneficial to all.

Conclusion

During the period 1890–1913, political economy interpreted in a wide sense was a very significant component of social scientific discourse in Russia. Themes like the possibility of the growth of Russian capitalism, the best way to encourage industrial development, the significance of the peasant commune, and the nature of various forms of non-capitalist economy were debated in detail; but no decisive victory that was accepted by all participants in the fate of the capitalism debate was won by either side at any time before 1913.

In terms of the impact of Russian economics overseas, the work of

Tugan-Baranovsky was certainly influential in the West, although its full impact took some time to work itself through to the academic mainstream. Struve and Bulgakov had much less effect outside Russia. Kropotkin was influential in the UK as a result of his lecture tours and many English-language publications. In the next chapter, aspects of the development of more abstract economic theory in the period 1890 to 1913 will be examined, as a counterpoint to the varied currents of political economy just discussed.

5 Economic theory in late Tsarism, 1890–1913

It would be wrong to suggest that overtly political issues such as the destiny of Western capitalism continually dominated economic theory in Russia in the late Tsarist period. Other areas of interest such as mathematical economics and statistics also received much attention, and this chapter focuses on these more technical aspects of economic discourse in detail. Of course, the many varied issues in Russian political economy were not completely separate from those examined in this chapter, but the more analytical approach sometimes actively distanced itself from political issues, and this makes for a convenient point of subject demarcation.

Mathematical economics

In the West the pioneers of mathematical economics in this period were people like W.S. Jevons and Leon Walras, advocates of a marginal utility approach to understanding value, but it is of course possible to combine mathematical rigour with approaches other than that of the neoclassical school. In Russia at the end of the nineteenth century, pure mathematics in itself was a highly developed and important subject, with famous names like N. Lobachevsky (non-Euclidian geometry) and P.L. Chebyshev (probability theory) making key contributions to new developments. The economic and statistical use of mathematics might thus be thought a natural progression in the Russian context, and various individuals made this fruitful connection in a number of ways, as discussed below.

V.K. Dmitriev (1868–1913)

Born in Smolensk, Dmitriev had first studied medicine at Moscow University before transferring to political economy. His major work was the *Economic Essays on Value, Competition and Utility*, first published separately in 1898 and 1902. These essays explored various different topics such as David Ricardo's theories of value and rent, the theory of monopoly prices, Augustin Cournot's theory of competition, and the consequences of technical progress. They anticipated various later ideas such as Paul Samuelson's non-substitution theorem and Piero Sraffa's work on the composition of prices of production. Dmitriev has been called Russia's first mathematical economist and he was also interested in the historical evolution of neoclassical doctrine.

For example, Dmitriev emphasised that all the information that was needed for the construction of a complete theory of marginal utility was actually found in the work of F. Galiani, whose major work *Della Moneta* was published in 1750. Dmitriev quoted the following passage from Galiani:

> I understand that others say that a pound of bread is more useful than a pound of gold. My answer is: this is a disgraceful play of words, deriving from the lack of realisation that *more useful and less useful are relative notions*, and that they are measured according to the different conditions of individuals.[1]

This contextual conception of value – it depended on the specific circumstances of the individual evaluating the goods in question – meant that the use value of a commodity was not invariable, but dependent on many factors which changed over space and time. According to Dmitriev, very little that was new was provided by the Austrian school, although Galiani's theory went unnoticed by most in the classical school.[2]

Another component of Dmitriev's analysis of the concept of marginal utility was his conviction that existing psychophysical laws borrowed from psychology could not provide a general foundation for marginalist doctrine. For example, the law of logarithmic relation between stimulus and sensation could not be used, as it could apply only to the utility curves of products whose consumption (and not merely use) arose from their effect on external sense organs. This meant for Dmitriev that it was possible to establish only that, as the quantity of a product obtained increased, the utility of the next unit declined, but that this relationship was different for each good.[3]

Perhaps one of the most famous elements in Dmitriev's essays was the argument that unrestricted free competition tended to raise production costs above their essential level, that is above the lowest possible level for any given state of technique. According to Dmitriev, in the competitive battle for sales, accumulating stocks of commodities played the same role as a military arms race between opposing powers did during peacetime. Under free competition, the non-productive expenditure on commodity storage was higher than under monopoly, due to the need for competing producers to maintain significant levels of dead stock, in fear of others stepping in and gaining market share. Hence free competition (at least as modelled by neoclassical theory) had additional economic costs in terms of wasted output, excess inventories and also in redundant advertising.[4] Through this analysis Dmitriev undermined the idea that unfettered competition ensured greatest productivity.

Dmitriev's work on calculating expended labour was taken up by economists in the Soviet period with regards to input-output tables, although Dmitrev himself died before 1917. His approach was also relevant to explaining periodic crises, which were seen as the result of the accumulation of too high a level of dead stock.

N.N. Shaposhnikov (1878–?)

The economist following most closely in Dmitriev's footsteps was Nikolai Nikolaevich Shaposhnikov. Shaposhnikov was born in 1878 and enrolled in the juridical faculty of Moscow University in 1901. In the second half of the 1900s he was posted overseas for two-and-a-half years, and after returning to Russia in 1910 he became a senior lecturer (*dotsent*) at the Petrograd Political Institute and then worked in the Moscow Communal Institute.[5] He understood some German and was described as a 'good organiser of scientific activities', as being 'authoritative', and as maintaining good relations with colleagues.[6] His most significant work from a policy perspective was conducted in Kondratiev's Conjuncture Institute in the 1920s, where he provided methods for the calculation of effective capital investment scenarios.

One source stated that the exact date of Shaposhnikov's death was unknown, suggesting that he perished in the purges of 1937–38. It described him as a specialist in the field of value and distribution, a typical 'bourgeois' Russian economist who attempted to synthesise the labour theory of value with marginal utility. In the theory of distribution he propagated the approach of John Bates Clark, considering that the marginal labourer determined wages. Shaposhnikov's methodology was described as 'eclectic', although his work on foreign trade was described as 'of significant scientific value'.[7] In this chapter, Shaposhnikov's work only up until 1914 will be discussed, as his work during the war will be briefly considered in the next chapter.

Shaposhnikov's early work

Shaposhnikov's first economic article was 'Free Competition and Commodity Prices' of 1905. He published a study of *Bohm-Bawerk's Theory of Profit* in St Petersburg a year later, and a study of *The Teachings of Thunen on Natural Wages* in Yaroslavl in 1909. He also wrote a general analysis of new developments in economics called *The Theory of Value and Distribution*, and in 1914 he wrote a study of *The First Russian Economist-Mathematician V.K. Dmitriev*.[8] Shaposhnikov was very interested in recent developments in Western economic theory and also in the Russian tradition of mathematical economics. In 1917 he published a translation of a paper by Frank Taussig on socialism, adding his own thoughts on capitalism to the finished work.[9]

The First Russian Economist-Mathematician V.K. Dmitriev was written in September 1913 for the memorial meeting in honour of Dmitriev held by the Chuprov society. Shaposhnikov began by stressing that for Dmitriev, exchange value depended on subjective as well as objective factors. Conditions of consumption (subjective) determined the demand for a good, whilst the conditions of production (objective) determined the supply.[10] Thus for Dmitriev, the theory of costs of production and the theory of marginal utility were not mutually exclusive as theories of value, rather they were complementary. Shaposhnikov noted that although at the beginning of the twentieth century this view was not widely held in Russia, it was prevalent in many foreign states, and hence Dmitriev's approach was not completely original.

Dmitriev had asserted that cost of production always depended on consumption conditions and the utility of the good traded. Moreover, not knowing the level of demand for a good meant that its price could not be determined. According to Shaposhnikov this was the first original feature of Dmitriev's work. Dmitriev was concerned to show that even in the case of constant costs of production, knowledge of the conditions of demand were necessary for determining price. Shaposhnikov outlined this point as follows. It was usually assumed that there was one case when price would be determined independently from demand, that case being constant costs of production despite changes in the level of production. Since with constant costs, no changes in demand could be reflected in changes to costs of production, there could not be any influence on price. In such conditions price was determined solely by the objective conditions of production. Shaposhnikov showed how Dmitriev rejected this reasoning as follows.[11]

It was often believed that competition acted to reduce prices to the level of costs of production. Dmitriev argued that this idea was incorrect. Instead of prices falling to the level of necessary costs, costs of production actually rose to the level of prices. Competition, like all forms of struggle, created a series of non-productive outlays which were inevitable and which served to increase production costs, and which left every producer with a supply of unrealised goods. The price of goods must take this unproductive outlay into account. Hence Dmitriev had shown how prices could not be determined independently from demand under any set of conditions.[12] For Shaposhnikov this was a key element of Dmitriev's contribution to economic theory, which clearly had implications for any notion that an economic system based on competition was optimally efficient. Shaposhnikov concluded that in the history of economic thought, Dmitriev had a secure and honourable place.

Statistical theory

As noted in the introduction, both the theory of statistics and statistical description were highly developed fields in the late Tsarist period. The development of Russian statistics was a long and complicated story in itself, the more theoretical aspects of which might be out of place in this book, and hence only a brief selection of some aspects of this topic is presented here. Of most immediate relevance to economics in this period was the statistical work of A.A. Chuprov and E.E. Slutsky. Slutsky's work eventually overlapped many thematic areas and periods of time – pre-revolutionary, Bolshevik and Stalinist – but he is presented in this section as a statistical theorist. A.A. Chuprov was the son of A.I. Chuprov, who was discussed in detail in Chapter 3.

A.A. Chuprov (1874–1926)

Alexander Alexandrovich Chuprov graduated from Moscow University in 1896 with a thesis on probability and statistics, and then headed for Germany in order to study political economy. From 1897–1901 he was a student of L. Bortkiewicz and G.F. Knapp, then in 1902 he became a member of the St Petersburg Polytechnic Institute where he taught statistics. In 1917 he left Russia, never to return. In terms of the work itself, Chuprov made important contributions to the theories of sampling and of dispersion, laying the groundwork for a stochastic conception of statistical theory that employed the law of large numbers, which would be built upon by subsequent Russian mathematicians like Slutsky.

For Chuprov, a characteristic feature of human thought in the epoch at the end of the nineteenth century and the beginning of the twentieth was the striving to give knowledge a statistical form in relation to collective phenomena. For example, the statistical point of view rejected the exclusive focus on individual events and instead considered the overall outcome of many different actions. Questions of balancing supply and demand over a broad range of the division of labour, the numerical balance between the sexes and the frequency of births and deaths were, according to Chuprov, matters best comprehended through the law of large numbers. Thus Chuprov promoted a 'macro' view of the outcome of human behaviour through statistical analysis. Connecting this to physics, the introduction of the statistical point of view had changed everything, since processes were now conceived of in a probabilistic sense, rather than in an absolute one, Chuprov implying that this approach might also be relevant to other subjects of academic inquiry.

Slutsky's early statistical work

Slutsky's initial academic interest and training was squarely in the fields of mathematics and statistics, but as a consequence of a significant period of time spent overseas (in Munich) between 1902 and 1905, Slutsky became interested in economics, or more specifically in the application of mathematical and statistical concepts to economic theory. Consequently, as a

Table 5.1 Slutsky's main publications, 1912–1916

Year	*Publication Title*	*Subject*
1912	*The Theory of Correlation* (a book)	Statistics
1913	'The essence of cooperation and its forms'	Political economy
1914	'An essay on the economic views of William Petty'	History of economics
1914	'On the criterion of goodness of fit of the regression line and on the best method of fitting them to the data'	Statistics
1915	'On the theory of the budget of the consumer'	Economics
1916	'On a mistake in the use of the formula of the theory of correlation'	Statistics
1916	Review of a book by A.A. Kaufman	Statistics

student at the University of Kiev in 1911 he wrote a paper on 'The Theory of Marginal Utility'. His first book, published in 1912, focused on correlation analysis, but he was also pursuing research of direct relevance to economics at this time, such as that on cooperatives as discussed in Chapter 4. Table 5.1 lists Slutsky's main publications between 1912 and 1916.

This demonstrated that Slutsky originally came to economics topics from statistical origins, and suggested that even before 1917 statistics was interconnected with economics in Russia in an important way. A biographical article explained that:

> Whilst still a student, Slutsky decided not to be limited to the area of purely theoretical construction, and thought to write works on the eight-hour working day. He studied factory accounts deeply, established links with factories, and studied the production and labour conditions of workers. Having obtained various data on factories, Slutsky distributed the injuries obtained in manufacture according to the hours in the working day, and established a dependence of the degree of fatigue of workers.[13]

Slutsky was thus a pioneer in terms of applying statistical concepts to economics-related concerns, an approach that he would continue to pursue in various original ways in the 1920s and even later in the 1930s.

Moreover, Slutsky actively participated in debates about the methodology of statistics that occurred in Russia at this time. For example, some participants in this debate (such as A.A. Chuprov) argued that statistics was quite separate from mathematics, in that statistics had its own separate tasks and its own separate methods. The focus of statistical analysis in this view should always be concrete investigation, and in this sense the tasks of statistics contradicted those of mathematics. Slutsky disagreed with this position fundamentally, arguing instead that statistics must be at heart a mathematical science, i.e. it must be a science where the mathematical method played an essential role. For Slutsky the limits of probability theory did not depend on the concrete structure of reality, but instead on a formal structure on the one hand and on the tasks that such a theory had to solve on the other.[14] As well as being relevant to the 1927 paper on business cycle (discussed in Chapter 7), Slutsky's mathematical work was also important regarding the later development of econometrics.

Public finance

Public finance was a very important topic within the general economics remit in the late Tsarist period, given the scale of the Russian national budget and the various attempts at encouraging economic development that had occurred throughout the nineteenth century. Within the field of public finance, various individuals specialised in certain branches of the subject, for example Ozerov on taxation and Migulin on monetary and banking policy. This section discusses aspects of their work of relevance to both economic theory and policy, being in no sense an exhaustive account of this topic.

P.P. Migulin (1870–?)

Petr Petrovich Migulin was a money, banking and finance specialist whose work invariably contained a major historical component. After studying law at Kharkov University and then teaching at this institution he worked in various government-related posts such as in the Russian Ministry of Finance. Although Migulin was by no means a socialist sympathiser, Russian financial policy was nearly always discussed by him in historical perspective, as well as in comparison with the financial history of other countries. For example in 1899 he published a book entitled *Russian State Credit, 1769–1899*, which bore the subtitle 'Experiences of a historical-critical review'. Quoting P.A. Storch's work on the history of Russian monetary units, Migulin documented how the Russian budget deficit had increased from 12.1 million rubles in 1787 to 29.1 million in 1790, partly as a consequence of war. This led to a subsequent fall in the exchange rate of recently issued banknotes from 97 for 100 in 1787 to as low as 68.5 for 100 in 1795.[15] Migulin also published a book on *The Economic Growth of the Russian State, 1613–1912* that examined a very broad sweep of economic development over three centuries.

Migulin wrote a great deal of analysis on policy-related questions, publishing books such as *The Reform of Monetary Circulation in Russia and Industrial Crises, 1893–1902* in 1902 and *Our Banking Policy, 1729–1903* in 1904. Both of these works were highly detailed accounts of the history of Russian financial policy in the periods specified, with major concern for highlighting potential improvements in the policies discussed. Moreover Migulin campaigned actively for the proposals he supported both in print and though his government-related activities. For example in 1909 he published an article 'In Defence of Russian Finances' in which he argued that attacks on the state of Russian finances were misplaced, given that while some sources of state revenue had in the past been renounced, these had been adequately replaced by others.[16]

Also in 1909 Migulin published an article on 'Necessary Reform of the State Bank', where he discussed various reform options such as making the State Bank independent of the Ministry of Finance, converting it into a joint-stock bank and increasing the basic capital on which it was founded. Migulin pointed out that almost all countries in the world had a national central emission bank, the primary task of which was to regulate monetary circulation. He argued that the State Bank as it existed in Russia was in fact not owned and controlled by the state, but instead by the government, and hence it did not always show adequate leadership in matters relating to the arrangement of commercial credit. What existed in Russia was a commercial state bank, rather than a central emission bank, which served private individuals and institutions first and foremost. Migulin also suggested that the experience of Western Europe demonstrated that only a bank which was independent and autonomous and which acted in strict conformity with its statutes could effectively reduce the cost of credit.

As a result of this analysis, Migulin recommended that the State Bank should be clearly separated from the Ministry of Finance, which could be accomplished by transferring regulatory rights to a special Supreme Observation Committee that held responsibility for drafting a new set of statutory regulations.[17] The new State Bank should be primarily a central emission bank concerned first of all with the regulation of monetary circulation. It should have the right to issue its own paper currency in the form of bank notes, i.e. currency of the State Bank rather than state credit notes, and small gold coinage should be withdrawn from circulation. As in Western Europe and America, gold should be held only in bank vaults. Migulin's work demonstrates that liberal economics had a definite presence within Russian borders before 1913, and also that socialists did not have a monopoly on using historical analysis as support for their economic policy proposals.

I.Kh. Ozerov (1869–)

Ivan Khristoforovich Ozerov was head of the department of financial law at Moscow University where he specialised in analysing the tax systems of England and Germany. Ozerov's courses on public finance were characterised by the close coordination of general financial problems with the more concrete questions relating to taxes, tariffs, budgets, state credit and so on. Their connection to the task of developing the Russian national economy was also emphasised, and specific problems were illustrated with concrete material on Russia and other states.[18] In theoretical terms,

Ozerov was eclectic, combining the standard financial authorities with ideas from the subjectivist school of Friedrich Wieser and Carl Menger, the historical approach of Wilhelm Roscher and Werner Sombart, and various ethical concerns, without much concern for the purity of the mix.

An example of Ozerov's social and historical approach to public finance could be found in his 1898 work *Income Tax in England*, which bore the subtitle 'The economic and social conditions of its existence'. Here Ozerov wrote:

> All systems of taxation reflect on the social structure on which they are built, as the geological structure tracks the life of its epoch, and as geology can establish from what remains the living conditions of the past, so the history of the tax system can be read as a sign imprinted by the tax structure of a given country.[19]

Examining the history of land taxation in England for example, Ozerov saw the replacement of feudal privileges with indirect taxes and consequently the imprint of class conflict. In another case, the introduction of income taxes, a struggle was provoked in which arguments against the imposition of such a tax – it would cause the emigration of capital and the disruption of industry and so on – were deployed not from the point of view of objective logic, but were created *ad hoc*, solely from the position of defending particular group interests.[20] This structural conception of the development of the tax system and its associated ideology was clearly of historical school inspiration.

In his textbook *Foundations of Public Finance*, Ozerov gave a short account of how the work of the historical school influenced the study of financial matters, for example the concerns of the historical school with legal conduct and financial law were highlighted. Adolph Wagner, an important member of the younger German historical school, had nominated four factors influencing the development of the tax system. The first was the organisation of the economy and property rights, the second was political structure, the third was economic groupings, and the fourth was social groups, especially the relation between those who owned property and those who did not. Ozerov could be interpreted as using aspects of this approach in his study of the tax history of England discussed previously. Moreover, Ozerov explained that Wagner divided the financial history of states into two periods. The first was when countries were dominated by purely fiscal concerns, tax being viewed as only a tool for collecting state income. The second was when countries were dominated by socio-political concerns, in which the societal function of taxation was a major concern.

In general, Ozerov highlighted how the historical school viewed financial institutions not merely as the mechanical legacy of various legal acts, but as developing in close connection with all economic, political, legal and other circumstances.[21] Ozerov and Migulin displayed representative contrasts as to the nature of public finance in Russian economics at this time, with Ozerov taking a historical school approach and Migulin a more mainstream liberal attitude.

The theory of markets

In the Marxian context, the question of the development of markets was important in relation to deciding to what extent capitalism could actually develop in Russia, a topic that was central to the debate between the Legal Marxists and the *narodniki* covered in Chapters 3 and 4. For example, in 1893 V.I. Lenin had written:

> the concept 'market' is quite inseparable from the concept of the social division of labour. . . . The 'market' arises where and to the extent that the social division of labour and commodity production appear.[22]

In this sense of the term, the spatial extent and prior conditions of capitalist markets were being considered, but there were other quite distinct conceptions of markets that were also being investigated in Russia at the end of the nineteenth century, for example by talented young economists such as W.S. Woytinsky.

W.S. Woytinsky (1885–1960)

Woytinsky was born in St Petersburg and went on to read law at St Petersburg University, although his first book *Market and Prices: The Theory of Consumption, Market and Market Prices* published in 1906 was actually written whilst the author was still at high school. This work has been described by some as 'respectable but unremarkable' except for its schoolboy authorship.[23] In fact it was in some respects quite original, particularly in the general method adopted and in the anti-essentialist approach to neoclassicism that underpinned it. Woytinsky sent the unpublished manuscript to Tugan-Baranovsky, who penned an enthusiastic introduction that praised the author for grounding his theoretical abstractions in historical soil.

In methodological terms, Woytinsky used some elements of the psychological approach of the marginal utility school, but rejected the idea of a single universal guiding spirit of self-interest. Instead of this, each specific economic grouping was said to have particular characteristic motivations, which were dependent on place, time and economic system for validity. Hence Woytinsky tried to make the psychological approach more empirically orientated by combining both the psychological and historical methodologies into a unified historico-psychological framework.[24]

In *Market and Prices*, Woytinsky analysed innovatively the structure of markets. He proposed a cellular structure, defining markets as being composed of many individual shops, each with a given circle of buyers. Every shop together with its circle of buyers was defined as a cell of the market, with the system of market cells changing over time. In selecting a market cell to operate within, a consumer was guided by various different considerations such as cheapness of goods, comfort of shopping, utility differences of products, prestige of use, ethics of purchasing and so on. In analysing the structure of market cells, the distance from consumer to store was very important, but others factors played a role in defining market borders, given that differences between stores were common.[25] Another idea proposed was that of the market ladder, in which a good moved from producer to consumer through a whole line of intermediaries such as the primary retail market and the primary wholesale market.

Woytinsky outlined very different motivating drives for merchants and consumers in a capitalist system, in line with his idea of specifying characteristic motivations for various groups. The merchant was seen as an individualist solely concerned with obtaining profit, and such people viewed both commodities and their buyers only as a means of acquiring additional money. The consumer, on the other hand, was seen as a hedonist, with money being viewed by them only as a means of satisfying specific life-enhancing desires.[26] From this perspective, the merchant knew no passions except the love of accumulating money, whilst the consumer was only satisfied by spending money on goods and services, although it should be noted that Woytinsky appeared to derive these categorisations from common everyday perceptions rather than from detailed scrutiny of the groups concerned.

Furthermore, Woytinsky suggested that in fact goods were not sold in 'the market' in abstract terms, but in concrete stores, and hence what should be analysed by economists was store prices and not market prices. Individual dealers established store prices themselves, and the most advantageous price level was the one that obtained maximum proceeds for all the stock of a given commodity, i.e. that at which the demand for a good in the particular cell was just met by the supply in the warehouse. Prices differed among stores because strict proportionality between the supply of a good in each store and its share as a percentage of total sales was impossible.[27] There existed no perfect market that corresponded to the abstract model of pure competition.

One particularly original feature of Woytinsky's analysis was a stress on the importance of fashion and advertising in determining economic behaviour, a feature that might be interpreted institutionally. For example, a change in fashion favourable to a particular good was said to raise demand and hence price for the given good, but also reduced the prices of some other related goods. Woytinsky believed that the price of a good changed in direct proportion to the impact of advertising and fashion, and hence prices were subject to constant manipulation.[28] Successful advertising enabled dealers to raise store prices, and a favourable impact of fashion on consumer sentiment forced some additional customers to buy the good in question. Fashion and advertising could be subjectively ruinous to the psychology of the consumer in that some desires were not satisfied due to individual budget restrictions, which made consumers feel poorer as a result.[29] Thus Woytinsky believed that some advertising and fashion had negative consequences by raising the marginal utility of certain goods and forcing a reduction in expenditure on other goods.

After the revolutionary events of 1905, Woytinsky became politicised and joined the Bolsheviks for a period, but after 1917 he fled to Georgia and then to Germany. Whilst his writings after 1920 were extensive, they were usually much more empirically orientated than his high school effort, which appears today to be rather fresh, at least in comparison with some abstract neoclassical ideas of the period.

Conclusion

Considering the accounts presented in chapters 4 and 5 together, economic discourse in Russia during the period 1890–1913 was extremely rich and diverse, with historical, socialist, liberal and conservative thinkers all contributing in various ways to new developments. Sometimes the distinctions between particular currents appeared less rigid and clear-cut at the time than perhaps they would in retrospect. The detached hardening of currents was something that was boosted by 1917. Of course there were many heated debates over specific questions within and between the various different currents, but the philosophical underpinnings of the competing views were perhaps a little less distinct than they would later become.

This was in part due to the fact that in Russia the neoclassical approach did not gain the academic dominance that it did in the West at this time, and perhaps also because some Russian economists were open to a range of possible influences, regardless of apparent ideological origin. A few were even open to changing their fundamental beliefs as well. The October revolution in 1917 was a divisive event for economics, as it was for Russia as a whole. It also made coexistence and mutual respect between opposing views more difficult to maintain. But what made 1917 possible was the outbreak of war, which had serious consequences for economic theory in general, as will be seen in the next chapter.

6 Interregnum – the Russian economic mind at war, 1914–1917

The causes of the First World War were various, but economic factors certainly played a major role in triggering the outbreak of the first widespread international conflict in modern times. Imperialistic rivalry had a multitude of political, social and economic dimensions, despite the Marxian notion that the economic base determined everything above it in the societal superstructure, and the Russian Empire was unquestionably a major player in the territorial machinations that led to war. Tsar Nicholas II had been somewhat ill equipped to helm the Russian state, especially at a time of national emergency, and the effects of the war on almost every aspect of Russian life were enormous.

One such aspect was the financial health of the country, which had been making good progress since the successful introduction of the gold standard in 1897, but which suffered a serious decline after 1914. The tradition of money, banking and finance in Russian economics before 1917 was not inconsiderable, with figures like P.P. Migulin and I.Kh. Ozerov making notable contributions to various aspects of financial analysis. However, academic experts were not always consulted or heeded by government officials, although sometimes they were employed with respect to specific issues of immediate concern. One such issue, the First World War, would test the theoretical mettle of Russian economists to the limit in an arena of international debate, a development that signalled a new era of intellectual relations across Europe and beyond.

Russian war finance

In the UK, economists like J.M. Keynes were in 1914 quickly co-opted into providing advice to the British government on urgent policy matters such as war finance, whilst in Russia, academic economists like M.I. Tugan-Baranovsky provided salient commentary from a respectful distance. The Russian Minister of Finance from the beginning of the war to the February revolution, P.L. Bark, attempted valiantly to defend the Russian position in difficult negotiations amongst the Allies – Russia, the UK and France – but the cards were sometimes stacked against the

Russian case. The consequences of the financial measures taken to fund the war were particularly heavy in Russia, with cover of the paper ruble by national gold reserves falling dramatically from just over 100 per cent at the start of the war to around 6 per cent in October 1917. In response to this dramatic situation, various Russian economists discussed policy-relevant aspects of the war as follows.

Migulin wrote a significant amount on currency policy and the State Bank in this period. For example in April 1915 he explained how the war had greatly constrained the Russian government, forcing it to extend the emission rights of the State Bank and also to suspend the exchange of credit notes for gold. A law of 27 July 1914 allowed the State Bank to issue notes up to a value of 1,200 million rubles, this entirely changing the character of the original law of 29 August 1897, which had specified that credit notes were to be issued by the State Bank on a strictly limited basis. They should be secured by gold at a level of 50 per cent up to 600 million rubles and 100 per cent above this level, thus ensuring that no more than 300 million rubles of unsecured notes were in circulation. The new 1914 law did not specify the necessity for a gold guarantee of credit notes at all.

Moreover, according to Migulin, before the war the Russian currency was in perfect order, unlimited gold exchange being affected without impediments and currency reserves held by Russia in foreign banks reaching 500 million rubles. The latter served to guarantee international exchange despite the balance of trade turning against Russia. Migulin wrote:

> . . . the character of the active operations of the State Bank has very materially altered, and moreover for the worse. The fact is that the law of 27 July 1914 permitted the State Bank to discount short-term Exchequer bonds to any degree called for by the needs of wartime; in other words, to extend aid to the State Exchequer for military requirements in the same manner as the Banque de France.[1]

An additional expansion of emission rights of the State Bank of 1000 million rubles was authorised on 4 March 1915. Migulin advised in conclusion that the Russian government should quickly adopt a series of technical measures to improve the currency situation. These included the cessation of the issuing of notes of small denomination (one, three and five rubles), of which there were around 1,000 million rubles in circulation, to be replaced by notes of the State Exchequer. This would assist in preserving the gold guarantee of the State Bank by curtailing note issue. Moreover, the issue of small gold coins should also be stopped, and the exchange of paper for gold should be undertaken only with the imperial, which was the basic gold coin specified in the existing law. Finally, Migulin encouraged a more exact formulation of the law of emission in correspondence with accepted Western European practice.

P.L. Bark (1869–1937)

The necessity of funding the Allied military campaign led to Keynes recommending strongly that Russian gold should be used for this purpose.[2] The Russian response to the idea that part of its gold reserve be transferred overseas was to protest and to request that additional credits be provided in return. Keynes had some responsibility for resolving this question in September 1915 when Russian representatives arrived in London. He composed a 'Note on the Finance of Russia' for this meeting in which he wrote:

> So far M. Bark has been extremely moderate in his calls upon the Bank of Russia; and the available evidence goes to show that the degree of inflation of the Russian economy is not yet serious. . . . Thus Russia has depended from bank notes to a somewhat less extent than France. Yet the economic condition of Russia permits a far greater amount of internal absorption of notes, before any harm is done . . .[3]

For Keynes this meant that the Russian gold reserves could be further depleted without serious danger of hyperinflation, even that note issue could proceed apace.

In response to the British position, Minister of Finance Bark attempted at least initially to argue the Russian position against the transfer of gold overseas. His first line of defence was to maintain that Russian creditworthiness was beyond any doubt and hence to link the opening of lines of credit to the transfer of gold was unnecessary.[4] He also warned of the potential dangers of the physical shipment of gold overseas during wartime.[5] As one account explained:

> Bark described in detail and with great energy the dangers to which Russia was exposed if her gold reserve was impaired . . . While Russia was not stinting her sacrifices on the field of battle, it was essential for the common interests of the Allies that nothing be demanded of her which might threaten her economic system.[6]

For Bark, the question of supporting the exchange rate of the ruble was one of three key concerns that he took into a 1915 meeting in Paris. He linked this concern directly to increasing the export of Russian goods, and it might reasonably be connected also to the level of gold held in reserves.[7] That Bark explicitly made this connection is apparent from a document dated 9 August 1916, in which Bark described the gold reserve as the 'last anchor' (*poslednii yakor'*) of Russian monetary circulation.[8] Another account related that before the meeting in Paris between Bark, Lloyd George and the French Minister of Finance Ribot, Bark was 'determined not to transfer any further gold outright to Britain'.[9] However, when the

French agreed to transfer some of their gold reserves overseas and the UK stood firm on the need for Russian gold, Bark's outright opposition became an untenable position and further Russian transfers were agreed.

Bark's opposition to the transfer of Russian gold was eventually tempered by the reality of the situation, and he came to partially concede Keynes's view that the altered context had made the question of Russian gold reserves less crucial.[10] However, in order to permit the reserves of the State Bank to fall below 1.4 milliard rubles, Bark was forced to disregard the direction of the State Duma.[11] This Ministerial change of view on gold reserves was apparent at the second and third conferences with the British Chancellor of the Exchequer in September 1915 and June 1916.[12] Nonetheless Bark was still concerned with currency depreciation in these meetings, as his attempt to obtain special credit from the Allies to support the exchange rate of the ruble demonstrated.[13] In May 1916, Bark spoke of the possible catastrophic influence of the devaluation of the ruble on the Russian economy.[14]

Overall, Bark's initial opposition to the transfer of gold can be viewed in two ways. A sympathetic interpreter might see it as arising from a genuine concern about the economic stability of Russia, whereas a less favourable interpretation would view it simply as an attempt to minimise the cost of the war to Russia. In reality it was probably a mixture of the two. After 1917 Bark assisted in arranging financial assistance from the Allies to the White government, but when this government collapsed, he moved permanently to London. In the 1920s Bark worked freelance for the Bank of England and various other financial institutions.

Tugan-Baranovsky and war finance

Although not employed in any official governmental capacity, Tugan-Baranovsky published a number of works on various aspects of the First World War. For example he wrote a general analysis of the economic consequences of the war under the title 'The Influence of the War on the National Economies of Russia, England and Germany' which was published in 1915. In this he wrote:

> The more wealthy a country is, the more capital it possesses, the easier it can cover war expenditure. And since war expenditure by necessity has a monetary character, then this outlay must with greater ease be covered by countries with developed monetary economies than by countries with semi-natural economies. Trade-industrial countries are richer in capital than agricultural states, and money markets are more developed in them. Therefore in relation to covering the costs of war trade-industrial countries are in a better position than agricultural.[15]

Since Tugan-Baranovsky characterised Russia in 1915 as an agricultural economy rather than a trade-industrial state, he appeared to be contradicting

Keynes's view that Russia was in 'at least as sound a position' as developed monetary economies such as England to cover war expenditure.

In a newspaper article entitled 'Paper Money and War' published in January 1915, Tugan-Baranovsky argued that the issue of paper currency as a means of Russian war finance was a necessity given the grandiose scale of the war. Financing the war solely by loans was impossible since the free capital needed for this exceeded that which was accumulated in the Russian economy in any given year. There was according to Tugan-Baranovsky only one country that possessed the colossal wealth required to conduct the war through loans and without the need to issue paper money, and that was England (*sic*). Even so he warned that a regime of paper money was not only dangerous for state finances but also disastrous for the economy itself.[16] How this danger would manifest itself was not clearly explained.

Tugan-Baranovsky wrote a further analysis of Russian war finance in 1915 under the heading 'War and the National Economy'. Here, he again advocated the idea that paper money was the single most important source of war finance, but in this article he recognised that this would lead to the dramatic devaluation of the ruble in relation to gold.[17] However at this time it was Tugan-Baranovsky's expectation that the war would continue for approximately one year, and that it would cost Russia between five and six milliard rubles.[18] Significantly, he recognised that confidence was the crucial factor in respect to currency emission in Russia. This was why the French central bank had been able to pursue a course of emission without provoking a corresponding scramble for gold, as confidence in the French monetary system was high. A favourable international balance of accounts had also helped.

Thus, Tugan-Baranovsky implied that Russia did not possess this intangible quality to the same degree as France, as witnessed by the decline in the exchange rate of the ruble that had already occurred. He was suggesting that Russia should expect a more volatile experience in this area than France, and hence that the Russian financial system was not fully comparable to that of advanced Western states. This was a view that was held by many Russian financial specialists at the time, although convincing Western economists of its significance proved a difficult task.

Tugan-Baranovsky and war loans

In 1917, Tugan-Baranovsky published an edited volume with the title *War Loans*.[19] This book revealed a change in his attitude to war finance, in part conditioned by the war continuing beyond the initial expectation of its duration. Tugan-Baranovsky now emphasised that loans differed from other methods of covering war expenditure in that the element of compulsion was absent. Out of the three basic ways of paying for war – taxation, the issue of paper money and loans – the latter was by far the best.

However, since the war was being waged on such a large scale, all three methods were being used to some extent.[20]

Regarding the issue of paper money, Tugan-Baranovsky still admitted in 1917 that this was necessary given the huge scale of the war. Nevertheless he now stressed that this method was extremely dangerous and should only be used sparingly. Even given the limited use of increased taxes and currency issue, loans must be recognised as a rational and desirable means of war finance. The advantage of loans was that the population voluntarily participated in the burden of war, which acted to strengthen the link between the people and the state. Tugan-Baranovsky speculated that there was an especially fast accumulation of free monetary capital occurring in Russia. He suggested:

> It is beyond doubt that the Russian money market can provide the state with 3 milliard rubles, which composes the nominal amount of the new war loan. The success of the new loan is guaranteed if Russian society and the working masses correctly understand their patriotic duty.[21]

Such a partisan attitude might suggest that Tugan-Baranovsky had moved a long way from his Marxian roots, although in fact he had distanced himself from only one particular interpretation of Marx's legacy.

In the autumn of 1916, Tugan-Baranovsky had written a book on monetary theory entitled *Paper Money and Metal*. At this time he did not appear to know the full extent of Russian gold transfers overseas, as is apparent from the following passage:

> The gold supply of the State Bank inside the country at the current time equals 1,554 million rubles. For full cover of credit notes the gold required would be an increase of between 900–1,500 million rubles. Would an increase in our gold supply by this amount be possible? ... only very slowly, over many years.[22]

The fact that by May 1916 the actual level of cover of currency by gold was nowhere near what it had been at the start of the war was acknowledged, Tugan-Baranovsky suggesting that a doubling of the amount of gold held was needed for full cover to be restored. He concluded *Paper Money and Metal* by stating that the preservation of a large metallic reserve in Russia was certainly necessary. Tugan-Baranovsky's work on war finance demonstrated that his contribution to economics was not limited to abstract concepts – business cycle theory for example – but was equally at home in the more applied fields of operation, the range of his interests being very broad. Moreover in such areas the approach adopted often differed little from that of many mainstream economists of the day.

Economic theory in wartime

In the purely theoretical realm, European economics as a discipline continued to develop immediately after 1914 in the traditional manner, albeit in more difficult historical circumstances. For example D.H. Robertson's *Study of Industrial Fluctuation* and E.E. Slutsky's 'On the Theory of the Budget of the Consumer' were both published in 1915, and neither had any direct link to wartime concerns. Slutsky's 1915 article was first published in Italian, and it took some period of time before its relevance to the theory of consumer demand was recognised in the West. Slutsky had become interested in the theory of marginal utility as a student as early as 1911. The 1915 article was intended to follow on from Pareto's work on a similar theme, as well as (to a lesser extent) to contribute to the Russian tradition of studying peasant budgets; for example A.V. Chayanov published a book called *Experience of Elaborating Budget Data for Farms in Kharkov* also in 1915.

However in the practical realm, the war had great significance for the development of both Western European and Russian economics, although for somewhat different reasons. In the West, mainstream economists such as A.C. Pigou became directly concerned with the consequences of the war in both financial and real terms, and in Russia more orthodox thinkers experienced similar concerns. Marxist economists however saw the war as a valediction of their prognoses regarding imminent capitalist collapse, and hence their contribution to wartime economics was very different from that of most mainstream thinkers. Even more significantly, exactly how Marxist economists theorised the war in relation to imperialism as an advanced stage of capitalism had great significance for how the Bolsheviks initially conceived of the transition to socialism, as will be seen in what follows.

Tugan-Baranovsky on cooperatives

Two specific topics that Russian economists pursued during the war that were not directly related to military concerns were cooperatives and foreign trade. For example, Tugan-Baranovsky wrote a detailed account of cooperatives entitled *The Social Foundations of Cooperation*, a substantial treatise on the topic that was published in 1916, which had a different emphasis from Slutsky's account discussed previously. As opposed to the 'natural' development of capitalism, Tugan-Baranovsky outlined that cooperatives were created 'artificially', as a means of transforming the social-economic structure. Cooperatives arose in connection with the socialist movement but it would be wrong to confuse the two.

The first step towards understanding the essence of cooperation was to distinguish it from the socialist *obshchina* (commune). The latter was a tool for social transformation that renounced the idea of profit. Cooperatives on the other hand were economic enterprises and hence they appealed to the economic interests of specific groups. In this limited sense cooperatives were similar to all other capitalist economic organisations.[23] However, while cooperatives were certainly enterprises, they were enterprises of a non-capitalist nature. Tugan-Baranovsky defined an enterprise as an economic organisation pursuing the private profit of its members and achieving this aim through exchange. But what distinguished a capitalist enterprise from a non-capitalist one? According to Tugan-Baranovsky it was not the presence of hired labour, rather it was obtaining a non-labour income through the circuit of capital. Such income arose from the exploitation of labour, although not always of that labour employed in the particular enterprise in question.

A capitalist enterprise aspired to the unlimited expansion of turnover through the circulation of capital. This was in contradistinction to a cooperative enterprise, in which obtaining a yield on capital was not the primary aim. Cooperatives attempted to hold payments on capital to a minimum; for example a consumer cooperative would rather distribute any gains to consumers through lower prices than to shareholders through dividends.[24] Tugan-Baranovsky provided a definition of a cooperative as follows:

> A cooperative is an economic enterprise comprising several voluntarily combined people which has as its aim not obtaining the greatest profit on capital expended, but rather increasing the labour income of its members or reducing the outlay of members on their consumer necessities.[25]

Cooperatives were the offspring of two contradictory social systems, capitalism and socialism, the psychological motivation of those participating being a combination of egoism and altruism. But cooperatives were also an organisation that represented the interests of the labouring classes, against capitalist enterprises representing the ruling classes; these two forms of economy competed with each other.

The vast majority of theorists of cooperation in Russia were obviously of a socialistic bent, although they were often quite distinct from those within the Marxian variety of socialism, who looked down upon theorists of 'petty-bourgeois' institutions like cooperatives with disdain. Lenin, for example, held particular contempt for Tugan-Baranovsky, whose morality-based and anti-class struggle conception of socialism was anathema to most hardened Social Democrats. Consequently, when Lenin initially obtained control of the Russian state in 1917, developing cooperatives was not seen as a high priority at all. Ironically, near the very end of his life, Lenin had a dramatic change of heart in this respect, suggesting that only everybody in Russia participating in cooperatives would finally produce socialism. But even then, theorists like Tugan-Baranovsky who had worked on this topic in detail before the Bolshevik revolution, were simply ignored.

Shaposhnikov and foreign trade

As noted in the previous chapter, Shaposhnikov achieved the height of his influence in the 1920s as an important member of Kondratiev's Conjuncture Institute, but before 1917 he produced work on foreign trade that was a useful barometer for the general attitude of many liberal economists to this topic in the pre-revolutionary period. He continued working on this topic after 1917, publishing a book on *Tariff Policy in Russia Before and After the Revolution* in 1924, but Shaposhnikov's first book on foreign trade was entitled *Protectionism and Free Trade* published in 1915. What was particularly valuable about this work was that it was written before the Bolshevik revolution, thus removing any doubts that Shaposhnikov was deliberately modifying his views to prevent conflict with the Bolshevik government, a possibility that arises after 1917. The task that Shaposhnikov set himself in the 1915 book was to investigate the pure theory of international trade, ignoring the concrete tariff policy of any individual country.[26]

Shaposhnikov began by pointing out that before the state in the modern sense existed, and hence before a foreign trade policy could be developed, similar policy concerns had arisen in response to inter-city trade. For Western Europe from the beginning of the sixteenth century, when the state began to take on the function of determining economic policy, much attention began to be given to trade policy. Roughly coincident with this was the development of the first theoretical system devoted to international trade – mercantilism. Mercantilism proposed a whole arsenal of measures – duties (*poshliny*), premiums (*premia*), prohibitions (*zapreshcheniya*), trade agreements, monopolies, navigational acts and so on – the aim of all these being to encourage exports and to make imports more difficult.[27] For mercantilists foreign trade was regarded as the most useful means to enrich a country, and in order to accomplish this a surplus of exports over imports must be achieved.

Shaposhnikov related that mercantilism was the dominant force in the seventeenth and eighteenth centuries, but in the nineteenth century it was eclipsed by free trade ideas. Adam Smith used arguments based on the achievement of maximum labour productivity and individual freedom to justify free trade, whereas David Ricardo argued that it would be rational for countries to specialise in producing those goods in which they had a comparative advantage.[28] From a theoretical point of view, Shaposhnikov did not have any objections to free trade ideas. However, from a practical point of view this theory was based on simplified presuppositions that might not be appropriate for all real-world situations.[29] Shaposhnikov outlined that theoreticians of free trade supposed that the productive resources of a country were always fully utilised. If this was accepted and if the possibility of an influx of capital from overseas was ignored, then their critique of protectionism was irrefutable. But these suppositions were incorrect.

The actual degree of utilisation of resources was very diverse and fluctuated wildly, and capital certainly did flow over international borders. Consequently, Shaposhnikov argued that customs duties could, by artificially increasing prices, provoke an inflow of extra capital into protected branches, encourage better use of existing resources, and increase the total level of national production. This assumed that not all capital and labour was initially being utilised. Shaposhnikov continually stressed that at the heart of the theory of free trade was the idea of fully-employed capital and labour. He pointed out that since the theory of international trade had rejected this excessive simplification, it should accept that protection could, in certain circumstances, bring positive results. Customs duties could increase the level of production by encouraging the use of idle resources.[30]

Shaposhnikov then distinguished between customs duties designed as a temporary support for infant industries (*molodoi promyshlennosti*) and those used for the creation of an enterprise that required permanent support. Not all new industries required artificial support. Shaposhnikov quoted Frank Taussig to the effect that in a country with a developed paper-cotton industry, the creation of enterprises for the production of flax materials did not require tariffs. However, the creation of a textiles industry itself from scratch might indeed require artificial support.[31]

Finally, Shaposhnikov turned his attention to analysing agrarian protectionism, beginning with the idea that agricultural tariffs could have different effects to industrial tariffs. This was due to the fact that demand for agricultural goods was often less elastic than demand for industrial goods, causing the effects of price rises to differ. In order to evaluate agrarian protectionism Shaposhnikov asked, do grain tariffs increase the overall level of production? He responded that agricultural duties more than their industrial equivalents led only to increasing the income of one group of the population at the expense of all the others. Thus agrarian protectionism led to a fall in demand for labour and hence it aggravated the conditions of the working classes.[32] It was apparent from this that Shaposhnikov was more sympathetic to industrial protectionism than to agrarian protectionism, allowing that the former could in certain circumstances lead to positive results. This was clearly an ambiguous position, and could be seen to favour industry against agriculture, a position in direct opposition to what many critics accused members of the Conjuncture Institute of doing in the 1920s.

The economics of imperialism

The economic aspects of imperialism were obviously significant to both the general analysis of advanced capitalist development, and also to understanding the political conflicts generated by imperialistic control. The First World War was a prime example of such conflict. Nikolai Bukharin's 1915 work *World Economy and Imperialism* had set out a Social Democratic approach to the purely economic aspects of this problem, but had left the political interpretation of this topic rather undeveloped. It was V.I. Lenin who took the next step in the analysis as follows.

V.I. Lenin (1870–1924)

Lenin's important work *Imperialism as the Highest Stage of Capitalism* – important from the point of view of the development of Marxist economic theory at least – was written in the spring of 1916 in Zurich, Lenin explicitly acknowledging the significant influence of J.A. Hobson on his approach to the topic. In this work Lenin outlined five basic features of imperialism as follows:

1 The concentration of capital had developed to a new monopolistic stage.
2 The merging of bank and industrial capital into finance capital had created a powerful financial oligarchy.
3 The export of capital rather than commodities had acquired great significance.
4 The formation of global monopolistic associations had occurred.
5 The territorial division of the world amongst the capitalist powers was completed.[33]

These features were all interpreted by Lenin as showing that the economic apparatus created by monopoly capitalism was the perfect tool for use by socialist politicians in creating a new economic system, in that the methods of international accounting had made conscious planning a real possibility. For example, the capitalist financial oligarchy that was created through monopoly had formed an expansive network of relations across all the institutions of society, a network that could by implication be used by socialists for planning control.

In addition to the five basic features outlined by Lenin, other important elements of the new imperialism were the prevalence of holding companies structured into principal and subsidiaries, which were used to disguise various types of dubious financial operations, and the development of cartels and trusts as organisational forms of imperialistic control. Lenin argued that it was the ongoing concentration of production itself, something that had been emphasised by Marx, which led directly to the monopoly phase of capitalism, and hence Lenin attempted to demonstrate that his analysis was simply Marx's approach extrapolated into the present day.

The motivating drive of imperialist expansion was, according to Lenin, the struggle for spheres of favourable deals, concessions and monopoly profits, i.e. to obtain a greater return on capital than would be available domestically. Thus the drive for geographical extension was explained economically, as the need to continually offset the tendency within developed capitalism of the rate of profit to fall. This rationale for imperialism has been questioned by some, who emphasised the lack of social overhead facilities (roads, railways, power plants and so on) often found in less developed countries and the greater risk associated with investing overseas, as being serious hindrances to the supposedly superior yield on capital obtained outside domestic frontiers.[34] Some have identified other motives for imperialism such as naked power politics, although Lenin might have responded that politics was simply economics in an alternative guise.

In terms of economic concepts, there was nothing really new in Lenin's account of imperialism, it simply brought together various existing elements from authorities such as Rudolf Hilferding, Hobson, Gerhardt Schulze-Gaevernitz and many others, within a framework critical of 'revisionist' accounts of the topic such as Kautsky's, and concluding that the imperialist phase of capitalism had demonstrated that the time was ripe for transmuting into socialism, regardless of the political situation. Hence *Imperialism as the Highest Stage of Capitalism* was really a political interpretation of the facts of imperialistic development, an interpretation that was of course open to question, and might be seen to follow directly from Lenin's ultimate career goal of the immediate revolutionary overthrow of capitalism, with himself as the new socialist leader.

Whether capitalism was really ripe for transformation into socialism in the economic sense suggested by Lenin might easily be disputed, especially given the reality that unfolded after 1917. For example, the network of relations said by Lenin to have been created by the imperialist financial oligarchy might be forecast to evaporate quickly in a revolutionary situation, rather than be taken over intact for use by socialists, not necessarily by any deliberate acts of sabotage, but simply through collapsing contacts and personnel turmoil. Lenin appeared unaware of this possibility, or at least if he was aware of it, he downplayed its very serious consequences. Thus Lenin's economic analysis in 1916 was the theoretical expression of a vastly over-optimistic political evaluation of the historical situation that presented itself in Russia via the First World War. The fact that Lenin appeared to be proved right through 1917 was really a chimera. After all, the monkeys who (given enough time to make numerous attempts) accidentally type the collected works of Shakespeare are still only monkeys.

Conclusion

Russian economists reacted to the outbreak of war in various diverse ways. Marxian Social Democrats saw first and foremost a political opportunity, in which capitalism might be encouraged to break at its weakest link. Financial specialists and even some Legal Marxists were occupied with more immediate day-to-day concerns, such as covering wartime expenditure and protecting the Russian financial system. In terms of abstract theory, the war went some considerable way to confirming the Marxian idea that capitalism was inevitably antagonistic in nature, with imperialistic rivalry quickly spilling over into military conflict. However, it must be recognised that not all socialists of the day adhered to this cataclysmic interpretation. Tugan-Baranovsky, for example, had a more fine-tuned analysis that allowed him to support the Russian cause against Germany, although his move away from orthodox Marxism had begun well before 1914. Nevertheless, it is beyond doubt that the consequences of the war itself for Russia generally, and for Russian economics in particular, were huge. In the next chapter some of these post-war consequences are explored in more detail.

7 The Russian economic mind under Bolshevism, 1917–1929

The Bolshevik assumption of power in Russia in October 1917 has often been described as a political revolution. Without question there certainly was a revolutionary situation in existence in Russia at this time, but the fact that the Bolsheviks eventually took absolute control of the Russian state could be interpreted as a historical accident, given that other left-leaning groups such as the Socialist Revolutionaries had much greater political support amongst the Russian population than the Bolsheviks ever did. But the Bolshevik leadership possessed that iron constitution often necessary for success in these types of situations, and they subsequently acted ruthlessly to quell various oppositional movements at the appropriate times. In terms of the state of Bolshevik economic theory in 1917, this would soon be found to be rather inadequate, as is documented in detail in the chapter that follows.

In the West after 1918, issues of national immediacy such as monetary reconstruction came to prominence in Western economics, J.M. Keynes's *The Economic Consequences of the Peace* of 1919 and *Tract on Monetary Reform* of 1923 being key examples of works written as a direct consequence of apparent post-war requirements. Other important areas of progress were in business cycle theory – A.C. Pigou and D.H. Robertson in the UK for example – and also in institutional economics – J.R. Commons and Wesley Mitchell in the USA. In terms of specific national currents, Austrian economics developed through the works of F.A. Hayek, whilst in the UK, the beginnings of the Keynesian system were starting to coalesce at Cambridge.

The period between the two world wars has been described generally as one of interwar pluralism, with different currents coexisting in economics to a significant degree, without there being a single dominating approach; at least this was the case in the USA. In Soviet Russia the situation was different to some extent, although the 1920s were also a period of relative pluralism in economic theory, at least in relation to what was to follow in the 1930s. Some similar thematic concerns were apparent between Western and Soviet economics in this period, monetary reconstruction being one such common thread, although in other areas of the discipline, Soviet economics developed along a very different trajectory.

The consequences of Bolshevik control

The Bolshevik assumption of power in October 1917 radically changed the context and framework in which economic thought was developed and utilised in Russia. Before 1917, economics was seen as an activity devoted to understanding and describing the past and present reality of that specific entity called 'the economy' and to gauging specific government interventions for promoting faster development, or was seen as a means of evaluating critically the position of human subjects within existing economic systems. After 1917, economics was fundamentally transformed into the means and tool by which an entire economic system was to be constructed from scratch, and new economic policies based on apparently people-centred goals were to be created and implemented; or at least this was one interpretation of how 1917 might have changed the function of economics, if that annoying nuisance 'currently existing reality' had not sometimes gotten in the way.

Of course, the situation for economics in Soviet Russia was far more complicated than this, in that reality was not suspended until the new economic system had been perfected *a priori*, rather it continued to develop without any direct input from 'rationalising' economic thought after the Bolsheviks had first assumed control, as no replacement economic system had yet been fully conceived of by the new ruling authorities. Even given this subtler context, the role of economic ideas did change dramatically after 1917. The Bolsheviks had come to power on a platform that claimed economic analysis to be a central component determining its worldview in a way unlike any previously existing government before it. The wholesale transformation of the social and economic system was the ultimate goal, and economic ideas were to be the underlying guide. The exact degree to which purely economic concerns, rather than political, ideological, or career-advancement motives were involved in creating the new economic system, is a complicated question to answer fully, but at least some attempt to resolve it should be made in this chapter, given the (on the face of it) exalted position of economics in the Bolshevik intellectual schema.

With this in mind, it is pertinent to remember that what was (and still is) regarded as Lenin's major work in economics, *The Development of Capitalism in Russia*, was first published in 1899, 18 years before Lenin took the helm of the Russian state. This book was the product of political debates occurring in Russia throughout the 1890s, and concerned only the precise nature of some of the economic formations that were then developing in the Tsarist economy. This context was radically different from that facing Lenin in 1917, when the immediate circumstances and general goals were very different.

Lenin had made a short attempt to outline some principles that might guide socialists in power, *State and Revolution* written in August 1917, but this was certainly not a detailed plan of action for creating an entirely new economic system. What it did contain was a short account of elements of the transition from capitalism to communism that included a strong emphasis on the dictatorship of the proletariat as the organisation of the vanguard of the oppressed – revealingly, not an organisation of all oppressed people themselves – and on crushing any resistance to socialist control by force.[1] In terms of economic systems, Lenin wrote of the significance of monopoly capitalism as follows:

> The trusts, of course, never provided, do not now provide, and cannot provide complete planning. But however much they do plan, however much the capitalist magnates calculate in advance the volume of production on a national and even on an international scale ... [it is] still capitalism. The 'proximity' of such capitalism to socialism should serve genuine representatives of the proletariat as an argument proving the proximity, facility, feasibility and urgency of the socialist revolution.[2]

This was a repetition (in modified form) of what Lenin had argued in *Imperialism as the Highest Stage of Capitalism*; he had added nothing new to this basic point in 1917.

Other leading Bolsheviks such as Leon Trotsky and Joseph Stalin had written even less on economic matters before 1917 than Lenin had. Perhaps the most significant pre-revolutionary Bolshevik contributor to economics was Nikolai Bukharin, who in works such as *World Economy and Imperialism* of 1915 had attempted to provide a more detailed and up-to-date account of capitalist economic reality. Even so, such works would turn out to be of only minor use in designing the new economic structures required for socialist development, and a significant gap in Bolshevik economics was revealed.

In the event, new economic theorists arose to fill the yawning gap in socialist thinking left by Lenin and Company after 1917, people like V.A. Bazarov, V.G. Groman, A.V. Chayanov and L.N. Yurovsky, the subjects of more detailed examination further on in this chapter. However, it was significant that these people were usually more flexible intellectually than many of the Bolsheviks, indeed they often were not Bolsheviks themselves prior to 1917, and had even opposed Bolshevik policies on many occasions. The potential for future conflict that this politically fractious situation created would be an important part of the story that would evolve after 1917.

Social democratic economics immediately after 1917

Various key themes came to dominate the immediate post-revolutionary period in relation to Bolshevik economics, for example the precise nature of socialised control of the productive forces, the role of non-monetary accounting in the planning process, the practicalities of monetary reform, and the importance of accommodating peasant economy in the construction of Russian socialism.

With respect to the nature of socialised control, in 1918 Lenin wrote a pamphlet entitled *Can the Bolsheviks Retain State Power?*, which gave significant prominence to the idea of workers' control of the production and distribution of goods. He suggested that workers' control could become a countrywide, all-embracing and precise means for accounting of the making and moving of commodities.[3] For example, workbooks for the entire population should be introduced, which documented the amount and quality of labour undertaken, and the principle 'he who does not work, neither shall he eat' should be applied. Crucially Lenin remarked that 'we shall not invent the organisational form of the work, but take it ready-made from capitalism'.[4] He was admitting that the managerial structure of capitalist work was to be simply taken over by socialists, i.e. that the form of labour in capitalism was not to be altered through the Bolshevik revolution, at least in its initial stages.

This very significant issue was glossed over by Lenin as though it was a minor matter, but in fact it went to the heart of the new economic system being created by the Bolsheviks. Lenin's underlying view was that socialist political control of the economic apparatus of already existing capitalism would yield a socialist economy. An alternative view, that socialist organisational forms would have to be designed and then created from scratch using non-capitalist principles, was not discussed by Lenin in either *State and Revolution* or *Can the Bolsheviks Retain State Power?*.

In terms of economic theory, this conception of socialism had important consequences, in that economists could have been employed to create new socialistic organisational forms, as Bolsheviks were now directing economic affairs. Leading economists did debate various specific issues, such as the possibility of non-monetary accounting and the unit of exchange to be adopted, but they did not discuss possible new organisational structures of socialist economy at the most fundamental level in anything like as much detail. There were a few books devoted to exploring new possibilities in this area, such as A.M. Kaktyn's *New Forms of Organisation of Industry* of 1920, but Kaktyn's works are little known today, and he wrote another more symptomatic book in 1920 entitled *A Single Economic Plan and a Single Economic Centre*.

It might be suggested that the initial idea of Russian socialists simply taking-over the existing structures of capitalism was quickly bypassed as reality unfolded after 1918, and new organisational forms were seen to be required. In fact, this notion was still prevalent amongst some Bolshevik leaders in the mid-1920s. For example, Trotsky wrote the following in December 1923:

> If the doctrines of the Brentanists … and the Bernsteinists, according to which the domination of the capitalist trusts 'regulates' the market

> … was radically false, it is entirely correct when applied to the workers' state considered as a trust of trusts and bank of banks.[5]

Here Trotsky still apparently conceived of the workers' state as the supreme culmination of the industrial and financial forms of capitalism – a trust of trusts and a bank of banks. It is not being suggested that the Bolsheviks brought no new economic structures into being after 1917 at all, but the view that political control of the already existing structures of capitalism would be the essential skeleton of the new socialist economy was widely held amongst the party leadership well into the 1920s. In this, they were faithfully following Lenin's conception as outlined in *Imperialism* of 1916 through *Can the Bolsheviks Retain State Power?* of 1918.

L.N. Yurovsky for and against the Bolsheviks

Whilst the concerns of the Bolsheviks dominated much economic thinking in Russia immediately after 1917, this dominion was certainly not complete. One of the most prominent examples of someone who opposed Social Democratic thinking in both theoretical and practical matters, yet had a prominent role in Soviet policy-making in the early 1920s, was L.N. Yurovsky (1884–1938). Yurovsky was born in Odessa and studied in St Petersburg before travelling overseas to Munich and Berlin, and after his return to Russia he wrote a dissertation on Russian grain exports at Kharkov University in 1913. In 1918 he was appointed to the Saratov Institute of National Economy and in 1919 he published his most significant work in pure economics entitled *Studies in Price Theory*.

This book analysed in detail the classical and neoclassical doctrines on price determination and interest rates as outlined by many leading representatives, as well as various aspects of the marginalist approach. For example, Yurovsky distinguished between static equilibrium prices and dynamic equilibrium prices. The former were average market prices under a given level of supply and demand, the latter were determined by the law of cost of production. In relation to Leon Walras's theory of marginal productivity, Yurovsky pointed out various real-world factors that complicated this approach, such as the inability of small firms to obtain capital for expansion even when it was rational to do so and the possibility of a less-than-full employment macroeconomic equilibrium. This concern with price theory had little direct impact or relevance in Bolshevik Russia, but after 1921 Yurovsky's expertise in the allied fields of banking and finance was much in demand; he quickly became an important member of NKFin and a leading theorist of the 1922–24 monetary reform.

In this respect Yurovsky supported the idea of creating a gold-backed parallel currency, the *chervonets*, which would replace the old massively depreciating ruble. In terms of stabilising the monetary situation in Soviet Russia, this policy was a definite success. Yurovsky also entered the debate over economic planning that occurred throughout the 1920s. In the War Communist period he had criticised the idea of replacing monetary accounting with other forms of calculation such as labour units as unworkable, and during NEP he criticised the teleological approach to planning articulated by some within Gosplan as unrealistic. It was in part this opposition to the expansion of imperative planning that led to Yurovsky becoming a target of the political purges after 1930: he was eventually executed in 1938.[6]

J.M. Keynes and Soviet Russia

As noted in Chapter 6, Keynes had been a very important policy adviser on financial matters to the UK government during the First World War. After the international war ended, but whilst the Russian civil war still raged on, Keynes continued to be involved in Russian economic affairs through his efforts to assist in designing a new currency for the Northern parts of Russia that were still under anti-Bolshevik control. The aims of the policy of the Allies at this time was recommended in a memorandum of the Russian Political Conference in Paris as being:

> For the reconstruction of Russia, the opening of foreign credits must be facilitated, to secure vital necessities to Russia, till her production is restored to the normal. This will go to strengthen the resistance against Bolshevism and to consolidate future commercial relations.[7]

Moreover, it was suggested that all funds held in banks that belonged to agents of the Bolsheviks should be sequestrated, and that the Allies should cooperate with local governments in Russia in order to restore order.

In relation to such general aims, Keynes composed various versions of a 'Memorandum on Financial Arrangements of Northern Russia' in August 1918 in which he wrote:

> I believe that it will not be unduly ambitious to seek to establish a stable currency which may eventually develop into the permanent currency of Northern Russia. The existing issues of roubles are without intrinsic value and must certainly become worthless as soon as normal trade relations are established with Russia if not sooner. At present they are kept in circulation merely by sentiment and custom.[8]

Keynes went on to suggest that a good many conditions existed in Northern Russia for a recommended currency experiment, which he characterised as a 'sterling exchange standard regulated by an office of conversion'. The office of conversion would be Russian in constitution, being established as an appendage of local government, and it would issue new ruble notes in exchange for sterling (or possibly for gold) at a fixed rate of exchange of forty to the pound. Old rubles would also be exchanged at a rate to be established by the office of conversion at various intervals, and imported foodstuffs would be sold only in terms of the new currency. No sterling exchange operations would be permitted outside the office of conversion, which would be the principal source of the sterling reserve.[9]

Keynes gave various hypothesised possible difficulties in relation to this set of arrangements as follows. The new currency might prove unpopular at least at first, and/or it might go on to be hoarded. Moreover the premium of the new ruble over the old might lead to difficulties in terms of established wage levels. Keynes emphasised that it would be crucial to preserve a rigorous application of the rules of issue in order to guarantee currency stability. In the event, the anti-Bolshevik forces were defeated militarily, and Keynes's currency scheme collapsed along with them, but his general political loyalties were made clear through the affirmed allegiance of his currency proposals.

As a general backdrop to such schemes, Keynes's lack of understanding of the actual forces that had generated the Bolshevik revolution was made clear in a passage from *The Economic Consequences of the Peace* of 1919:

> the extraordinary occurrences of the past two years in Russia, that vast upheaval of society which has overturned what seemed most stable … may owe more to the deep influences of expanding numbers than to Lenin or Nicholas.[10]

As the Russian population had been expanding well before 1917 – Keynes himself noted the increased rate of growth from 1890 – and also given the vast size of the Russian territory itself, which might more easily cope with rapid population growth than a smaller country, it was likely that other factors rather than increased fecundity had caused the Bolshevik success. In fact Keynes confessed a rather extraordinary admission near the end of the book – he stated that about the details of the situation in Russia 'we know almost nothing authentic'.[11] Either he was being economical with the truth in this statement, or he was admitting that his own policy advice on Russian matters at this time was based on tenuous informational foundations.

From War Communism to NEP

In terms of a general sketch, Bukharin's work *The Economics of the Transition Period* of 1920 characterised the immediate post-revolutionary system of socialist dictatorship as the proletariat organised as state power, with all property transformed under collective-proletarian control. Municipalisation and communalisation were presented as only component parts of overall statification or proletarian nationalisation. The organising principle was declared to be bringing the working class into the production process, albeit in a militaristic manner due to the context of the civil war. In terms of economic theory, Bukharin forecast a transition to a naturalistic approach as occurring in the near future, as the ideological categories of capitalism were said to be breaking down.[12] The concept of expanded negative reproduction was proposed by Bukharin as characterising the general collapse that had followed 1917, drawing on Marx's own reproduction schemes (in inverted form) for inspiration.

Noticeably absent from most of this work however were the majority of Russian citizens, the peasantry, who appeared to be excluded from the socialist dictatorship, at least as it was defined by Bukharin in 1920. Soon after *The Economics of the Transition Period* appeared – this work perhaps being the supreme ideological expression of the economic ideas of War Communism – Bukharin made a dramatic *volte face* to become the leading advocate of the re-introduction of 'the market' as a category of commodity economy into the socialist system, otherwise known as NEP. Bukharin's theoretical enthusiasm for both War Communism and NEP was infectious to many around him, and later in the 1920s a group of Bukharinite economic theorists would emerge to flesh out Bukharin's general pronouncements of exactly how the market was to be employed within Soviet socialism.

One of Bukharin's main ideological opponents within Soviet Marxism, E.A. Preobrazhensky, also produced a key work of the War Communism period, *Finance in the Epoch of the Dictatorship of the Proletariat* of 1921. Here Preobrazhensky wrote that the issue of paper money by a proletarian government was necessary:

> for both countries with a highly developed capitalism and for predominantly agrarian economies with only one difference, that in the first group of countries the liquidation of paper-money circulation can occur quicker than in the second.[13]

Preobrazhensky also wrote of the need to 'close all apparatuses of paper emission and to allow the monetary system to die a natural death'.[14] In the War Communist period the notion that non-monetary accounting would eventually replace monetary forms of control was repeatedly declared, although various difficulties in accomplishing this endeavour were discussed and reluctantly accepted. With the transition to NEP the idea of promoting the death of the monetary system was abandoned, and monetary stability was instead enshrined as the new goal.

Some of the financial problems that faced Soviet Russia at this time were not unique. For example, the German economy also required large-scale monetary reconstruction after the First World War, although the political context in which this reconstruction occurred was very different to that in Russia. Some Russian theorists looked to Western economic theory for guidance in monetary questions. Irving Fisher's *Purchasing Power of Money* was translated into Russian and published in 1925, and provided inspiration for A.A. Konyus within the Conjuncture Institute. The quantity theory of money was employed in modelling the effects of paper money emission by people as diverse as Yurovsky, Katsenellenbaum and even Preobrazhensky, suggesting that it was regarded by many in Russia at this time as simply a technical tool of monetary analysis, rather than the more ideological concept it became through Milton Friedman's reformulation in the USA in the 1950s.

L.D. Trotsky (1879–1940)

Trotsky is often held up as a heroic figure for those socialists who strongly opposed Stalin's ascent to power, yet believed that an alternative Bolshevik platform of more democratic or more inclusive planning could have been developed from within the Social Democratic current in Russian socialism. Politically, there is little doubt that Trotsky was indeed a key alternative to Stalin, but what about in the realm of economics? Did Trotsky have an alternative programme for the economic development or the planning structures of Russia?

In the early 1920s Trotsky played an important role in relation to economic affairs within Russia, being People's Commissar of the Army and Navy, member of SNK and also of the Politburo. Moreover, Trotsky was a hugely charismatic figure within Russian Social Democracy, and cultivated a very close association with Lenin. Hence the opportunity for suggesting alternative economic policies regarding planning methodology was certainly present. To what extent did Trotsky take up this opportunity in the early and mid-1920s, when he was not yet the victim of a concerted campaign against him orchestrated by Stalin and his lieutenants?

In December 1923 Trotsky discussed a controversial order (no. 1042) regarding the repair of locomotives, an order that was seen as involving a transportation plan of repair operations that had not been 100 per cent fulfilled in certain areas of application. This failure had been seen by some as indicating faulty planning methods. Trotsky however came to the defence of order no. 1042, suggesting that modifications of plan targets should be expected. The checking of a plan according to Trotsky was one of the most important points in its realisation, and periodic alterations that were suggested by experience should be seen as normal. It was easy to poke fun at plans for long periods that later proved to be 'soap bubbles', in that in order to reach a point of being able to create fully rational plans, it was necessary to begin with primitive and rough plans.[15] This analysis does not sound like someone who was deeply critical of the Soviet planning system as it was developing in 1923.

In April 1926, Trotsky commented on a draft resolution on economic matters presented by A. Rykov. Here Trotsky acknowledged the changing definitions of planning that had occurred over time. For example, he stated that until recently, planning had meant the attempt to foresee the movement of the essential elements of the Soviet economy for the year to come, and to coordinate them harmoniously. However, a new definition of planning was now required, one that encompassed the planning of very large industrial units and projects over a number of years, and hence a temporal extension to five years was in order.[16] This demonstrated that the content of Soviet planning developed in piecemeal fashion over time, and that Trotsky's views on the matter followed the flow of the majority in this particular instance.

Sometime later, in September 1927, Trotsky composed his famous 'Platform of the Opposition', which contained his alternative programme for socialist political and economic development. In terms of the five-year plan that was then being created and debated for the period 1926–27 to 1930–31, Trotsky was quite critical, suggesting that the figures projected for the annual increase in industrial production of between 4 and 9 per cent were low, merely the rate of growth in capitalist countries during boom periods.[17] However, the overall system of planning or alternative socialist industrial structures were not really discussed by Trotsky at all. Perhaps the most radical difference that Trotsky proposed in economic terms concerned the monopoly of foreign trade and the isolationist stance of Stalin. Trotsky wrote:

> The aim of economic management ought to be not a closed-off, self-sufficient economy … but just the opposite – an all-sided increase of our relative weight in the world economy, to be achieved by increasing our rate of development to the utmost.[18]

Note, however, that Trotsky wanted increases in the planned rates of industrial growth, not changes to the structures of socialist economy themselves. Trotsky did call for the gradual involvement of the working population in the work of state administration and a rural cooperative structure whereby participants enjoyed maximum independent initiative. He also advocated an end to bureaucratic abuse and warned of the political dangers of allowing private capital free reign in the countryside. Hence it can be concluded that on many issues Trotsky advocated only minor changes to Soviet planning techniques whilst he was still within Soviet borders, although in one important area – foreign trade – his position was very different to that of Stalin's. Whether this amounted to a fully elaborated alternative programme, or was simply tinkering at the rough edges, is disputable.

Keynes calls short on Russia

In 1925 Keynes published an analysis of various aspects of the Soviet experiment entitled *A Short View of Russia*, the consequence of a brief visit to Russia in September 1925. His attempt to create an alternative currency in North Russia in the autumn of 1918 appears to have been forgiven by the Soviet authorities. In his short account of Russia, Keynes outlined that in his view, Leninism itself was made up of two elements – religion and business – with the latter being subordinate to the former. The Bolsheviks possessed a fanatical zeal that dominated the experimental technique of new economy that was being constructed, and Keynes found it unfathomable how a patently erroneous book (as he saw it) such as Marx's *Capital* could inspire such religious fervour. He was also critical of what he saw as the exaltation of the proletariat over the bourgeoisie and the intelligentsia, and the destruction of liberty and security in everyday life.

In terms of the new economic system that was being constructed, Keynes explained that in Soviet Russia, it was intended that the career of money making as such would disappear, and the love of money would come to an end. He believed that whilst the Soviet system was inefficient, it was not fatally so, and hence its immediate survival prospects were good. As to its long-term prospects, Keynes was uncertain, as it depended on the precise degree to which capitalism was more efficient. In terms of economic theory, Keynes commented:

> I cannot perceive that Russian Communism has made any contribution to our economic problems of intellectual interest or scientific value. I do not think that it contains ... any piece of useful economic technique which we could not apply ... in a society ... of British bourgeois ideals.[19]

He was thus overwhelmingly negative about the possibility of Soviet economists contributing anything of much original value. Even so, he concluded that he would rather contribute his quota of labour activity to Soviet as against Tsarist Russia.

Keynes's admitted lack of comprehension of the appeal of Marxist (and subsequently Soviet) economics was revealing of his corresponding difficulty in understanding capitalism as a historical creation rather than as a universal type. Keynesian economics viewed capitalism as a fixed system that could be modelled mechanically, with variations in one particular variable – interest rates, investment and so on – causing variations in other variables such as employment levels and inflation. This assumed that the structure that was being modelled was to a large extent constant over time; it was just a question of getting the model as accurate as possible. The idea that the economic system itself was constantly evolving, and hence that historical factors were very important to understanding system operation, was downplayed in Keynesian-type modelling of capitalism, and hence was also lacking in an understanding of the appeal of non-capitalist systems of economy.

Agricultural economics in NEP

As the development of agriculture was a crucial policy issue throughout the 1920s – perhaps even the single most important issue – the development of agricultural economics in Soviet Russia was a major area of innovation and originality. A plethora of significant names still remembered today – A.V. Chayanov, N.D. Kondratiev, L.N. Litoshenko, N.P. Makarov – made important contributions to the progress of the theory of peasant economy, and to conceptualising the role of agriculture in a socialist system. Moreover, even economic thinkers who were not really agricultural specialists – people like Preobrazhensky and Bukharin – realised the major significance of agriculture in the USSR, and attempted to characterise peasant affairs theoretically. All of this attention paid to agricultural economics resulted in many new inventions of significant relevance even to non-socialist systems of economy.

A number of separate currents within Soviet agricultural economics in the 1920s can be distinguished. For example, an organisation-production school led by Chayanov and including Makarov and A.N. Chelinstev; a group of agrarian Marxists led by L.N. Kritsman; Kondratiev and his co-workers (Vainshtein for example) in the Conjuncture Institute; and right-wing agrarian specialists like Litoshenko can be quickly identified as distinct currents. The organisation-production school analysed the nature of peasant farms by highlighting the psychology of peasant farmers, identifying such farms as forms of household economy in which the balance between effort expended and goods consumed was fundamental to determining production. The agrarian Marxists highlighted the class structure prevalent in the countryside, with hired labour and peasant proprietors being crucial points of reference. Kondratiev focused on the nature and function of agricultural markets, and how various types of farm reacted within market and non-market structures of control to outside events.[20] The following section discusses a few of the debates that occurred within and between these various currents of agricultural economics.

The essence of Soviet agricultural debates

One crucial point of conflict between various currents of agricultural economics emerged with respect to the economic function of agricultural entrepreneurs. Some on the centre-right like Kondratiev argued for the need for a class of prosperous peasant farm-holders who would enable new techniques of farming and more efficient forms of production to develop. To some on the far left this approach was anathema, as it was precisely this type of class differentiation that the Bolshevik revolution had been fated to overcome. Instead of an entrepreneurial approach, the need for collective forms of farming was highlighted by many Marxists, but with the concomitant modernisation of machinery and tools. This basic conflict permeated all the debates over agricultural policy that occurred in the USSR in the 1920s, and was only finally resolved in 1929 with the acceptance of the notion of the annihilation of the *kulaks* as a class.

Throughout the 1920s, echoes of this basic difference of approach were found in many agricultural debates. For example, one of Litoshenko's original arguments vis-à-vis Russian agriculture, presented in *The Evolution and Progress of Peasant Farms* of 1923, was that the most dominant theory (by which he meant Chayanov's labour–consumption balance account) of the nature of peasant farms was fundamentally incorrect. For Litoshenko, peasant farms should be considered not as units of household management (*domovodstvo*), but as units in which the notion of acquisition (*priobreteniya*) was central. The aim of all acquisitive activity was maximising the difference between outlay and earnings, and peasant farms should be viewed in this context. Litoshenko accepted that household management elements did exist within farms, but denied that the consumer-balance factor was the leading principle of regulation. For Litoshenko, Chayanov's *narodnik*-inspired conception had relevance to natural economy, but not to the contemporary monetary economy. This error was traced to a mistake in the underlying theory of economy being posited, in which only labour was seen as the single source of wealth, rather than it being only one of three sources.[21]

Other forms of dissent with Bolshevik agrarian ideology also existed. After the revolutionary events of 1917, the statistician A.A. Chuprov studied the agrarian policies of the Soviet government with much interest. In 1921 he wrote an introductory essay to his father's book *Small-Scale Farming and its Needs*, in which he analysed aspects of the agricultural ideology of the Bolsheviks. According to Chuprov, the socialist programme of the proletariat encompassed a struggle on two different fronts, against the bourgeoisie and also against the labouring peasants, as contemporary 'scientific' socialism (as it was called by its proponents) was inextricably linked to the growth of large-scale industry. However, not only peasant-proprietors, but small-scale farmers and the landless rural proletariat, refused to comply with the sermon in favour of collectivism as it was preached to them by Social Democrats. Collectivism as an ideal was the product of capitalistic concentration, and as such was often alien to rural interests, as well as to small independent enterprises of many types. Where a powerful labouring peasantry was in existence, rural workers shared the ideology attached to this social group rather than that of the urban factory proletariat.[22] Hence the question of the role of individual peasant entrepreneurs against that of the collective totality was an underlying concern for Chuprov, as it was for Kondratiev and Litoshenko.

The economics of planning

Throughout the 1920s, debates on the techniques and methodology of planning were a major component of Soviet economic discourse. Together with agriculture, planning was the other 'great theme' of the decade. The debate had in fact begun even before the Bolshevik assumption of power in October 1917, as Tugan-Baranovsky had developed his account of the application of marginalist techniques to the planning process in the summer of 1917. The Bolsheviks ignored such off-field thought experiments, but the topic itself was universally accepted as being of central importance to future socialist economic success by most left-leaning economists.

It might be argued that after 1917, those who tackled the task began with a completely blank sheet (at least as regards theory), a fact that had both positive and negative ramifications. On the positive side, a unique opportunity for the creation of an entirely original economic theory of planning shorn of the vestiges of the past had arisen, which need not pay any undue respects to previous doctrines, but might be focused solely on unlocking all human potential. On the negative side, little (if any) guidance to this monumental task could be found in previous socialist theory, except for vague aspirations and general statements of projected superiority.

It is worth presenting an account of the individual people who first tackled this task in outline. Groman, Bazarov, Ginzburg, Yurovsky, Kondratiev, Ognovsky and Strumilin all contributed to the debates on planning which developed in the 1920s, although from quite different perspectives. The Gosplan economists Groman, Bazarov and Strumilin were generally favourable to the extension of imperative planning techniques, although debates occurred between them over the precise nature of such imperatives. NKFin economists like Yurovsky were in principle hostile to the idea of planning itself, providing ideological support for the extension of market forms of control, although they conceded that some form of planning was inevitable in the Soviet context. Agricultural economists like Kondratiev and Oganovsky were not necessarily against planning in principle, but were careful to delineate a moderate and indicate planning methodology only, and to allow ample room for manoeuvre within any concrete plans that had actually been outlined.

As the decade of the 1920s unfolded, these various different approaches to planning came into and went out of favour. As NEP was being introduced, economic planning was of only minor concern to policy-makers, as others matters such as currency reform were much more urgent. By the middle of the decade, Kondratiev's moderate genetic approach to planning was being explored in detail, but by the end of the decade, Strumilin's more comprehensive and imperative attitude prevailed. These shifts in approach were determined mainly by political factors outside the direct control of individual economists, and hence are of only peripheral concern to this book. But underlying the debates over particular forms of planning were more fundamental philosophical differences about the possibility of accurate prediction in any area of human social activity. Kondratiev, for example, was sceptical about the precision of planning techniques required for a system of national economic control to function smoothly, instead favouring a more open-ended and approximate approach that would allow for constant planning revisions. Opponents to this methodology argued that this was a concession to capitalism that allowed the spontaneous market in through the back door.

In general, there is no doubt that as the 1920s progressed, the planning techniques that were outlined by Soviet economists improved considerably, and that by 1929, at least some of the problems inherent to conscious projection of economic control had been at least partially solved. For example, Kondratiev's plan for agriculture and forestry, 1924–28, developed the idea of projecting total sown area of crops and livestock levels, with corrections to grain statistics for pre-war comparison.[23] In terms of results the Kondratiev plan targets were eventually over-fulfilled, but not by as much as its critics made out. Furthermore, A.M. Ginzburg and a group of VSNKh economists had prepared a draft five-year plan for the period 1927–28 to 1931–32, in which the basic indicators for future industrial production were given in great numerical detail, and agricultural yields were presented in the form of raw material balances using a method that had been promoted by Groman.[24]

Such preparatory exercises enabled much experience about the type of information required in the planned process to be accumulated, and also began to build-up the institutions that would be required to supervise the implementation of actual imperative plans. However, the general context of such preliminary planning operations was so thoroughly permeated by political and personal fractiousness that, not infrequently, the genuine lessons that might have been learnt from such plan mock-ups were lost amidst an avalanche of ill-founded recriminations. The pre-revolutionary Bolshevik *modus operandi* often spilled over into some post-revolutionary planning practices.

The balance of the national economy

One of the most significant precursors to the full-blown imperative plan from the point of view of ideas was the notion of an economic balance, an idea that was closely associated with the work of P.I. Popov (1872–1950) from the Central Statistical Administration (TsSU). Before 1917, Popov had been a local government statistician. After becoming chairman of the TsSU in 1923, Popov and his team began to prepare a detailed balance of the Soviet national economy that attempted to provide a *post-factum* account of the process of the existing connections of production and consumption in the entire economy for 1923–24, i.e. both total manufacture and distribution measured in terms of a statistical census. On the income side of the balance, the total amount of goods at the disposal of the economy for the year was listed; on the expenditure side, how the income of the economy was distributed and used over the year was indicated.

Various distinctions were employed with regards to groups of products such as consumption goods, raw materials, fuels and tools of production, as well as branches of production such as industry, agriculture and construction.

Popov's balance was a significant development in economic techniques in general, not just in the Soviet context, and it was subject to detailed scrutiny from various sources. One very noteworthy source of discussion was W.W. Leontief (1906–1999), who published a short critique of Popov's balance at the end of 1925. Leontief's work as an émigré is discussed in more detail in the next chapter. In his 1925 balance critique, Leontief recognised that the problem that Popov had tackled was one of the most interesting and complex that required a solution by contemporary economic statistics, but advanced a basic criticism of part of the methodology as follows. With regards to preparing the balance, two points of view for accounting purposes were possible to adopt. These were firstly a technical point of view, in which the various stages of production were looked upon as separate subjects of calculation. For example, the production of fabrics in the various textile industries was calculated by branch such as cotton and silk, which could then be compared with each other as total turnovers for a given period of time.

However, according to Leontief this method was inapplicable when comparing branches of production that did not have anything in common, branches such as paper and machinery, and hence he recommended the employment of a second point of view instead, the economic. In this method, the calculation was made in value terms, with goods sold on the free market by individual enterprises, and hence a common denominator was available for all goods, no matter from what branch of industry they originated.[25] This 'economic' approach to preparing a national balance was subsequently taken up in detail by Leontief after leaving the USSR permanently. Other criticisms of Popov's efforts were provided by Groman, who complained that Popov's balance did not show class divisions, outlays of manpower or mechanical energy. Groman instead proposed selecting six forms of economy as broad headings, these being state and cooperative socialist; state and private capitalist; small-scale commodity; and semi-natural production. Calculation of human and mechanical power outlays would then be listed, together with material values of outlay on capital and wages, interest and taxes.

There was of course a close relationship between the construction of such economic balances and the preparation of imperative plans, in that plans required balances as a point of entry for preparing suggested production targets. Without an indication of the existing state of economic affairs, planning future states of such affairs might be very difficult. But in the context of the USSR in the mid-1920s, a conflict between the balance method and planning itself simmered beneath the surface for a number of years, before erupting at the end of the 1920s into a full-scale battle of views. Paying too much attention to past economic regularities came to be seen as a political crime, and the balance method as a separate approach fell completely out of favour. Even so, Popov survived the purges of 1936–38 and worked in the RSFSR Gosplan until his death in 1950.

A.A. Bogdanov (1873–1928)

One of the most genuinely original thinkers to emerge from the Russian revolutionary tradition was A.A. Bogdanov (real name Malinovsky), a medical doctor who became a prominent philosopher, economic theorist and political agitator. A well-known opponent of Lenin on various issues, Bogdanov became most famous for his inventive work on tektology, this being a general science of organization, which was (or could have been) directly relevant to matters of economic planning. Bogdanov also wrote two accounts of economic principles in short course form, as well as various philosophical and natural science-related works, all of which were connected with his work on organisation. The specific aspects of tektology that were of relevance to economic thinking in general, and planning matters in particular, are surveyed in what follows.

Tektology can be seen as the study of complex structures and their interrelation with other multi-level forms. In his general account of the science of organization Bogdanov explained:

> The self-organization of humanity is a struggle with its own internal biological and social primordial forces; for this humanity needs tools just as much as for its struggle with external nature, although different tools, namely the *instruments of organization*.[26]

Bogdanov listed these various tools as the word, the idea and social norms, and placed the organization of human forces alongside the organization of external forces (nature) and of experience as the three basic types of organizational activity with which he was concerned. The principles through (and ways that) organization occurred both within and without particular entities were thus the main focus of tektological research.

In relation to economic structures in particular, the principle of organization was said by Bogdanov to be of crucial relevance as follows:

> ...the exchange of goods is an expression of the organizational relations among people in a society; it is a system of production; and the activity of separate psychics with its subjective valuations reduces to an adjustment of a given individual with his economy to the objective, independent conditions of social organization... It consists of an investigation of the conditions of mutual exchange under which enterprises are able to maintain and increase their share of work in the general system of production.[27]

For Bogdanov, capitalist society was structurally heterogeneous, with a gradation of the most varied existences, each part being in continued mutual interaction with all the others parts. The way particular elements interacted was to be investigated by tektological analysis, which included the concepts of conjunction, ingression, equilibrium and selection. More particularly, a crisis was defined as a change in the organizational form of a complex, with equilibrium being broken and then re-established in a new organizational formation. In a crisis, a tektological boundary between two complexes was broken up, and a new system structure was created that included reformulated tektological boundaries.

Bogdanov was particularly concerned to stress multi-structural complexity and how the various systemic forms developed over time. He wrote that:

> Any complex, developing system represents a chain of groupings which are different in their age on the one hand, and in their connectedness and stability on the other. Historically, this represents a series of sequential layers: some layers were created earlier while others later 'superimpose' themselves (in the organizational sense) on the earlier layers . . . The development of any grouping is regulated by the mechanism of selection.[28]

The relative durability of such sequential historical layers depended upon the totality of conditions prevalent at any given time, as well as any destructive influences operating on them. Such a conception of both general historical development and particular economic structures was clearly antithetical to the mono-generative approach of neoclassical economics. In theory, this should have made Bogdanov's work attractive to many Bolshevik thinkers, but in practice Lenin's hostility to Bogdanov's philosophical views made the use of Bogdanov's work on tektology unacceptable to Communist Party personnel.

Business cycle analysis

It might reasonably be claimed that, within 'conventional' mainstream economics, the area of business cycle analysis was the field that Russian economists contributed most to developing in the period 1890–1930. Certainly in Western accounts of the history of economics, Tugan-Baranovsky, Kondratiev and Slutsky are the Russian names most likely to be encountered. Before 1917, the Russian contribution to trade cycle theory had been spearheaded by Tugan-Baranovsky, as discussed in Chapter 4. After 1917, a number of other Russian economists made very significant contributions to expanding the field of business cycle analysis, including Kondratiev (Tugan-Baranovsky's pupil), Slutsky and Pervushin. Whilst these people all contributed to the same general topic, each of their individual approaches was quite different, sometimes even a little contrary. Aspects of their work are discussed in what follows.

E.E. Slutsky and random cycles

As evaluated by most mainstream Western economists, Slutsky's work was an outstanding contribution to business cycle analysis in the 1920s that had very important ramifications for cycle theory in a number of different ways. However, Slutsky's contribution to economics widely considered was much greater than is sometimes acknowledged, in that he worked on many diverse topics such as currency emission, the foundations of economics and the theory of cooperatives, in addition to the well known work on the statistical analysis of business cycles. Before 1926, when Slutsky moved to Kondratiev's Conjuncture Institute in Moscow, he had worked at the Kiev Institute of Commerce. After the Conjuncture Institute was closed at the end of the 1920s, Slutsky moved to various mathematical centres and pursued work on the theory of probability and statistics, an aspect of his work that will be covered in more detail in the next chapter.

Table 7.1 lists Slutsky's main publications for the period 1922 to 1927, when his interest in economics was at its height. Five out of the 13 papers listed were squarely in the field of economics.

Table 7.1 Slutsky's main publications, 1922–27

Year	*Publication title*	*Subject*
1922	'On the question of the logical basis of calculating probability'	Mathematics
1923	'On several schemes of correlation'	Statistics
1923	'On a new coefficient of average population density'	Statistics
1923	'On the question of calculating the income received by the state from currency emission'	Economics
1923	'Mathematical notes towards a theory of currency emission'	Economics
1924	'On an attempt to construct a theory of averages without the assistance of a theory of probability'	Statistics
1925	'On the question of the "law of large numbers"'	Mathematics
1925	'On the stochastic asymptote and limit'	Mathematics
1926	'On the spontaneous cyclicity of a sequence of pairs of equal elements'	Mathematics
1926	'On the formal phraxeological foundations of economics'	Economics
1927	'The summation of random causes as the source of cyclic processes'	Economics
1927	'On a limit theorem related to a series of random quantities'	Mathematics
1927	'Towards a critique of Bohm–Bawerk's conception of value'	Economics

As can be seen from examining the temporal sequence of articles give in Table 7.1, the 1927 business cycles paper was an attempt to apply some of Slutsky's recently developed understanding of mathematical and statistical phenomena to economic matters, conditioned by his move from Kiev to Nikolai Kondratiev's Conjuncture Institute in Moscow in 1926. Slutsky had been working on various related statistical and mathematical topics such as stochastic convergence, the theory of averages, the law of large numbers and the foundations of probability theory throughout the 1920s. Slutsky would have been keen to demonstrate his abilities and usefulness to the economists he was working with in Moscow, and the 1927 paper was an impressive way to do so.

Slutsky's 1927 article on random cycles

It is likely that Slutsky first absorbed the more empirically orientated business cycle work of other members of the Conjuncture Institute, such as Kondratiev on long-run price dynamics and T.I. Rainov on trends in scientific discovery; Slutsky then supplied in addition what no-one else could provide, a deep theoretical re-interpretation of cycle theory based on his profound knowledge of mathematics and statistics. Slutsky's basic thesis in the 1927 article was that the summation of random causes could generate a cyclical pattern in a time series, which would imitate for a number of cycles a harmonic series, but this imitation would not last forever. After a number of periods this cyclical pattern would become disarranged, and the transition to another regime (series pattern) would occur around certain critical points. Fundamental to Slutsky's analysis was harmonic analysis, or the expression of the irregularities in the form and spacing of real cycles in terms of the summation of a number of separate regular sinusoidal fluctuations, an area of mathematics that had been developed by Jean Baptiste Fourier.

Slutsky reasoned that the probability of a value in a series remaining above or below the trend for a long period was negligible; hence values would pass from positive to negative deviations from the trend quite frequently. This would inevitably give rise to an undulatory appearance. However, this cyclical pattern might not be strictly periodic. In order to prove strict periodicity, Slutsky had to provide a second stage of argument which was much more complicated than the first. This second stage involved the idea that the decomposition of a wave pattern into various Fourier series revealed with greater distinction the regular wave pattern desired.[29] For example if a curve was represented as the product of two sinusoids, then these sinusoids according to Slutsky separated on a graph the regions that corresponded to definite regimes or series patterns. The point where such a sinusoid cut the axis of the abscissas was the critical point beyond which one regime was replaced by another one with different parameters.

Slutsky related that any given curve could be represented by the sum of a series of sinusoids, provided a large enough number of terms was taken. The approximately regular waves apparent in even the crude series which Slutsky presented were made much more distinct when the sum of the first five harmonics were deducted.[30] Slutsky took this as evidence that random waves could contain sections of apparently periodic movement. It should be stressed again that Slutsky's analysis was purely hypothetical, and he made no attempt to prove that any actual economic cycles were the outcome of random factors.[31]

One of the main consequences of this work of Slutsky's was taken to be that an oscillatory series could be generated from a random series by taking a moving sum or difference; that is, if a moving average of a random series was taken, for example to determine trend, then a (spurious) oscillatory movement in the series might be generated where none had existed originally. This fact was discovered independently by Yule, and is usually referred to as the Slutsky-Yule effect. This effect was related to but was not identical with the idea that the summation of random causes could be the source of actual cyclic processes, these processes displaying approximate regularity. Slutsky's analysis also implied that a time series might contain structural breaks, in which a regularity that had previously acted on the series was replaced by a new regularity with different parameters.[32]

Slutsky's work was very different in approach to either Kondratiev's in the USSR or Wesley Mitchell's in the USA at this time. Slutsky argued that Mitchell's denial of the periodicity of business cycles was a result of Mitchell's purely descriptive methodology. Using Slutsky's more sophisticated Fourier-series analysis, periodicity was discovered, albeit confined to definite regions of a series. Slutsky named the tendency of random series to possess periodicity 'the tendency to sinusoid form'.[33] Therefore according to Slutsky a key difference between randomly generated cycles and genuinely periodic cycles was that in the former, periodicity would not extend to the entire series under consideration, whereas in the latter it did.

The uniqueness of Slutsky's approach within the USSR is emphasised by examining the range of authors on which his work drew. Slutsky footnoted Arthur Schuster 'On the periodicities of sunspots'; G. Yule's 1926 paper on nonsense correlations; L. von Bortkiewicz's work on iteration; E. Husserl's work on the philosophy of phenomenology; V. Romanovsky's work on the sinusoidal limit theorem; W. Thorp's business annals; R. von Mises on probability; K. Pearson's statistical tables; and A. Lyapunov's analysis of the limit properties of integrals. This list demonstrated that Slutsky's theoretical approach to cycles was not influenced to any large extent by the normal economics authors which other Conjuncture Institute members were more familiar with, people such as M.I. Tugan-Baranovsky, G. Cassel, A. Pigou, A. Aftalion and so on. The impetus for the new approach of the 1927 article had originated from Slutsky himself.

Other Russian economists on business cycles

If Slutsky's 1927 article was the most famous single article published on business cycle analysis in the USSR in the 1920s, it was not at all typical of most of the other work done in this area by Russian contributors. The other very well known article was Kondratiev's 1925 paper on long cycles, which was later expanded into book form in 1928, and Kondratiev's predominantly empirical approach to detecting the long cycle was different in many ways to Slutsky's more statistically rigorous approach. These two influential articles went alongside the publication of a great deal of lesser-known work on topics such as the relation between the harvest and business cycles, monetary policy and cycles and the national as against the international synchronisation of cyclical movements.

For example, S.A. Pervushin adopted a Mitchell-type approach in terms of plotting cycles in Russia, the UK and the USA in long-run comparison, and A.L. Vainshtein examined various theories linking meteorological phenomena and cyclical turning points and their possible relevance to the Russian data.[34] Other economic thinkers such as Bazarov compared the long-run secular dynamics of capitalist development as against those in the Soviet economy. The connection between cycles and growth was also indirectly raised in various ways, for example in G.A. Fel'dman's (1884–1958) model of economic growth under socialism, and through the general question of whether the Soviet economy would actually experience cyclical patterns of development itself. In classical Marxist theory, business cycles were often seen as indicative of capitalistic waste, but the realities of the Soviet system meant that phenomena such as the economic restoration process that occurred after the civil war might usefully be conceived of as a particularly strong cyclical upturn.

Kondratiev's Conjuncture Institute was the most famous and intellectually rigorous governmental body devoted to the study of business cycles and economic analysis in general in this period, but it was not the only place where interesting work was undertaken in this subject area. Gosplan had its own conjunctural department, and Chayanov's Institute of Agricultural Economics also produced work on related topics. In terms of comparing Russian business cycle analysis with its Western counterparts, it was generally true that the Russian work was a little more empirically-orientated that that in the UK, bearing more comparison with the work of the NBER in the USA. Comparing the post-revolutionary work with the pre-revolutionary Russian heritage, Tugan-Baranovsky's approach of combining disproportion, maldistribution and loanable funds was not directly employed after 1917, although the question of the extent of harmonisation of Russian cycles with international movements was still a relevant concern for some.

Institutional economists on socialism

The creation of the Soviet system of economic management in Russia after 1917 attracted a great deal of attention from overseas, including the attention of some American institutional economists. For example, Thorstein Veblen was well known for proposing the idea of a Soviet of Technicians as a superior alternative to the existing vested interests for managing industrial production in America. He favoured the idea of an 'industrial republic', or an economic order devoted first of all to making goods instead of making profit. However, Veblen was pessimistic as to the possibility that an American Soviet would actually be formed.

One of Veblen's earliest articles was entitled 'Some neglected points in the theory of socialism'. In some ways it was particularly insightful and honest. For example, although Veblen was sympathetic to the general goal of overcoming vested business interests and the power of absentee owners, he was perceptive enough to write about the motivation of some socialists that:

> The ground of the unrest with which we are concerned is, very largely, jealousy, – envy, if you choose: and the ground of this particular form of jealousy, that makes for socialism, is to be found in the institution of private property.[35]

Veblen was implying that although the general goal of the abolition of private property was one which he sympathized with, the reasons why at least some socialists supported this goal was not always that they believed it would improve overall human well-being, but rather that they thought there was 'something in it for them'. Self-interest backed by jealousy was sometimes a motive for socialists, just as it was for supporters of conspicuous consumption, and presumably Veblen thought that this might be a fault-line for attempts at creating a socialist society in the future.

Regarding Russian Marxism as a political movement, before the Bolshevik assumption of power Veblen had written:

> In practical politics, the Social Democrats have had to make up their account with the labor movement, the agricultural population, and the imperialistic policy. On each of these heads the preconceived program of Marxism has come in conflict with the run of events, and on each head it has been necessary to deal shrewdly and adapt the principles to the facts of the time.[36]

This passage suggested that Veblen believed the 'preconceived program of Marxism' to be incomplete, even though he was sympathetic to the revolutionary cause. After 1917 Veblen was quite enthusiastic about the Bolshevik experiment. His analysis of accomplishments in Russia emphasised that:

> the Soviet owes this measure of success to the fact that the Russian people have not been industrialized in anything like the same degree as their western neighbors. They have in great measure been able to fall back on an earlier, simpler, less close-knit plan of productive industry.[37]

By implication, in America this 'falling back' would not be possible, and hence Soviet success in America would have to follow a very different form. According to Veblen's suggested definition, Bolshevism was primarily a form of economic organization based on Soviet control of industry, which replaced capitalist control through absentee owners. For John Commons however the Soviet Union's dictatorship of the proletariat had originated in one-sided collective action.[38]

Regarding the early development of the USSR itself, Veblen defended the fledgling Soviet Russia against perceived imperialistic attack. For example, in a 1920 review of Keynes's *The Economic Consequences of the Peace* Veblen wrote:

> The events of the past months go to show that the central and most binding provision of the Treaty (and of the League) is an unrecorded clause by which the governments of the Great Powers are banded together for the suppression of Soviet Russia.[39]

In the review Veblen stressed that the Bolsheviks were a threat to absentee ownership, the maintenance and extension of such ownership being the major purpose of all the contemporaneous political traffic of the Great Powers. In the event the 'Red Terror' that occurred in America in 1919–20 pushed Veblen's pro-Soviet teachings on the USSR into obscurity.[40] In general the reaction of American institutionalism to the creation of the USSR was a little ambiguous. Whilst some institutionalists like Veblen were keen to highlight the non-capitalist nature of Soviet economy, they were often pessimistic as to its application in the wider world.

Conclusion

This chapter has only skimmed the surface of the contributions made by some Russian economists of the period, yet it should be apparent even from this outline that the 1920s were a high point of the development of original socialist economic theory in the USSR, with relative freedom being bestowed on many diverse currents and eddies. Many genuinely unique ideas and approaches were developed by people like Kondratiev, Slutsky, Chayanov and Preobrazhensky, ideas that began to challenge the West in terms of leadership of the direction of international economic research in a few areas of speciality. Moreover, the diversity of economic thinking that flourished in this decade was truly remarkable, ranging from

Yurovsky's neoclassicism to Trotsky's Marxism, a range that is perhaps unparalleled when also allied with the innovation that was displayed. But all good things usually come to an end, and by 1929, the fragile political truce that had been developed after the end of War Communism finally collapsed. The consequences of this for Soviet economic theory were immense, as will be seen in the next chapter.

8 The Russian economic mind under Stalinism, 1929–1940

The year 1929 was without doubt a decisive turning point in Soviet history. A campaign for the mass collectivisation of Soviet agriculture was developed and the first national five-year economic plan came into operation. These two events marked the initial peak of Stalin's 'left turn', away from the relatively open mixed economy of NEP, towards the creation of a fully centralised 'administrative-command' economy that would later become characterised as communism by both Stalin's supporters, and by many virulent anti-socialists. Of course, whether the actual Soviet system was the only possible interpretation of socialist planning that it was possible to create in the USSR at this time remains a controversial question. It could reasonably be maintained that, whilst the material conditions of Soviet Russia were indeed an important limiting condition on possible interpretations of socialism that could have been implemented at this time, so was the underdeveloped theoretical understanding of many leading Bolsheviks, the rigid and authoritarian attitude of whom sometimes discouraged flexible thinking in this regard.

On the political plane, the level of general Communist Party concern over apparent threats from 'bourgeois' counter-revolutionary forces grew dramatically in the USSR at the end of the 1920s, and this had a major effect on the attitude of the authorities to economists and economic theory in Russia. Whilst ever since 1917 economists had always been regarded with more than a little suspicion by the Soviet authorities, after 1929, a campaign to ruin many of them personally and destroy their influence on policy-making developed in earnest. This campaign had a decimating effect on 'conventional' economics in general and on some economists as individuals, but its effect was not simply to destroy. Rather in some instances its effect was to dramatically transform or to fundamentally shift the existing trajectory of existing currents and eddies, and to create a new partition of management science appropriate to the Soviet system of planning. These various developments will be explored more fully as this chapter unfolds.

Intellectual exile

In 1930, a number of key figures in economics were arrested, including Nikolai Bukharin, N.D. Kondratiev and L.N. Yurovsky, and propaganda designed to smear and discredit their work was published concertedly across many Soviet newspapers and journals. They were portrayed as intellectual puppets of foreign capitalist interests and as desiring and actually trying to organise a counter-revolution in the USSR. Kondratiev for example was verbally interrogated in order to try to get him to confess to various ideological and actual crimes, and although he admitted to proposing economic policy that sometimes contradicted that of the government, he refused to confess to the more severe charges of treasonable activities or sabotage. Even so he was sentenced to a long jail term, before being finally executed in 1938. Apart from the actual murder itself, which was a secret affair, this type of rough handling was a very public event, and served to provide a forceful lesson to those who might have thought of acting in any way against the Stalinist system of power.

The effect of such treatment of 'star' economists like Kondratiev, and an associated purging of various institutes and government bodies of any independently-minded individuals, meant that after 1929, the nature and content of economic theory in the USSR changed dramatically. In large measure it became simply the ideological expression of current Communist Party policy, with little scope for true individuality or the genuine discovery of new ideas. This is not to say however that no original or interesting developments occurred in Soviet economics in the 1930s. In fact there were two main sources of original work in this period: the detailed and technical aspects of economic planning, which was often carried out at a level that had no great ideological significance, and hence was relatively free from day-to-day interference; and areas of study tangentially related to economics, such as statistics and mathematics, which were either too abstract for ideology to permeate fully, or had no direct political significance at all. Hence this chapter will examine these two areas of originality in detail, as well as sampling the more conventional yet overwhelmingly ideological 'mainstream' of Stalinist economics in the 1930s.

Joseph Schumpeter's characterisation of the nature of the historical break that occurred while moving from Russian to Soviet economics was that Soviet Russia inherited an excellent tradition of work in statistical methods and their probabilistic foundations that survived and continued to flourish even after 1929.[1] One very prominent example of this was the work of E.E. Slutsky, who managed to continue actively working in an intellectual capacity until his death from natural causes in 1948.

Slutsky's research programme in the 1930s

After 1930, Slutsky was forced to significantly modify his research programme as a response to the closure of the Conjuncture Institute and the arrest of some of its leading members. Slutsky moved decisively away from economics and back to his original corpus of research interests in mathematics and statistics, by transferring institutionally to a centre devoted to the study of meteorology and then to various mathematical institutes. Table 8.1 lists Slutsky's most important publications in the period 1930–37, none of which were devoted to clearly economics topics.

Despite the absence of economic papers, some definite continuity with Slutsky's research in the 1920s can be detected in the continual appearance of the notion of the chance function in his work in the 1930s, and some (lesser) continuity with his work before 1917 in the reappearance of correlation analysis. Hence although Slutsky was forced to modify significantly his research programme after the closure of the Conjuncture Institute, he did not completely abandon all of the topic areas in which he had been working before 1930, rather he simply removed the economic component from them. This thematic subtraction was possible because most of Slutsky's economics-related work in the 1920s involved the pioneering application of statistical techniques to economic themes, rather than the straightforward development of economic topics within themselves.

In this period, Slutsky continued operating on statistical problems relating to cyclical phenomena, working at the Central Institute of Meteorology between 1931 and 1934. As Table 8.1 demonstrated, a specific area of

Table 8.1 Slutsky's main publications, 1930–37

Year	*Publication title*	*Subject*
1932	'On the error distribution of correlation coefficients in a first-order correlated series'	Statistics
1932	'On the random compact function'	Mathematics
1933	'On the question of the connection between sunspot periodicity and temperature'	Geophysics
1934	'On the question of sunspot periodicity'	Geophysics
1934	'Ten years of working for geophysical statistics'	Geophysics
1934	'Several applications of Fourier's coefficient to the analysis of random stationary functions'	Mathematics
1935	'Statistical experiment as a method of investigating concrete problems'	Statistics
1935	'On the question of extrapolating the chance function in connection with the problem of prognosis'	Mathematics
1935	'On the 11-year periodicity of sunspots'	Geophysics
1937	'Several propositions on the theory of chance functions'	Mathematics

statistical research that Slutsky found particularly interesting was sunspot cycles. It was W.S. Jevons and Henry Moore who had first pursued the connection between sunspots and economics cycles in the West, evoking some ridicule in response. In the USSR in the 1920s, A.L. Vainshtein had investigated the influence of sunspot activity on economic phenomena, and this topic did therefore have some direct resonance with Soviet economics. Vainshtein had reviewed two Moore books on economic cycles in 1925: *Economic Cycles: Their Law and Cause* of 1914 and *Generating Economic Cycles* of 1923. Moore had attempted to connect meteorological patterns to economic cycles by associating rainfall with harvest. According to Moore, periodic meteorological fluctuations had a decisive effect on the production of goods dependent on climatic and natural conditions, namely raw materials.[2]

Moore, like Slutsky after him, used Fourier analysis to search for cyclical patterns, and to distinguish real cycles from spontaneous random cycles Moore had used the method of the periodogram. Vainshtein criticised the periodogram methods as used by Moore for a 'purely formal, statistical analysis of the question' and for ignoring the economic meaning of the problem. Vainshtein also criticised Moore for his inability to provide a mechanism of influence for the connections he assumed in the statistical methods utilised.[3] However, Slutsky's work on sunspot cycles in the 1930s was purely statistical in approach, making no reference whatsoever to economic theory, which was by then a minefield of possible political infringements.

Slutsky and sunspot periodicity

Slutsky's three papers on this topic from the 1930s were 'On the question of the connection between sunspot periodicity and temperature' of 1933, 'On the question of sunspot periodicity' of 1934, and 'On the 11-year periodicity of sunspots' of 1935. In these papers Slutsky took up the line of investigation undertaken by statisticians such as G.U. Yule and Arthur Schuster. Schuster had pioneered the use of the periodogram to detect hidden periodicity, and Yule had shown that Schuster's periodogram method was only reliable when eliminating superposed fluctuations from a time series, not when eliminating truly random disturbances. While most of the examples used by Schuster and Yule were taken from meteorological and astronomical time series, the results were readily applicable to economic time series, something that Slutsky must have been aware of.

Slutsky's 1934 paper 'On the question of sunspot periodicity' was a direct response to a paper by C.G. Abbot entitled 'On periodicity in solar variation' published in 1922. Abbot had attempted to detect periodicity in solar variation by comparing the solar constant for each day with those of one, two and subsequent days up to 40 days later. To do this he simply calculated correlation coefficients between the values of the solar constant for a given day with those of one, two, three and so on days later. Abbot explained that, if periodicity was present in the given series, it would be revealed by positive and negative runs of the correlation coefficient.[4] In fact, no clearly defined periodicity in solar variation persisted throughout the eight years of investigation. With respect to individual years, regularity was clearest in 1915, with a period of about 27 days being indicated. For 1916 a period of 3.5 days was indicated.[5] The years 1909, 1910 and 1914 showed similar results. The years 1908, 1911 and 1913 showed no similarity to each other or to any demonstrated pattern. Abbot therefore concluded that there was no periodicity in solar variations in the years examined, and hence that each season was a law unto itself.[6]

However, in 'On the question of sunspot periodicity' Slutsky suggested that Abbot's work was based on faulty methodology, pointing out that the data on sunspot constants was autocorrelated. He described the graph of sunspot constants as containing waves of a number of different lengths, such as a few days, monthly, and also yearly. In these conditions it would be hopeless to attempt to detect periodicity through the use of correlation coefficients between members of the series without a sufficiently large sequence of data.[7] If too few observations were used, then any waves that were detected might be interpreted as a secular component, not as proper cycles. Consequently, Slutsky suggested that it would be more appropriate to 'rework' the existing series to form a new series. After performing this process Slutsky obtained several new series that were of sufficient length.[8] These series related to the periods 1924–27, 1928–31 and 1924–31, and contained 400, 400 and 800 observations respectively. Correlation coefficients were calculated for a lag of one observation up to a lag of 143 observations in each series. The resulting graph showed how the correlation coefficient r was connected to previous values of r from r_1 to r_{143}, i.e. how much autocorrelation there was in the series.

According to Slutsky, this graph showed that there was a noticeable level of correlation between members of the series, as a cyclical pattern was clearly visible. There were minima at values for r of 11, 40–1, 68, 93–5 and 115–16, and maxima at values for r of 30–1, 49–54, 83–5, 103–5 and 124–5. These maxima corresponded to time periods over the eight years of t = 31, t = 226, t = 328, t = 426 and t = 525, which according to Slutsky suggested a very plausible hypothesis: that the fluctuations in the correlation coefficients reflected the period of rotation of the sun around its axis.[9] The synodic period of rotation of the sun was generally accepted to be 27.28 days, and for Slutsky this gave a material base for the observed fluctuations.[10]

Slutsky's use of the sun's synodic period to explain the observed periodicity matched Abbot's original attempt to detect runs of high and low values for the solar constant of approximately 27 days.[11] However, Abbot's conclusion that a constant periodicity for the years 1908–16 could not be detected was contradicted by Slutsky's claim to have found evidence of exactly such periodicity for the years 1924–31. This demonstrated that Slutsky did not use statistical techniques only to bring the existence of cycles into question, but also used them (when appropriate) for confirming the existence of cycles that had been queried. This reversal of technique was also apparent from Slutsky's next article on this topic entitled 'Concerning the 11-year periodicity of sunspots' from 1935, where the results obtained were declared as being unlikely to have been found purely by chance.[12]

Slutsky and statistics in the 1930s

Whilst it is clear from the above account of one particular aspect of Slutsky's work in the 1930s that he had changed the direction of his research in a significant way, he still kept faith with some underlying themes of his research from the 1920s. An example of something at least indirectly related to Slutsky's 1927 article on random cycles issued by Slutsky in 1935 was a paper entitled 'On the question of extrapolation in connection with the problem of prognosis', which was published in the Soviet *Journal of Geophysics*. In this article, Slutsky investigated the use of the extrapolation method in relation to determinate random processes, suggesting that the effectiveness of this method depended on the probability structure of the process under review. The possibility of extrapolation was proved by the existence of limiting cases such as the law of the sinusoidal limit, and Slutsky referred to his 1927 paper in this respect directly.

After describing various methods based on a number of different regression equations, Slutsky recommended that the best way of testing a particular method was by comparing it with a real application. He thus presented as a practical example a prognosis of the water level of the river Volga at Saratov over 95 days in 1925, outlining that an accurate forecast for two days ahead was possible through the use of a specific equation that was given.[13] While in no sense as significant for economics as the 1927 article, Slutsky's work in the 1930s was still in a limited sense a continuation of some of the themes that were articulated there. Thus while Stalin's ascendancy to power drastically altered the trajectory of Soviet economic discourse, a few elements of previous concerns still remained.

Officially sanctioned economic discourse

After the arrest of the leading 'bourgeois' economists such as Kondratiev and Yurovsky in 1930, economic discourse continued to occur in the USSR, but in a dramatically modified form. It became very general on the one hand and very technical and specific on the other, i.e. in the former the abstract principles on which the Soviet economy was allegedly based were articulated by bureaucratic decree, in the latter the minutiae of the various methods for establishing planning targets were elaborated through engineer-like methods. The content of economic discourse thus became polarised towards ideological and technical extremes, with the middle ground of traditional 'mainstay' economic analysis being forced to close shop. This was not simply because the Soviet economy itself had dramatically changed its nature, as it was readily acknowledged by all concerned that some so-called 'petty bourgeois' elements still existed within Soviet borders.

For example, in 1931 a debate occurred in the trade section of the Institute of Economics in Leningrad, the record of this discussion being published as *The Object and Method of the Economics of Soviet Trade* in 1932. The main paper under discussion – by V.V. Smushkov – distinguished in general terms between trade (*torgovlya*) and goods circulation (*tovarooborot*), the process of goods turnover in capitalism being circulation but the organisational form of this process was trade.[14] In the Soviet context, trade still existed in relation to the three existing sectors of the economy – the socialist sector, the petty-commodity sector and the capitalist sector. When full communism was achieved, planned natural distribution of all goods would occur, but before this time commodity–money forms of distribution still existed in the non-socialist sectors of the economy. The process of transforming from commodity–money forms of trade to direct product exchange was seen as a 'growing in' process, i.e. an organic transformation over a period of time.[15]

In response to Smushkov's paper, other authors raised various questions and additional considerations. For example, S.E. Gorelik differentiated between the general theory of Soviet economy, the economics of Soviet trade and the techniques of planned calculation in trading enterprises. In the theory of Soviet economy the laws of movement towards socialism and the methodological foundations of planning were established. In the economics of Soviet trade, planning methodology was used in the specific areas of goods circulation, the balancing of supply and demand and price determination. With respects to the techniques of planned calculation, planned accounts to fulfil the national economic plan for various enterprises were constructed.[16] A general theoretical characterisation of Soviet trade in the 1930s was made by G. Neiman as follows:

> As opposed to capitalist trade, Soviet trade is not the sphere of action of spontaneous laws. The movement of the goods mass in the Soviet system is determined not by the play of market forces … but by a proletarian state plan. … Soviet trade limits the alienating feature of capitalist trade, competition; its place is taken by socialist emulation between trading enterprises.[17]

Such discussions revealed the very general and rather low intellectual level of such debates that were held at the abstract plane, abounding with vague terminology that was imprecisely defined. This was in part due to a dramatic decline in much of the personnel associated with economic discourse, but also it reflected the ambiguous status of concepts such as trade in an allegedly socialist economy. If trade occurred in capitalism, what then was the socialist form of trade? In the early 1930s the tendency to try to distinguish every aspect of socialist economy from its capitalist forebear was at its height, a tendency that sometimes produced awkwardly contorted results.

With regards to the minutiae of planning methodology, numerous articles appeared in journals such as *Plan*, *Bol'shevik* and *Planovoe khozyaistvo* in the 1930s that were devoted to specific aspects of plan construction. Discussions about topics like measuring the population purchasing fund, the construction of trading plans, the use of budget data for measuring demand and the use of preliminary orders for demand planning flourished, the dry technical content of such articles being a world away from the heated ideological conflicts which had permeated many Soviet economics journals in the 1920s. Newspaper articles such as those in *Ekonomicheskaya zhizn'* discussed topics like improving the efficiency of trading units, the reform of trading organisations and the improvement of trading links. In general they followed Communist Party pronouncements and party policy on most matters, although occasionally a low-level debate might arise on a specific topic. This indicated that economic decision-making now occurred behind closed doors, and economic discourse accessible to the general public was thus dramatically transformed. There was certainly an element of Orwellian newspeak in such discourse, but also of simple-minded fact-worship.

J.V. Stalin (1879–1953)

Stalin's bogus omnipotence stretched from politics to nationalities to constitutional matters and even to economic doctrine. In general terms it can be stated that Stalin's apparently theoretical writings were usually just the convenient expression of the particular policy that he was currently favouring in whatever particular realm, be it economics, politics or some other field of influence. The flavour of some of Stalin's ideas in economics can be gleaned from the following quotations. In a speech from April 1929 Stalin declared:

> The difference between Soviet society and every other society lies in the very fact that it is interested not in any kind of increase of productivity of labour but in such an increase as will guarantee the supremacy of socialist forms of economy over other forms.[18]

This apparently clear distinction related to the conflict between the socialist and capitalist sectors of the Soviet economy, but Stalin was tacitly acknowledging that it was a political decision that was being made to support the socialist sector, not an exclusively economic one. This might be seen to conflict with Lenin's notion from the early days of NEP that the socialist sectors of the Soviet economy must gain victory over the non-socialist parts through purely economic means.

Stalin was keen to provide theoretical characterisations of current states of economic affairs. As a characterisation of the Soviet economy generally, Stalin wrote in February 1931 that:

> we are conducting a planned economy, systematically accumulating resources and properly distributing them among the different branches of national economy. ... The superiority of our system lies in that we have no crises of overproduction.[19]

Whereas in capitalism such crises were apparently overcome by reducing the wages of workers and through mass unemployment, in a planned economy the absence of production anarchy meant that, according to Stalin, such problems did not arise. This view of the causes of economic crises owes a significant debt to the disproportionality component of Tugan-Baranovsky's account of trade cycles, although Tugan-Baranovsky himself was of course never mentioned in Soviet economic literature from this period.

Stalin was later keen to propound what he called the 'economic laws of socialism', which in truth were merely vague phrases that characterised his currently favoured policies. Examples of such 'economic laws' were the law of the priority development of means of production and the law of the harmonious development of the national economy, which were obviously not 'laws' in any genuinely scientific sense, rather they were simply practical policy aims. In terms of the results of the first five-year plan, Stalin wrote in January 1933 that:

> The results of the Five-Year Plan have shattered the thesis of the Social-Democrats that it is impossible to build socialism in one separate country. ... The results of the Five-Year Plan have refuted the assertions of bourgeois economists that the capitalist system of economy is the best of all systems.[20]

Maintaining doctrinal righteousness was an important element in Stalin's personal authority, socialism in one country being a key plank of his own policy programme at the end of the 1920s.

Stalin sometimes personally entered the ideological battle against individual economic specialists directly. For example in December 1929, Stalin attacked Groman by name for suggesting that 1917 brought no advantages to the peasantry, this idea being taken up by the 'Trotsky-Zinoviev opposition'. Bukharin's heretical ideas were the subject of a long invective by Stalin entitled 'The Right Deviation in the CPSU' from 1929. Moreover, Stalin took a keen personal interest in the fate of pro-market economists such as Kondratiev and Yurovsky who had been arrested on his orders in 1930. While Stalin also intervened in many other areas of intellectual endeavour, special attention was given to the fortunes of economists in the late 1920s and early 1930s, when Stalin was consolidating his personal dictatorship, as economists possessed that specialist knowledge which might have served to undermine Stalin's pretensions to theoretical precision. In general it can be concluded that Stalin's economic pronouncements had no genuine originality or theoretical worth to them at all, except as an indication of his own over-inflated ego. Whilst undoubtedly a skilled bureaucratic manipulator, as a theorist he was a resounding dud.

L.V. Kantorovich (1912–1986)

The idea of an optimal plan was initially suggested by the economist L.V. Kantorovich in a work first published in Leningrad in 1939, an idea that later contributed to his receiving the Nobel Prize in economics. Up until this time the idea of an economic optimum had been negatively associated with neoclassical economics in the minds of most Bolsheviks, the neoclassical approach being dismissed by them as the supreme folly of vulgar apologetics. Kantorovich explicitly acknowledged that deficiencies in existing Soviet planning procedures existed, due to the fact that economic science lagged behind the requirements of a socialist system, and also that existing plans were not necessarily fully efficient. The 1939 study actually proposed a method for solving various technical problems such as the least wasteful allocation of work to machines and the shaping of materials with minimum loss. The initial problem was to distribute the manufacture of parts to available machine tools so as to produce the maximum number of complete sets of parts, or a method of machine loading to obtain the highest productivity, but Kantorovich soon realised that the method outlined had more general application to the planning process.[21]

The notion of an optimal plan that Kantorovich proposed was a plan in which the proposed product assortment was optimally distributed amongst firms at the lowest possible cost of production. Within the optimal plan, the principle of profitability was observed, that is each factory was assigned the production of that type of good on which it had the highest net product.[22] Using a system of so-called objectively-determined valuations (or shadow prices) and economic indices, in which resources were categorised with respect to their scarcity, Kantorovich devised specific methods for ensuring the maximum fulfilment of the programme task in terms of the given assortment of goods. The shadow prices were objective in the sense that they were the result of mathematical operations performed on data, rather than simply the subjective evaluations of planning officials. The significance of all this in general was that a method of finding the solution to problems involving a large number of different input factors and planned variants – from which the best variant had to be selected – had been developed.

Later Kantorovich expanded this idea into a more general approach to economic planning, and also added other elements that flowed from the initial idea. He specified the two main tasks of planning in a socialist society as being first, the correct choice of method in the production of a given output, and second, the best allocation of the plan programme amongst individual enterprises.[23] Significantly, Kantorovich distinguished between short-term planning, when methods of production were fixed – i.e. over a year, a quarter or a month – and long-term planning, when it was possible to develop new factories, transport links, training schemes and so on.[24] Such long-term investments were part of general political decision-making, although the efficiency of capital investment should still be considered as part of long-term planning procedures. Thus an optimal long-term plan certainly existed, which used a dynamic system of evaluations, but Kantorovich implied that the methods used for long-term planning were somewhat different than that for generating short-term plans.[25] Solving a short-term problem was mainly a technical task, but outlining the goals of a long-term plan was not something that could be accomplished solely through mathematical calculations.

Thus the notion of an optimal plan referred only to the most rational path between two already-selected points; the end-state of a particular plan had to be selected by criteria outside of Kantorovich's method. Hence although on the face of it, Kantorovich's invention of optimal planning was revolutionary in the Soviet context, it was only revolutionary in a technical sense; its still implicitly accepted that existing political methods of setting overall planning targets should be maintained. Kantorovich admitted that in his method, a number of important problems had been ignored, for example adjustments to the composition of final output on the basis of demand studies, but he implied that his methods might be of use in these areas also.

As the most significant example of its type, it is necessary to ponder a little further on the exact significance of Kantorovich's optimal planning ideas. Schumpeter suggested that the task of Soviet economists after 1929 was really to smuggle concepts like interest and marginal productivity into Soviet economics in such a manner as to hide their identity with the corresponding capitalist concepts.[26] In a very general sense this was often true, but did Kantorovich himself fully understand that this was what he was doing? Put another way, was Kantorovich fully conscious of Schumpeter's task, or did he believe that the idea of an optimal plan was not simply a black market copy of capitalist techniques? Given the intellectual origins of Kantorovich's work in a very technical problem, it is unlikely that he realised the full ideological significance of his invention, at least at the beginning.

Another answer fashioned along institutionalist lines would be that, since real market economies themselves were not actually described by the theorems of neoclassical economics, then Kantorovich's work was not a copy of actually existing capitalism, but only of its theoretical misrepresentation. An institutionalist account of the Soviet economic system would then have to be developed that located the notion of an optimal plan in parallel with the same role as played by mainstream economics in the West, and then actual plans would have to be explained as the result of a multitude of institutional forces such as conflicts of interest between producers, consumers and Communist Party personnel. The idea of an optimal plan would then be only one amongst many conceptual factors that functioned as a point of debate between the various participants in the ongoing development of the planning process in Soviet-style economies.

Émigré economists

The scope for disagreement and dissent within Soviet economics declined dramatically after 1929, but one extra-national avenue for the expression of dissent still remained – the work of émigré economists. After 1917, some economic thinkers had felt it necessary to leave the USSR for safer political climates overseas, and even for some who decided to remain within Soviet borders, the decision to stay had been a difficult one. These émigré economists can legitimately be considered as a geographically stray branch of Russian economics widely considered, and their work provided a unique point of supply for information about Soviet economics from a resolutely non-Party source. In political terms, these émigrés often bore a grudge against the Bolsheviks for forcing their expulsion, but this does not necessarily mean that their work contained no genuine insights.

One of the most prominent émigré economists was S.N. Prokopovich (1871–1955), who in the 1930s published a 'Bulletin of the economic cabinet of Prokopovich' that subjected Soviet economic analysis and statistics to detailed scrutiny from overseas. Prokopovich also provided an interesting theoretical account of Soviet economy but it was more for his on-going empirical analyses that he was known. In the late 1890s, Prokopovich had been a young socialist who came under the influence of Bernstein's revisionism, and he had consequently criticised Plekhanov's conception of a revolution that was to be controlled by a very small party, preferring instead to encourage workers to learn to organise for themselves.[27]

Prokopovich worked for a time in the Provisional Government but left Russia in 1922. Subsequent to this exile, Prokopovich's 'economic cabinet' was set up first in Berlin and then transferred to Prague, and in addition to the 'Bulletin' it also published a journal on Russian economics. As an example of the empirical approach taken, the 'Bulletin' questioned figures for the level of goods turnover that had been provided in the USSR between 1932 and 1935 that were given in rubles, which Prokopovich suggested only measured the monetary receipts obtained for goods, rather than the level of actual physical turnover.[28] Prokopovich's work in this respect is still a useful point of reference even today.

Prokopovich's underlying theoretical argument regarding the state of the Soviet economy throughout Bolshevik control was expressed in relation to analysing the principles of communism that had been implemented by 1922. He wrote:

> The whole history of the three years of communist reign proves that the dislocation of industry was due to the principles themselves and not to the inexperience and mistakes in the application of these principles.[29]

By 'the principles themselves' Prokopovich meant the nationalisation of industry and the centralisation of economic control, which had, according to Prokopovich, yielded unambiguously negative results. A decline in labour productivity and the destruction of labour incentives had occurred together with a waste of industrial capital caused by a failure to continue re-investment. Prokopovich's solution was to reinstate private property in the means of production, which would serve to re-awaken economic initiative. In this conception, the introduction of NEP in 1921 did not go far enough towards dismantling the principles of communism that had apparently been implemented after 1917. Prokopovich was one of the most significant of the émigré economists in that his work engaged with Soviet economics at a very detailed level, and hence it was at the time a key source for alternative information about the precise state of Soviet development.

Another prominent émigré economist was P.B. Struve, whose work before 1917 was discussed previously. Struve's post-1917 economics were far less significant than that which he had published before 1917, and also less significant than that of Prokopovich, but he did provide some interesting general commentary on Stalin's 'economic revolution'. Struve's attitude by 1930 was ambiguous, sometimes mocking the 'blockade mentality' of a closed economy, but also recognising that the five-year plans could result in increased industrial growth. He was particularly concerned to stress that the Soviet planning system could only function in association with political despotism and the use of continued coercion, and he described the five-year plan as a 'pump for accumulation and a machine for exploitation'.[30] Like some other émigrés, dislocation from his homeland led Struve to a position of total hostility towards Soviet Russia, an attitude that sometimes blinded such people to the nuances of the Soviet position, and often made their post-revolutionary economics less original than their pre-revolutionary efforts. There was, however, one very prominent exception to this rule.

W.W. Leontief (1906–1999)

Another very important émigré economist, but one not at all in the same category of ideological dissident as Prokopovich and Struve, was W.W. Leontief. Leontief had attended Leningrad University between 1921 and 1925 and his work in the USSR in the 1920s, mentioned in the previous chapter, had a likely influence on his later work on input-output analysis. Leontief's work after emigration was less obviously anti-Soviet than that of either Prokopovich or Struve, although this does not necessarily mean that Leontief's personal political views were any different to those of many other émigrés.

In the introduction to *The Structure of American Economy*, first published in 1941, Leontief explained that this work was an attempt to apply the idea of general interdependence to an empirical study of a specific national economy.[31] This description might apply equally to the various Soviet attempts at creating a balance of the national economy that had occurred in the 1920s, such as that of P.I. Popov, and that Leontief was certainly fully aware of. Of course, the general idea of mapping all the various connections in an economy went back to Francois Quesnay, but the idea was pursued with such vigour and determination in the USSR in the 1920s that it would seem difficult to accept the notion that this context had no influence on Leontief's intellectual development at all.

In Leontief's method, three sets of equations served to make up the scheme of general interdependence characterising the entire economic system in stationary equilibrium. The first set described total output of each industry equalling total consumption, the second demonstrated that the value of the product of each industry equalled the value of all goods and services absorbed by it, and the third showed the relation between physical output and input cost elements or the production function for any given industry.[32] Leontief then added consideration of saving and investment by means of a savings coefficient and an investment coefficient, together with consideration of ongoing technical change. Coefficients identifying the level of raw materials and intermediate goods needed for each unit of product in each sector of the economy were also employed. Leontief was awarded the Nobel prize in economics in 1973 for his work on the input-output approach.

Unlike some of his émigré colleagues, and perhaps prefigured by the type of work that he pursued, Leontief was not totally opposed to some forms of economic planning in market-type systems. As late as the 1970s, Leontief advocated the creation of a planning board in the USA that would use input–output techniques to develop indicative plans for various economic growth possibilities, and he accepted that the final choice in such a process would always be political. Leontief was the Soviet émigré who achieved the most in relation to mainstream Western economics, but the national origins of his work should not be forgotten.

Western economists on the Soviet system

Developments in the Soviet economy in the 1930s attracted the prickly attention of Western economists for contradictory reasons. Some wanted to demonstrate the unreserved futility of attempting to create an economic system based on non-capitalist principles – F.A. Hayek for instance – while others wanted in their hearts to show how the genuine achievements of the Soviet economy were progressing, even if their heads told them to be more sceptical. Very few (if any) were dispassionately divorced from the politics of the situation, perhaps due in part to the paucity of accurate information about what exactly was happening in the USSR at this time. In the absence of the full facts, ideology sometimes went into overdrive.

Discussion of the principles behind creating a planned economy even reached the pages of the *Economic Journal* in the 1930s, with authors such as A.C. Pigou and E.F.M. Durbin contributing articles and reviews on related themes. Pigou for example reviewed the influential book *Soviet Communism* by Sidney and Beatrice Webb, suggesting that their attempt to band together 'the economists of the Western world' as arguing that a free price mechanism secured maximum consumer satisfaction was far too simplistic. Pigou wrote that:

> The Communist replies [to the Western economist] by pointing out that, as between rich people and poor people, equal money demand cannot reasonably be taken to represent equally urgent desires. … The Communists' words have so close a resemblance to those of Marshall, the words of his colleagues of the Western world so strongly suggest a Mad Hatter's Tea Party![33]

Pigou highlighted a key feature of the Soviet system as being planning from the centre of all the nation's production, distribution and exchange in the general social interest, a system that he believed would inevitably 'creak and groan and lag'. Pigou only semi-humorously characterised the shock brigade approach to work as introducing the 'sport spirit' into Soviet industry.

Other Western economists were more positive in their evaluations of Soviet economy. E.F.M. Durbin argued for the theoretical possibility of an accurate pricing system in a planned economy and that the rational calculation of relative productions could be done. This would be possible by first calculating the marginal productivity of all mobile resources and then allocating them to the positions of highest calculated product.[34] Many would undoubtedly respond that this theoretical possibility could not ever be realised in practice, even ignoring the fact that marginal concepts were doctrinal heresy in Soviet economics at this time. It was Oscar Lange who provided the most well-known attempt at theorising planned price calculations in a socialist economy in the West.

Outside the pages of the *Economic Journal*, various authors wrote books on aspects of the Soviet economic system, including a book by M. Polanyi entitled *The Contempt of Freedom* of 1940. Promoting a state totalitarian-type understanding of the Soviet system, Polanyi analysed collectivist planning as being based on the forethought of engineers, applied to society as a whole. Military in inspiration and including extreme mechanisation and an emphasis on large-scale construction, collectivist planning was directed from one central authority. In contrast to such planning, Polanyi proposed an alternative method of ordering human affairs that he called supervision, which relied on a multitude of individual initiatives rather than one unified will.[35]

Polanyi outlined in detail how the Soviet militarist conception of planning arose out of the need to direct all members of an army to a single purpose, which included planned manoeuvres of assault and engagement. The essence of this comprehensive planning was the action of hundreds of thousands of people being directed by the mind of one single person, and strict discipline based on vertical lines of authority was essential to the success of such planning. According to Polanyi this type of planning had its genuine purpose, but it was not meant for controlling all and every human action. In contrast to such a collectivist planning system, a system of supervision was based on the notion of human activities being initiated from a multitude of points within the system, which were merely regulated from above in line with their inherent purpose and in line with various legal and other socially established rules. For Polanyi, such supervision was much superior to planning, in that it enabled the expression of human liberty rather than suppressing it.[36] Polanyi's account was not particularly influential but it was characteristic of a common response from many in the liberal tradition.

Conclusion

Were there any genuine achievements in Soviet economics of the 1930s? Certainly Kantorovich's work on linear programming must be one such achievement, and the detailed work on elaborating exactly how various economic plans should be composed and implemented deserves recognition as being a pioneering effort in this field, if not a long-lasting or currently influential one. And whilst Slutsky was forced out of economics after 1929, his contributions to mathematics and statistics in the 1930s were still significant. But a basic point must be that a world-historical opportunity was actually lost in the USSR in the 1930s, if the high intellectual calibre of the economists present in the USSR in the 1920s was considered as potential human capital.

If, instead of imprisoning some leading figures like Kondratiev and Yurovsky, and forcing the exile of others such as Struve and Leontief, all these people could somehow have been involved creatively in the attempt to design and implement new economic mechanisms and structures in the USSR after 1929, then it is just possible (but by no means certain) that the outcome of the first experiment at creating a planned economy might have been somewhat different. Of course, in the political environment of Stalin's Russia, such an alternative was not possible to engineer, and the fractured circumstances of the day were victorious. But if it is recognised that the Soviet economic system after 1929 was constructed without the efforts of many of Russia's finest economists, a system that after all is said and done survived for over 70 years in the face of continued international hostility, it might be wondered what could actually have been achieved with their active participation.

9 Conclusion – evaluating the Russian economic mind

It is first of all hoped that an understanding of the richness and international significance of Russian economic thought in the period under review has been clearly demonstrated, at least in some specific topic areas. The detail that has been surveyed should, if the task has been well accomplished, segue into an overall impression of original and worthwhile success. Russian economists from 1870 to 1940 were certainly not always second-class citizens in the world ranking of social scientific thinkers, but sometimes stood shoulder-to-shoulder with their Western counterparts, proudly and deservedly so; often they had a different focus to their work, and at times they performed in more difficult circumstances, but their achievements were of lasting relevance and their importance has occasionally been unduly maligned.

It is also hoped that, through the diverse range of materials surveyed, readers might begin to appreciate more that in the Russian context at least, no one-sided political philosophy can fully explain all the observed nuances and developments in intellectual history, in that such a reality is very often complex and contradictory. In fact, some Russian economists themselves appreciated this general truth, with the continued co-evolution and hybridisation of multifarious economic doctrines being a notable feature of Russian economic discourse in both the pre- and post-revolutionary periods (at least up until 1929). For example, the special place of Ukrainian economists in the history of 'Russian' economic thought broadly conceived was noted in the introduction. Two of Russia's most well known economists – Slutsky and Tugan-Baranovsky – were both born in the Ukraine, only later moving to Moscow and St Petersburg. When Tugan-Baranovsky's intellectual evolution took him some distance away from orthodox Russian Marxism, a switch of allegiance back to the Ukraine followed sometime later. Hence the entity identified as 'Russian' economic thought should be seen as being akin to Wittgenstein's thread, composed of many overlapping fibres. What runs through the entire length of thread is not any one single fibre, but rather only the continuous overlapping of many separate strands.

One question raised in the introduction was whether Russian

economics as a whole had actually 'progressed' across the periods covered in this book. Adopting a more functional and pragmatic approach, it is more appropriate to understand Russian economics evolving in relation to developments in the economic system itself, and in relation to changes in the role of economics within governmental and academic institutions. Given that the economic system changed radically through 1917, whether Russian economic ideas became more 'accurate' or 'truthful' over time can only be judged in relation to the period in question. For example there is little doubt that planning techniques improved in a technical sense between 1921 and 1929, but asking whether the economics of Soviet-style planning was an improvement over Tsarist economics is not a useful comparison. The complexity of such a question is such that, economics 'better' for whom and in what context and for what purpose, and how is 'better' defined anyway, make any simplistic evaluations of this question redundant.

Returning to another related issue posed in the introduction, there is certainly an element of truth in the notion that the peak in terms of originality in Russian economics occurred in the period 1890–1913 – but only with respect to pre-revolutionary economics. A second peak with very different characteristics was also reached in the 1920s, when agricultural, planning and methodological questions gave a new twist to pre-existing concerns. Moreover, the two peaks were connected, in that without the significant pre-revolutionary work in areas such as business cycles and agrarian development, it is doubtful as to whether the post-revolutionary efforts in areas such as economic forecasting and industrial development could have been so successfully accomplished.

Finally, the question of the degree of originality in Russian economics before 1890 needs now to be addressed. Certainly, the influence of various currents of Western economics was extensive in Russia before 1890, and no single indigenous figure can claim anything like the status of 'giants' like David Ricardo or Karl Marx. But exactly how Russian economists copied, adapted and utilised Western economics was itself a unique process, and in this respect their work was indeed inventive, if only imitatively original. In fact it was Stalin's 'left turn' in 1929 that was the most fundamental turning point in terms of charting the secular decline of Russian economics, proving to be a structural break of monumental significance.

The tragedy of Russian economics

However, even under the extreme ideological pressures of high Stalinism, some Soviet economists were able to produce work of genuine interest and merit, such as Slutsky and Kantorovich for example. The McCarthy-inspired witch-hunts in the 1950s have often been portrayed as having a devastating effect on many Americans, the careers of some of the victims never fully recovering from the red baiting charade. But in fact, the Soviet witch-hunts of the 1930s were many orders of magnitude worse than their later American echo; no US citizens were executed by the state for their ideological pseudo-crimes, yet thousands were thus dispatched in the USSR. Could any US economist claim to have produced a work on economic methodology as uplifting as Kondratiev did in similarly horrendous circumstances in jail in the 1930s?

The individual tragedy of American economic thinkers such as John Nash has received much attention, but the collective tragedy of Russian economists has so far been only partially recognised. The roll call of names that were dispatched on Stalin's paranoid orders included Kondratiev, Bazarov, Litoshenko, Bukharin, Yurovsky and Preobrazhensky, the crème-de-la-crème of Russian economic expertise at the time. Perhaps even more surprising was that politically, those arrested ranged from the far right (Litoshenko) to the far left (Preobrazhensky) – 'far' being used here only relatively – and hence Stalin's ignorant cull appeared indiscriminate: except of course that it was targeted at anyone who might have threatened Stalin's personal power mania. The turning point in Russian economics was thus engendered not by any genuine intellectual development, but through the dull thud of personal greed. Stalin was at root jealous of the powerful potential of those who had gained their positions through genuine ability and intellectual brilliance; Stalin's counter was intrigue and back stabbing machinations of the basest sort. In the short term Stalin triumphed, but his posthumous reputation is sealed in black.

Without a doubt, the 1930s began the secular decline of Russian economic thinking, which reached its nadir in the period of Brezhnevite stagnation in the 1970s, never again (thus far) reaching the comparative heights it did in the period under review in this book. Hence the period 1890–1930 should be characterised as a 'golden age' of Russian economics, in terms of both the international stature and the intellectual originality of the thought being conducted. Whether a new first class infusion of Russian economics might develop in the twenty-first century cannot yet be known, but the 'wild 1990s' certainly produced much of interest regarding the economic development of Russia itself. The jury is still out as to whether the cerebral expression of such change was as spectacular as the change itself.

The currents and themes of Russian economics

The story of the development of the various different currents in Russian economics was in some ways at least quite different to that of the development of currents in economics in the West in the period under review. While in the West in the period from 1870–1913, neoclassical theory dominated many of the official academic positions, in Russia the reality was more diversified. And while in the West the period from 1918–39 has been classified as one of interwar pluralism, in Russia after 1917 Marxism gained state-sponsored dominance, and from 1929 onwards, it was the only set of political beliefs that were officially allowed. Thus Russian economics was often out of temporal step with its Western counterpart, this perhaps in part explaining its only limited recognition amongst contemporary historians.

With this in mind it is apparent that the Western-originating labels given to the various currents in Russian economics – classical, historical, Marxist and so on – were only partially accurate in describing their unique character. As noted in the introduction, in Russia the importance of political considerations meant that a different type of classification scheme based on class allegiance also had some definite relevance. Hence more complex descriptions such as 'historical economist with some liberal sympathies' might be more accurate for someone like A.I. Chuprov, and 'historical economist with Marxian sympathies' for someone like Tugan-Baranovsky. Moreover, some Russian economists underwent significant changes in their approaches to economics over time, which meant that they moved from one category to another. Kondratiev for example evolved from a youthful socialism to a moderate pro-market stance through 1917, whilst Struve developed from a Legal Marxist into an ideological opponent of the Soviet system in exile.

In terms of identifying the most important reoccurring themes in Russian economics, a number have suggested themselves in the previous chapters. The precise relationship between industry and agriculture in the development process; the relation between the development of Russian industry, business cycles in Russia and the world economy; the continuously shifting balance between efficiency and egalitarianism in the political priorities of ruling elites; and the role of economics as a discipline in defining the legitimacy of state and bureaucratic control, have often been seen to be significant. In more precise terms, the importance of the labour theory of value, the encouragement or discouragement of foreign investment, the nature of management institutions and an ambiguous attitude towards profit and interest as categories of necessity have also been explored in the Russian context.

In terms of the importance of the previously acknowledged 'giants' in Russian economics – Tugan-Baranovsky, Slutsky, Kondratiev – it has been demonstrated that their work was even more significant and diverse than had in the past been admitted. Moreover, the work of many lesser-known figures such as Chuprov, Ozerov and Litoshenko and others have been shown to be of more interest than previously recognised. In their own time these Russian economists were recognised and respected by many economists in the West, they only faded from view as the Cold War progressed. Consequently, it is hoped that this book is just the beginning of the further exploration in the West of the life and work of the many nationally and internationally important and multi-thematically interesting economic thinkers who lived within Russian and/or Soviet borders. Their efforts deserve to be effectively and continually remembered.

10 Epilogue – the Russian economic mind after 1940

The looming shadow of the Second World War saw the Soviet economic system further pushed into adopting war economy-style principles of management and control, as exemplified by the appointment of N.A. Voznesensky as chief of Gosplan in January 1938. Voznesensky's approach has been characterised as 'disciplinarian' and his planning reforms as restoring previously lapsed central control functions.[1] Overall, the role of Gosplan and the importance of economic planning increased at this time, although the existing planning methodology had to be adapted to the particular circumstances of war such as major territorial losses and the increased importance of armaments production.

The Allied victory in 1945 and the subsequent political division of parts of Europe into spheres of influence for American and Soviet governments meant that Soviet-style economics could be enthusiastically exported into various East European states such as Poland, Hungary, Yugoslavia and Czechoslovakia. In these countries the theory and practice of economic planning as it had been created in the USSR was filtered through various existing national traditions and institutions, producing some notable East European variants on the original Soviet formulations. In terms of economic theory, individuals such as Janos Kornai (Hungary) and Michael Kalecki (Poland) made important contributions to improving both the theory of planning and to analysing the operation of economic dynamics in general.

For example, Kornai's work on the application of a systems theory approach to understanding economic forces was particularly original, although Kornai later turned into a fervent advocate of market reforms. But before this progression had occurred, in *Anti-Equilibrium* of 1971, Kornai had analysed the relations between organisational forms of economy in terms of information flows – price being only one particular type of information – as well as defining various institutional and decision-making structures that go to make up complex economic systems.[2] Stressing the importance of little-discussed factors such as conflict and compromise, aspiration, and adaptation and selection to understanding economic processes, Kornai's most famous notion of a shortage economy came out of his analysis of markets in terms of the pressure and suction exerted by trading participants. By the late 1980s, however, the general institutional elements of Kornai's approach had been downplayed, leaving only the analysis of Soviet-type economies as being based on bureaucratic coordination and soft budget constraints. The political consequences of this were eventually forthcoming.

Kalecki's early work was important to the modelling of business cycles, although his most celebrated book – the *Essay on Business Cycle Theory* – was published in 1933, before Poland had become a Soviet satellite state. Kalecki continued working on this topic from a quasi-Keynesian perspective after 1945, but also made important contributions to analysing planning methods and investment calculations within Soviet-style economies. Of course, neither Kalecki nor Kornai were Russian either by birth or by proxy political affiliation, but without the significant influence of the USSR on their respective nations, it is doubtful as to whether their work would have taken the particular direction that it did, or that East European economics in general would have been focused on planning concerns after 1945.

Soviet economics after Stalin

In the USSR itself, Stalin's death in 1953 paved the way for Nikita Khrushchev's thaw in both international relations and in Soviet domestic policy, and it also produced a concomitant thaw in economic theory that facilitated the re-introduction of some market-type elements under the banner of socialist reform. E.G. Liberman's article 'Cost Accounting and the Material Encouragement of Industrial Personnel' from 1955 started a new phase of the debate about the role of profit-like measures in the Soviet system, and was followed in the 1960s by articles with brash titles such as 'Are we flirting with capitalism?'.[3] However, the economic reforms that followed did not prevent Brezhnevite stagnation from subsequently occurring in the 1970s.

One of the most important developments in Soviet economic theory in the 1960s was the idea of a system of optimally functioning socialist economy (SOFE) that was developed in the Central Economic Mathematical Institute (TsEMI) by economists such as V.S. Nemchinov, V.V. Novoshilov and N.P. Fedorenko. This took Kantorovich's idea of an optimal plan a number of steps further by adding the notions that plans should be calculated using optimal prices and with concern for resource scarcity and incentive rewards. It also included the idea of an economy as a hierarchical structure in which decision-making should occur at various levels appropriate to the specific task being considered, such as the national economy, a given industry or an individual enterprise, rather than always at the apex of the pyramid.[4]

As a consequence of such ideas a significant debate occurred in the

USSR in the mid-1960s, in which old-style political economists such as A.I. Pashkov, who simply repeated the tired Stalin-inspired slogans of the past, opposed the new mathematical school of economists inspired by Kantorovich. In this debate Fedorenko supported the replacement of traditional Soviet political economy by a variety of economic cybernetics, an idea that Norbert Wiener might have warmly welcomed. By the early 1970s, the idea of using mathematical methods in economic calculations was more generally accepted in planning bodies.

Another aspect of Soviet-influenced economics after 1940 was the ongoing efforts of émigrés such as W.S. Woytinsky, whose early work was discussed in Chapter 5. An example of Woytinsky's later work was the volume *World Commerce and Governments*, written together with his wife and published in 1955. This was a comprehensive survey of the population, needs, resources, agriculture, industry, transport, trade and governmental systems of all nations of the world, and ran to 900 pages of impressively broad-ranging expanse. Declaring that the iron curtain had split the world in two, Woytinsky suggested that the goal of (Soviet) Moscow was to knit together a new super-empire by turning conquered nations into hinterlands, whereas the goal of the free world was to heal the wounds inflicted by the post-war split.[5] This suggested that Woytinsky had by the 1950s become a hardened cold warrior at least in principle, even though his pre-revolutionary economics had been quasi-institutionalist in spirit.

In general it would not be unfair to say that, whilst the 1950s, the 1960s and 1970s produced some inventive refinements and many controversies in Soviet economic theory and planned management practice, the post-war period did not produce many startlingly original or groundbreaking economic doctrines that really stand alone as being of major significance outside of the Soviet context. Of course, émigré economists such as W.W. Leontief certainly did produce work of great importance, in his case through the input–output approach, and since Leontief had experienced the Soviet economic debates of the 1920s first-hand, some credit for Leontief's work should be given to the context from which it first originated. However, even though the USSR itself produced little by way of truly original economic theory after 1945, this does not necessarily mean that its influence on economics in general was negligible. In fact, it could be argued that Western economic discourse after 1945 was thoroughly permeated by the reality of the existence of the USSR as a challenge to Western capitalism.

It was suggested in Chapter 3 that the appearance of the first volume of Marx's *Capital* in 1867 had a definite effect on Western economics, in that the impetus to prove the theoretical rationality of capitalist production, against the not totally ineffective criticisms of socialists, received a significant boost. In the same way, the founding of the USSR itself created an impetus to further strengthen the intellectual justification of capitalism, in that an actually existing competitor had now been created. However, after

1917 this effect was lagged to some extent by the particular circumstances of the time. First of all, the long-term stability of the USSR was not initially certain, and hence its status as a genuine challenger took some while to become fully recognised. Second, the USSR fought with Britain and America in the Second World War, and hence anti-Soviet propaganda was hardly the order of the day in this period. Only after 1945, when the USSR's long-term sustainability had become glaringly apparent, did the ideological gloves really come off.

Of course this effect worked at a very deep and sometimes unconscious level. Every economist in the West did not suddenly wake up at the end of the war and decide that the underlying theoretical justification of market control systems of economy required further effort. This effect might have operated more at an institutional level, or at a level of group selection, or even in terms of individual self-motivation. Nor does this mean that no dissenting currents in Western economics could exist in the post-war period, only that actually being such a dissenter was a somewhat more difficult choice after 1945 than it was in the interwar period. Moreover, it is only being suggested that this 'socialist challenger' effect was one amongst many varied factors influencing the development of Western economics after 1945, and that, in a nebulous contextual sense, the USSR certainly was an influence on the progress of economic discourse in general in the second half of the twentieth century. To precisely quantify such an influence on economic theory is very difficult, but the polarising effect of the existence of the USSR on political discourse in the West after 1945 is unquestionable.

The restoration of market forms of control

In the event, the efforts of many governments in the West to undermine the stability of the USSR eventually had a substantial effect, although internal factors also played a major part in eroding the perceived successes of the Soviet system. Mikhail Gorbachev's reforms after 1985 looked at least initially like a return to a NEP-style reintroduction of market elements into the Soviet system. For example, Abel Aganbegyan wrote in 1988 about 'market relations under socialism' being inherent to the Soviet social system and 'the socialist market' as a government-regulated market.[6] However, Gorbachev's reforms eventually accelerated away from him, leading to the 'wild 1990s', with full-scale privatisation, price liberalisation and the return of the free market with a vengeance, showing the way to the establishment of a successful market economy in Russia today. Or so some would undoubtedly argue. In a rather different view, the 1990s produced a mafia-infiltrated oligarch-controlled economy in Russia, combining the worst aspects of the administrative-command system – widespread corruption – with an extreme version of Western capitalism – unfettered survival of the fittest (best connected).

In terms of the influence of all of this on economic doctrines in general, various obvious but still very significant points can be highlighted as follows. The combination of the apparently successful Thatcher–Reagan emphasis on market-based values in the West throughout the 1980s, and the collapse of the Soviet Empire at the end of the 1980s/beginning of the 1990s, meant that mainstream Western economics became elevated to a platform of influence that it had rarely (if ever) been placed on before 1989 – that of providing a theoretical rationale for the construction of various new social and economic systems across Eastern Europe and in many former Soviet states. Economists from the West such as Jeffrey Sachs, David Lipton, Ronald McKinnon and Richard Layard provided detailed advice and guidance on how to create a market economy in various countries from scratch, and such advice was often implemented with the full force of governmental decree.

Whereas during many previous decades, Keynesian-type policies had achieved fame as the set of economic ideas that had 'rescued' capitalism from some of its most negative consequences, i.e. mass unemployment and industrial depression, in the very recent past, purely market-based policies were the underlying driving force behind the creation of entire national economic systems. The great irony of all this was that, whilst originally the creation of a socialist economy was supposed to elevate socialist ideas to the position of the key building blocks of a new society, in the medium term the effect of the existence of the USSR has been to enable mainstream market economics to become a blueprint for various new societies, as it had never really done before. From this perspective, Marx's historical predictions have not only failed to materialise, but their absolute opposites have been realised. Hegel would be proud, at least in his later right-of-centre incarnation.

In opposition to this approach however, it could be argued that, as is invariably the case, the economic ideas being presented as the primary generating force of the market reforms, were really only the theoretical expression of more fundamental material processes that were occurring 'naturally' and of their own accord – the stagnation and collapse of the Soviet economy and then its spontaneous privatisation – and hence that too much influence is being attributed to abstract ideas on their own in such an account of recent Russian history. And here a return to the general question of the relative importance of ideas in explaining human history is made, as against the role of naked self-interest or material factors.

This book cannot claim to definitively answer this question, but as with the question of the relative importance of genetic factors as against environmental influences on human behaviour, the latest research suggests that both are extremely important, and moreover that they are inextricably linked. Hence the economic ideas that have been the main focus of this book were simultaneously cause and consequence, base and superstructure, environment and content, process and result. The role of market economics in the very recent past was thus both as blueprint and reflection, plan and outcome, with mutual interaction between these two functions occurring continuously.

And what of the future of Russian economics itself? It has been fashionable in the last decade or so to stamp triumphantly on Marx's grave, and to pronounce that his long out of date ideas are finally dead. This is sometimes done by people who do not really understand Marx's ideas, except perhaps in their most vulgarised form. But in truth, the work of the Russian economists examined in the bulk of this book suggests that, the creative interpretation and development of economic ideas in Russia – ideas in part drawn from Marxian origins, but also originating in liberal, conservative, historical and socialist currents – is a never-ending process. Intellectual 'giants' such as Smith, Ricardo and Marx, never actually die, they are just reinterpreted or transformed as current needs demand. Thus the Soviet version(s) of late nineteenth century Russian Marxism that were mediated by the historical circumstances of the First and Second World Wars, Allied intervention, the Cold War and the material conditions of twentieth century Russia are unquestionably dead: long live the many present and future Russian interpretations of the entire ornate spectrum of economic ideas, including those of Adam Smith, Thorstein Veblen and Karl Marx.

Appendix I – the first Russian translations of the works of Western economists

The date of the first publication in the original language is given in brackets where possible.

Adam Smith	*The Wealth of Nations*, 1802–06 (1776)
	The Theory of Moral Sentiments, 1895 (1759)
J.B. Say	*Principles of Political Economy*, 1805 (1803)
	Catechisms on Political Economy, 1833
J.S. Mill	*The Principles of Political Economy*, 1860 (1848)
	Autobiography, 1874
William Roscher	*The Principles of National Economy*, 1860–62 (1854)
Jeremy Bentham	*Selected Works*, 1867
T.R. Malthus	*An Essay on the Principle of Population*, 1868 (1798)
Karl Marx	*Capital* vol. 1, 1872 (1867)
	Capital vol. 2, 1885 (1885)
	Capital vol. 3, 1896 (1894)
	Towards a Critique of Political Economy, 1896 (1859)
	Theories of Surplus Value, 1906
David Ricardo	*Selected Works*, 1873–75
	The Principles of Political Economy, 1895 (1817)
Emile Laveleye	*Primitive Ownership*, 1875 (1873)
	The Principles of Political Economy, 1895 (1882)
Friedrich List	*The National System of Political Economy*, 1891 (1841)
J.K. Ingram	*The History of Political Economy*, 1891 (1888)
Henry George	*Progress and Poverty*, 1896 (1879)
J.A. Hobson	*The Economics of Distribution*, 1903 (1900)
William Petty	*Selected Passages*, 1914
Irving Fisher	*The Purchasing Power of Money*, 1925 (1911)
	The Making of Index Numbers, 1928 (1922)
Wesley Mitchell	*Business Cycles: The Problem and its Setting*, 1930 (1927)
John Maynard Keynes	*The General Theory of Employment, Interest and Money*, 1948 (1936)
Paul Samuelson	*Economics* (5th edition), 1962 (1955)
J.K. Galbraith	*The New Industrial State*, 1969 (1967)
	Economics and the Public Purpose, 1979 (1973)
John von Neumann and Oskar Morgenstern	*The Theory of Games and Economic Behaviour*, 1970 (1944)
Joseph Schumpeter	*The Theory of Economic Development*, 1982 (1911)
Thorstein Veblen	*The Theory of the Leisure Class*, 1984 (1899)
Edward Chamberlin	*The Theory of Monopolistic Competition*, 1986 (1933)

Appendix II – dramatis personae

Russian economic theorists

I.K. Babst (1823–1881)	Initial transmitter of German historical economics to Russia.
P.L. Bark (1869–1937)	Russian Minister of Finance from the beginning of the First World War to the February revolution.
V.A. Bazarov (1874–1939)	Key economist within Gosplan, a close associate of Groman and (before 1917) Bogdanov.
V.V. Bervi-Flerovsky (1829–1918)	Analyst of the Russian working class.
V.P. Bezobrazov (1828–1889)	Economist and supporter of liberal reform.
I.G. Blyumin (1897–1959)	Leading analyst of Western 'bourgeois' economics in the USSR.
A.A. Bogdanov [Malinovsky] (1873–1928)	Uniquely original philosopher and economic thinker, inventor of tektology.
Nikolai Bukharin (1888–1938)	Leading economic theorist of Bolshevism; imprisoned and executed by Stalin.
S.N. Bulgakov (1871–1944)	Philosopher and economist writing on markets and agriculture in capitalism.
N.Kh. Bunge (1823–1895)	Russian Minister of Finance from 1881 to 1886.
A.V. Chayanov (1888–1939)	Theorist of peasant economy and director of the Institute for Agricultural Economics in Moscow.
N.G. Chernyshevsky (1828–1889)	Radical philosopher and social theorist.
B.N. Chicherin (1828–1904)	Liberal theorist and analyst of the peasant commune.
A.A. Chuprov (1874–1926)	Statistical theorist and son of A.I. Chuprov.
A.I. Chuprov (1842–1908)	Agrarian theorist and leading developer of historical economics in Russia.
N.F. Danielson ['Nikolai-on'] (1844–1918)	*Narodnik* theorist and translator of *Capital* into Russian.
V.K. Dmitriev (1868–1913)	Pioneer of mathematical economics in Russia.
G.A. Fel'dman (1884–1958)	Pioneer of the theory of economic growth.
S.L. Frank (1877–1950)	Interpreter of the labour and marginal utility theories of value.
V.G. Groman (1874–1837)	Leading Gosplan economist and theorist of planning regularities.

L.V. Kantorovich (1912–1986)	Originator of the theory of optimal planning.
V.N. Kokovtsov (1853–1943)	Russian Minister of Finance between 1904–5 and 1906–11/14.
N.D. Kondratiev [Kondratieff] (1892–1938)	Director of the Conjuncture Institute in Moscow and pioneer of long cycle analysis.
A.A. Konyus (1895–)	Specialist in index numbers, consumer demand and probability theory.
M.M. Kovalevsky (1851–1916)	Historian and economist, theorist of collective forms of ownership.
V.I. Lenin [Ulyanov] (1870–1924)	Leader of the Bolshevik wing of the RSDLP and Marxist investigator of the development of capitalism in pre-revolutionary Russia.
W.W. Leontiev [Leontief] (1906–1999)	Pioneer of input-output analysis and émigré to the USA.
L.N. Litoshenko (1886–1936)	Right-orientated agrarian economist.
D.I. Mendeleev [Mendeleef] (1834–1907)	Inventor of the periodic table of the elements and analyst of the industrial development of Russia.
P.P. Migulin (1870–?)	Money, banking and finance specialist.
N.K. Mikhailovsky (1842–1904)	Sociologist and philosopher.
V.A. Milyutin (1826–1855)	A socialist critic of the Russian agrarian system and classical economics in general.
N.S. Mordvinov (1754–1845)	Supporter of protectionism and member of the liberal nobility.
V.S. Nemchinov (1894–1964)	Mathematical economist and statistician.
V.V. Novozhilov (1892–1970)	Independent-minded Soviet economist of opportunity cost.
D.I. Oparin (1891–1978)	The most important critic of Kondratiev's long cycles within the USSR.
I.Kh. Ozerov (1869–?)	Specialist in financial economics and taxation.
S.A. Pervushin (1888–1966)	Innovator of empirical business cycle analysis.
G.V. Plekhanov (1856–1918)	Founding father of deterministic Marxism in Russia.
P.I. Popov (1872–1950)	Pioneer of the construction of balances of the national economy.
E.A. Preobrazhensky (1886–1937)	Leading Bolshevik economist and theorist of the transition from capitalism to socialism.
S.N. Prokopovich (1871–1955)	Analyst of the empirical development of the Russian and Soviet economies, he was later an émigré to Europe.
N.N. Shaposhnikov (1878–?)	Consultant of the Conjuncture Institute and specialist in foreign trade policy.
N.I. Sieber [Ziber] (1844–1888)	Interpreter of the ideas of David Ricardo and Karl Marx in Russia.
E.E. Slutsky (1880–1948)	Mathematical statistician, economist and political economist renowned for his innovative work on consumer budgets and the theory of stochastic processes.
G.Ya. Sokol'nikov (1888–1939)	People's Commissar of Finance between 1921 and 1926.
I.V. Stalin (1879–1953)	Totalitarian dictator and author of pseudo-socialist tracts.

P.A. Stolypin (1862–1911)	Instigator of pre-revolutionary agrarian reform and chair of the Council of Ministers, 1906–11.
H.F. Storch (1766–1835)	German-educated tutor to the son of the Tsar.
S.G. Strumilin (1877–1974)	Leading Gosplan economist and critic of the work of the Conjuncture Institute.
P.B. Struve (1870–1944)	Leading figure of the 'Legal Marxists' in Russia before 1917, later an émigré critic of Stalinism.
Leon Trotsky (1879–1940)	Leading political opponent of Stalin eventually expelled from the USSR.
M.I. Tugan-Baranovsky (1865–1919)	Pioneer of both theoretical and empirical business cycle analysis and investigator of the history of the Russian factory.
N.I. Turgenev (1789–1871)	Supporter of free trade and opponent of the peasant commune.
A.L. Vainshtein (1892–1970)	Deputy director of the Conjuncture Institute and specialist in national wealth estimation.
E.S. Varga (1879–1964)	Marxist theorist and specialist in the capitalist world economy.
I.V. Vernadsky (1821–1884)	Supporter of free trade and critic of socialism.
S.Yu. Vitte [Witte] (1849–1915)	Russian Minister of Finance between 1892 and 1903 and proponent of state assistance to certain strategic branches of industry.
W.S. Voitinsky [Woytinsky] (1885–1960)	Analyst of prices and markets, later an émigré to the USA.
V.P. Vorontsov ['V.V.'] (1847–1918)	*Narodnik* theorist and opponent of the development of capitalism in Russia.
I.A. Vyshnegradsky (1831–1895)	Russian Minister of Finance between 1886 and 1892.
L.N. Yurovsky (1884–1938)	Specialist in money, banking and finance and the mastermind of Soviet currency reform in the early 1920s.

Western economic theorists

Clarence Ayres (1891–1972)	Leading American Institutionalist and theorist of economic progress.
Jeremy Bentham (1748–1832)	English economist, utilitarian philosopher and advocate of a rational code of law.
Eugene von Bohm-Bawerk (1851–1914)	Leading Austrian economist and critic of Marx's theoretical constructs.
Gustav Cassel (1866–1944)	Progenitor of the purchasing power parity theory of the determination of exchange rates.
Colin Clark (1905–1989)	British analyst of Russian statistics and theorist of economic progress.
J.B. Clark (1847–1938)	American theorist of the distribution of wealth and monopoly.
J.R. Commons (1862–1945)	One of the founders of American Institutional economics and analyst of the legal foundations of capitalism.

E.F.M. Durbin (1906–1948)	Macroeconomic theorist of trade cycles and depressions.
Friedrich Engels (1820–1895)	Life-long friend and collaborator of Karl Marx.
Irving Fisher (1867–1947)	Pioneer of neoclassical economics in the USA and early formulator of the quantity theory of money.
Ragnar Frisch (1895–1973)	Founding father of econometric theory born in Norway.
J.K. Galbraith (1908–)	American Institutionalist analyst of the modern industrial state.
Henry George (1839–1897)	American radical politician and economist.
August von Haxthausen (1792–1866)	Analyst of the Russian economy and the Russian peasantry.
R.G. Hawtrey (1879–1975)	British exponent of the monetary explanation of business cycles.
F.A. Hayek (1898–1992)	Leading Austrian theorist and trenchant critic of socialist ideas.
E.F. Heckscher (1879–1952)	Theorist of international trade.
Rudolf Hilferding (1877–1941)	Marxist theorist of monopoly and finance capital and Minister of Finance in the Weimar Republic.
J.A. Hobson (1858–1940)	Theorist of imperialism and the evolution of capitalism.
J.K. Ingram (1823–1907)	Leading advocate of historical economics in the UK.
W.S. Jevons (1835–1882)	One of the leaders of the 'marginal revolution' in British economics and pioneer analyst of trends and cycles in financial data.
J.M. Keynes (1883–1946)	The doyen of Cambridge economists, founder of Western macroeconomics and theorist of state intervention in the economy.
Frank Knight (1885–1962)	Leading member of the Chicago school of economists and pioneer analyst of the role of the entrepreneur in economic life.
Simon Kuznets (1901–1985)	American analyst of the long-term movement of economic variables.
Emile Laveleye (1822–1892)	Quasi-socialist academic economist and supporter of bimetallism.
Friedrich List (1789–1846)	German theorist of protectionism as a tool to promote economic development.
Rosa Luxemburg (1871–1919)	Revolutionary Marxist and theorist of the accumulation of capital in imperialism.
T.R. Malthus (1766–1834)	Investigator of population growth and *bete noire* of Marx.
Alfred Marshall (1842–1924)	The most significant codifier of pre-war neoclassical economics in the UK.
Karl Marx (1818–1883)	German revolutionary thinker who began in the philosophical tradition of G.W.F. Hegel, but who turned to political economy to develop his system of thought.
Carl Menger (1840–1921)	Founding figure of Austrian economics and neoclassical value theory in general.

J.S. Mill (1806–1873)	The most important codifier of classical political economy in the UK.
Wesley Mitchell (1874–1948)	Creator of the National Bureau of Economic Research in New York and instigator of empirical business cycle analysis in the USA.
John von Neumann (1903–1957)	Mathematician and inventor of game theory.
A.C. Pigou (1877–1959)	Member of the UK Treasury and specialist in welfare economics.
Francois Quesnay (1694–1774)	French inventor of the tableau economique.
David Ricardo (1772–1823)	Originator of the theory of comparative advantage and (with Smith) a founding father of classical economics in the UK.
D.H. Robertson (1890–1963)	Cambridge economist (condemned to play second fiddle to Keynes) and specialist in the theory of industrial fluctuation.
Wilhelm Roscher (1817–1894)	Leading member of the 'older' school of German historical economists.
J.B. Say (1767–1832)	Creator of Say's law, which stated that supply creates its own demand.
Gustav Schmoller (1838–1917)	Leading member of the 'younger' school of German historical economists.
Joseph Schumpeter (1883–1950)	Theorist of capitalist development and business cycles.
Adam Smith (1723–1790)	British progenitor of free trade ideas and advocate of *laissez faire* in general.
Frank Taussig (1859–1940)	American economist, specialist in tariff policy and international trade.
Thomas Tooke (1774–1858)	Statistical investigator of price movements in the British economy, he was born in St Petersburg, the son of a historian of Russia.
Thorstein Veblen (1857–1929)	Leading American Institutional economist and savage critic of the pecuniary business elite.
Leon Walras (1834–1910)	Inventor of general equilibrium economics and proponent of the mathematisation of economic theory.
Max Weber (1864–1920)	Pioneer of economic sociology.
Knut Wicksell (1851–1926)	Leading monetary theorist and creator of the distinction between the market rate of interest and the real rate.

Notes

Preface

1 An ESRC-funded project entitled 'The Economic Mind in Russian Civilisation, 1880–1917' (R000239937) gave me the time necessary to complete this book. I owe an important debt of gratitude to the ESRC for their continued support.
2 When someone asked Michael Faraday what the point of his obscure research topic 'electricity' was, he responded by asking what the point of a baby really was.

1 Introduction: analysing the Russian economic mind

1 Such approaches are of course not considered as being ultimately true, only true to the period. When the ultimate end of history arrives, an infinite number of years in the future, we can then discover the finally correct position from which to judge all past developments. Until then, intellectual historians should always prefer relativism.
2 Mark Blaug, *Economic Theory in Retrospect* (Cambridge: CUP, 1985) p. 3.
3 J.K. Galbraith, *A History of Economics* (London: Hamish Hamilton, 1987) p. 187.
4 Max Weber, *The Russian Revolutions* (New York: Cornell, 1995) p. 60.
5 J.F. Normano, *The Spirit of Russian Economics* (New York: Day, 1945) p. 83.
6 Stepan Zlupko, *Ekonomichna dumka Ukraini* (Lviv: Lviv University, 2000) p. 480.
7 J.F. Hecker, *Russian Sociology* (London: Chapman and Hall, 1934).
8 V.I. Lenin, *Materialism and Empirio-Criticism* (Moscow: Progress, 1987) p. 117.
9 Judy Klein, *Statistical Visions in Time* (Cambridge: CUP, 1997) pp. 157–8.
10 I. Gerasimov, *A Short History of Geographical Science in the Soviet Union* (Moscow: Progress, 1976) pp. 12 and 70.
11 J.M. Letiche (ed.), *A History of Russian Economic Thought* (Berkeley: University of California, 1964) p. 16.
12 A.I. Pashkov (ed.), *Istoriya Russkoi ekonomicheskoi mysli* (Moscow: SotsEkon, 1966) vol. 3, pp. 15–129.
13 G.N. Sovina, 'Rossiiskaya shkola politicheskoi ekonomii', in Yu.V. Yakovtsa (ed.), *Rossiiskie ekonomicheskie shkoly* (Moscow: MFK, 2003) p. 30.
14 Joseph Schumpeter, *History of Economic Analysis* (London: Allen and Unwin, 1954) p. 36.
15 Ibid, p. 552.
16 I.I. Rubin, *A History of Economic Thought* (London: Ink Links, 1979) p. 118.
17 D. Mackenzie Wallace, *Russia* (London: Cassell, 1877) vol. 1, p. 437.

18 Hugh Seton-Watson, *The Russian Empire* (Oxford: Clarendon Press, 1967) pp. 534–5.
19 I. Zvavich (1943) 'Economic education and economic research in the Soviet Union', *Economic Journal*, vol. LIII: 415–16.
20 J.R. Commons, *Legal Foundations of Capitalism* (New Jersey: Kelley, 1974) pp. 215–16.
21 James Mavor, *An Economic History of Russia* (London: Dent and Son, 1925) vol. 1, pp. 524–5.
22 *Rossiiskoe zakonodatel'stvo X XX vekov* (Moscow: Yuridicheskaya, 1989) vol. 7, p. 44.
23 T.R. Malthus, *An Essay on the Principle of Population* (New Jersey: Kelley, 1986) 7th edn, p. 152.
24 Alfred Marshall, *Industry and Trade* (London: Macmillan, 1919) p. 162.
25 Ibid, p. 842.
26 Placido Bucolo, *The Other Pareto* (London: Scolar, 1980) p. 174.
27 Ibid, pp. 51 and 81.

2 Prelude: the Russian economic mind before 1870

1 E.F. Heckscher, *Mercantilism* (London: Routledge, 1994) vol. 2, p. 337.
2 J.M. Letiche (ed.), *A History of Russian Economic Thought* (Berkeley: University of California, 1964) pp. 290–1.
3 Ibid, p. 476.
4 I. Miklachewsky, 'Russian School of Political Economy', *Dictionary of Political Economy* (London: Macmillan, 1908) vol. 3, p. 338.
5 An expanded version of part of this section on Smith can be found in Vincent Barnett, 'Mr Smith Goes to Moscow: Russian Editions of *The Wealth of Nations*', *Research in the History of Economic Thought and Methodology*, vol. 20A, pp. 35–42.
6 I.G. Blyumin, *Ocherki ekonomicheskoi mysli v Rossii v pervoi polovine XIX veka* (Moscow-Leningrad: AN SSSR, 1940) p. 50.
7 J.F. Normano, *The Spirit of Russian Economics* (New York: Day, 1945) pp. 17–18.
8 Miklachewsky, 'Russian School of Political Economy' p. 338.
9 C. Lai, *Adam Smith Across Nations* (Oxford: OUP, 2000) p. xvii.
10 Andrzej Walecki, *A History of Russian Thought* (Oxford: Clarendon, 1980) p. 63.
11 M.I. Tugan-Baranovsky, *The Russian Factory in the 19th Century* (Illinois: AEA, 1970) p. 216.
12 Blyumin, *Ocherki ekonomicheskoi mysli v Rossii v pervoi polovine XIX veka*, p. 50.
13 Normano, *The Spirit of Russian Economics*, p. 24.
14 S.A. Fal'kner, *Proiskhozhdenie zheleznogo zakona zarabotnoi platy* (Moscow: Truda, 1925) p. 330.
15 Normano catalogued the various 'native' currents of social and economic thought in Russia in the nineteenth century as being Slavophiles (I.V. Kireyevsky); Westernisers (P.Y. Chaadayev, V.G. Belinsky); Pan-Slavists (Yu.F. Samarin); Social Democrats (G. Plekhanov); agrarian socialists (A. Herzen); and messianic anti-Westerners (N.Y. Danilevsky). See Normano, *The Spirit of Russian Economics*, pp. 82–113. Normano's categories related more to social and political considerations rather than to political economy more narrowly conceived.
16 J.K. Ingram, *A History of Political Economy* (New York: Kelley, 1967) p. 184.
17 J.K.I., 'Storch', *Dictionary of Political Economy*, vol. 3, p. 479.

18 Karl Marx, *Theories of Surplus Value* (Moscow: Progress, 1968) part 2, p. 99.
19 Quoted in ibid, p. 637.
20 Karl Marx, *Capital* (London: Penguin, 1981) vol. 3, p. 284. Marx's own view on this question was that both Storch and Ricardo were partially correct and partially wrong, in that they both failed to consider the average case or to distinguish conditions in which a majority of total commodities produced were made under better conditions or under worse conditions, where different laws became operative.
21 Karl Marx, *Theories of Surplus Value* (Moscow: Foreign Languages, 1958) part 1, pp. 101–2.
22 N.G. Chernyshevsky, *Izbrannye ekonomicheskie proizvedeniya* (Ogiz, 1948) vol. 3, part 1, p. 7.
23 J. Frankel (ed.), *Vladimir Akimov on the Dilemmas of Russian Marxism* (Cambridge: CUP, 1969) p. 208.
24 Some elements of this section have been taken from the various valuable entries in the *Ekonomicheskaya entsiklopediya politicheskaya ekonomiya* (Moscow: AN SSSR, 1972–80).
25 M.L. Tegoborski, *Commentaries on the Productive Forces of Russia* (London: Longman, 1855) vol. 1, p. 8.
26 Ibid, vol. 2, p. 155.
27 Ibid, vol. 1, p. 61.
28 August von Haxthausen, *Studies on the Interior of Russia* (Chicago: University of Chicago Press, 1972) p. 9.

3 The Russian economic mind under Tsarism, 1870–1890

1 Mark Blaug, *Economic Theory in Retrospect* (Cambridge: CUP, 1985) p. 295.
2 M.I. Tugan-Baranovsky, 'Smit, Adam', in *Entsiklopedicheskii slovar'* (St Petersburg, 1900) vol. 30, pp. 536–7.
3 Ibid, p. 539.
4 A.H. Brown, 'Adam Smith's First Russian Followers', in *Essays on Adam Smith* (Oxford: Clarendon, 1975) pp. 268–9, fn. 59.
5 David Rikardo, *Nachala politicheskoi ekonomii* (Moscow: Lashkevich, 1895).
6 S.A. Fal'kner, *Proiskhozhdenie zheleznogo zakona zarabotnoi platy* (Moscow: Truda, 1925) p. 330.
7 J.F. Normano, *The Spirit of Russian Economics* (New York: Day, 1945) p. 33.
8 Geoffrey Hodgson, *How Economics Forgot History* (London: Routledge, 2001) pp. 59–64.
9 An expanded version of this account of Babst and Chuprov is found in Vincent Barnett, 'Historical political economy in Russia, 1870–1913', *European Journal of the History of Economic Thought*, vol. 11 (2): 231–53.
10 A.M. Rumyantsev (ed.), *Ekonomicheskaya entsiklopediya politicheskaya ekonomiya* (Moscow: AN SSSR, 1972) vol. 1, p. 96.
11 A.I. Chuprov, 'I.K. Babst', in *Rechi i stati* (Moscow: Sabashnikov, 1909) vol. 1, p. 16.
12 N. Kablukov, 'A.I. Chuprov', in *Rechi i stati* (Moscow: Sabashnikov, 1909) vol. 1, p. xv.
13 Chuprov, 'I.K. Babst', in *Rechi i stati*, vol. 1, p. 475.
14 Max Weber, *Roscher and Knies: The Logical Problems of Historical Economics* (New York: Macmillan, 1975) p. 73.
15 I.K. Babst, *Izlozhenie nachal' narodnago khozyaistva* (Moscow: Shilovoi, 1872) vol. 1, p. 159.
16 Ibid, pp. 152–3.

17 A.I. Chuprov, 'Pis'ma iz Yuzhnoi Germanii', in *Rechi i stati*, (Moscow: Sabashnikov, 1909) vol. 2, p.4.
18 A.I. Pashkov, *Istoriya Russkoi ekonomicheskoi mysli*, vol. 2 part 1, (Moscow: SotsEkon, 1959) p. 143.
19 A.I. Chuprov, 'O sovremennom znachenii i zadachakh politicheskoi ekonomii', in *Rechi i stati*, (Moscow: Sabashnikov, 1909) vol. 1, pp. 7–8.
20 Pashkov, *Istoriya Russkoi ekonomicheskoi mysli*, vol. 2 part 1, p. 139.
21 A.I. Chuprov, *Istoriya politicheskoi ekonomii*, (Riga: Gliksman, 1924) pp. 209–15.
22 A.I. Chuprov, 'O snachenii statistiki dlya pravovedeniya i eya uspekhakh v Rossii za poslednee vremya', in *Rechi i stati*, (Moscow: Sabashnikov, 1909) vol. 1, p. 207.
23 Ibid, p. 210.
24 A.I. Chuprov, 'Znanie i narodnoe bogatstvo', in *Rechi i stati*, (Moscow: Sabashnikov, 1909) pp. 279–80.
25 Ibid, p. 282.
26 Ibid, p. 285 and p. 307.
27 A.I. Chuprov, 'Rol' lichnosti i obshchetva v sovremennom kooperativnom dvizhenii', in *Rechi i stati*, (Moscow: Sabashnikov, 1909) vol. 2, pp. 173–4.
28 Esther Kingston-Mann, *In Search of the True West: Culture, Economics and Problems of Russian Development* (Princeton: Princeton University Press, 1999) p. 129.
29 A.I. Chuprov, 'O tsentral'nykh" uchrezhdeniyakh" dlya melkago kredita v" Rossii', in *Rechi i stati*, vol. 2, pp. 295–7.
30 I.I. Rubin, *A History of Economic Thought* (London: Ink Links, 1979) p. 286.
31 G.V. Plekhanov, 'Novoe napravlenie v oblasti politicheskoi ekonomii', in *Sochineniya* (Moscow: GosIzdat, 1923) vol. 1, p. 170.
32 Ibid, p. 180.
33 Ibid, pp. 195–6.
34 Quoted in J. Frankel (ed.), *Vladimir Akimov on the Dilemmas of Russian Marxism* (Cambridge: CUP, 1969) p. 131.
35 G.V. Plekhanov, 'Our Differences', in *Selected Philosophical Works* (London: Lawrence and Wishart, 1961) pp. 261–6.
36 Ibid, pp. 272–309.
37 N.I. Sieber (2001) 'Marx's Theory of Value and Money', in P. Zarembka (ed.), *Research in Political Economy*, vol. 19, p. 18.
38 Ibid, p. 26.
39 M.C. Howard and J.E. King, *A History of Marxian Economics, 1883–1929* (Princeton: PUP, 1989) p. 167.
40 T.E. O'Conner, 'Voronstov, Vasilii', in *The Modern Encyclopedia of Russian and Soviet History* (AIP, 1986) vol. 43, p. 62.
41 Andrzej Walecki, *A History of Russian Thought* (Oxford: Clarendon, 1980) p. 224.
42 Ibid, p. 242.
43 N. Bunge, *Osnovaniya politicheskoi ekonomii* (Kiev, 1870) pp. 129–32.
44 B.V. Anan'ich, 'The Economic Policy of the Tsarist Government', in G. Guroff and F.V. Carstenson (eds), *Entrepreneurship in Imperial Russia and the Soviet Union* (Princeton: PUP, 1983) p. 129.
45 'The Years 1881–94 in Russia: A Memorandum Found in the Papers of N.Kh. Bunge', *Transactions of the American Philosophical Society*, vol. 71, part 6, 1981, pp. 59–68.
46 *Ministerstvo finansov 1802–1902* (St Petersburg: GosBumag, 1902) part 2, p. 100.
47 Oliver Hayward, 'Bunge, N.Kh.', in *The Modern Encyclopedia of Russian and Soviet History* (AIP, 1978) vol. 6, pp. 36–7.

48 P. Kovan'ko, *Glavneishiya reformy provedennyya N.Kh. Bunge* (Kiev, 1901) pp. 430–2.
49 CUSMC, Witte Papers, box 9, dela 6 (file 1) p. 131.

4 Socialism and development in late Tsarism, 1890–1913

1 Eugene von Bohm–Bawerk, *Karl Marx and the Close of His System* (New Jersey: Kelley, 1973) p. 101.
2 *The Encyclopedia of Philosophy* (New York: Macmillan, 1972) vol. 4, p. 266.
3 Richard Kindersley, *The First Russian Revisionists* (Oxford: Clarendon Press, 1962) pp. 166–8.
4 Quoted in ibid, p. 170.
5 An expanded version of this section on business cycles appeared in Vincent Barnett (2001) 'Tugan-Baranovsky as a pioneer of trade cycle analysis', *Journal of the History of Economic Thought*, vol. 23 (4): 443–66.
6 While Tugan-Baranovsky specified 'England' in the title, in fact this book focused on Great Britain as a whole, as the references attested.
7 M.I. Tugan-Baranovsky, *Izbrannoe: Periodicheskie promyshlennye krizisy* (Moscow: Nauka, 1997) pp. 85–6.
8 Ibid, pp. 149–206.
9 Ibid, pp. 90–5.
10 Ibid, p. 315.
11 M.I. Tuhan–Baranovsky, 'Periodic Industrial Crises', in *Annals of the Ukrainian Academy of Arts and Sciences in the United States*, 1954, p. 793.
12 Wilhelm Ropke, *Crises and Cycles* (London: Hodge, 1936) p. 100.
13 Gottfried Haberler, *Prosperity and Depressions* (Geneva: League of Nations, 1940) p. 83.
14 W.W. Rostow, *Theorists of Economic Growth from David Hume to the Present* (New York: OUP, 1990) p. 261.
15 Wesley Mitchell, *Business Cycles: The Problem and its Setting* (New York: NBER, 1927) p. 23.
16 M.I. Tugan-Baranovsky, 'Znachenie birzhi v sovremennom khozyaistvennom stroe', in *Bankovaya entsiklopediya* (Kiev, 1916) pp. 35–8.
17 M.I. Tugan-Baranovsky, *Periodicheskie promyshlennye krizisy* (Petrograd-Moscow, 1923) pp. 207–54.
18 Rosa Luxemburg, *The Accumulation of Capital* (London: RKP, 1951) p. 313.
19 S.A. Pervushin, *Teoriya krizisov M.I. Tugan-Baranovskago* (Moscow, 1914) p. 7.
20 For an account of Tugan-Baranovsky's work on the Russian factory see Vincent Barnett, *The Revolutionary Russian Economy, 1890–1940: Ideas, Debates and Alternatives* (London: Routledge, 2004) pp. 42–8.
21 A more detailed version of this section on methodology appeared in Vincent Barnett (2004) 'Tugan-Baranovsky, the methodology of political economy, and the "Russian Historical School"', *History of Political Economy*, vol. 36 (1): 79–101.
22 M.I. Tugan-Baranovsky, 'Metodologiya politicheskoi ekonomii', *Obrazovanie* no.12, 1908, p. 1.
23 Ibid, pp. 2–3.
24 M.I. Tugan-Baranovsky, 'Kant i Marks', in *K luchshemu budushchemu* (Moscow: Rosspen, 1996) p. 79.
25 Ibid, p. 78.
26 P.B. Struve, *Khozyaistvo i tsena*, in R. Pipes (ed.) *Collected Works* (Ann Arbor, 1970), vol. X, pp. 8–14.
27 Ibid, p. 16.

28 S.N. Bulgakov, *Istoriya sotsial'nykh uchenii v XIX veke* (Moscow, 1913) p. 5.
29 S.N. Bulgakov, *Ocherki po istorii ekonomicheskikh uchenii* (Moscow, 1913) pp. 2–3.
30 S.N. Bulgakov (1898) 'Nekotorykh osnovykh ponyatiyakh politicheskoi ekonomii', *Nauchnoe obozrenie*, pp. 1476–7.
31 S.N. Bulgakov, *Kapitalizm i zemledelie* (St Petersburg, 1900) vol. 2, pp. 442–3.
32 Ibid, p. 446.
33 Ibid, pp. 457–8.
34 Sergei Bulgakov, *Philosophy of Economy* (New Haven: Yale University Press, 2000) p. 121 and p. 217.
35 Ibid, pp. 248–50.
36 Ibid pp. 251–9.
37 Rosa Luxemburg, *The Accumulation of Capital* (London: Routledge, 1951) pp. 325–6.
38 Michael Gordin, *A Well-Ordered Thing: Dmitrii Mendeleev and the Shadow of the Periodic Table* (New York: Basic Books, 2004).
39 An expanded version of this section on Mendeleev appeared in Vincent Barnett, 'Catalysing growth? Mendeleev and the 1891 tariff', *Research in the History of Economic Thought and Methodology*, vol. 22–A: 123–44.
40 T.S. Kudryavtseva and M.E. Shekhter, *D.I. Mendeleev i ugol'haya promyshlennost' Rossii* (Moscow: UgletekhIzdat, 1952) p. 15.
41 D.I. Mendeleev, 'Osnovy fabrichno-zavodskoi promyshlennost', in *C dumoyu o blage rossiiskom* (Novosibirsk: Nauka, 1991) pp. 22–4.
42 Ibid, p. 36.
43 S.V. Kazantsev, 'Ot redaktora', in *C dumoyu o blage rossiiskom*, pp. 7–10.
44 F.H. Stackenwalt, 'The Economic Thought and Work of D.I. Mendeleev' (Unpublished PhD Thesis, University of Illinois at Urbana-Champaign, 1976) p. 108.
45 D.I. Mendeleev, 'Tolkovyi tarif, ili issledovanie o razvitii promyshlennosti Rossii v svyazi c eya obshchim tamozhennym tarifom 1891 goda', in *Sochineniya* (Moscow: AN SSSR, 1950) vol. XIX: 187.
46 D.I. Mendeleeff, 'Introduction: Review of the Manufactures and Trade of Russia', in J.M. Crawford (ed.), *The Industries of Russia, Manufactures and Trade* (St Petersburg, 1893) vol. I and II, p. vi.
47 D.I. Mendeleev, 'Opravdanie protektsionizma', in *Problemy ekonomicheskogo razvitiya Rossii* (Moscow: Sots-Ekon, 1960) p. 86.
48 Mendeleev, 'Tolkovyi tarif, ili issledovanie o razvitii promyshlennosti Rossii v svyazi c eya obshchim tamozhennym tarifom 1891 goda' p. 187.
49 Ibid, p. 207.
50 Mendeleeff, 'Introduction: Review of the Manufactures and Trade of Russia', vol. I and II, p. x.
51 'The Commercial Policy of Russia', in *The Anglo-Russian Literary Society*, Proceedings, May, June, July 1894, (7): 18.
52 Theodore von Laue, *Sergei Witte and the Industrialization of Russia* (New York: Atheneum, 1974).
53 Prince Kropotkin, *Fields, Factories and Workshops* (London: Nelson, 1912), p. x.
54 A more extensive version of this section on Slutsky appeared in Vincent Barnett, 'E.E. Slutsky: mathematical statistician, economist, and political economist?', *Journal of the History of Economic Thought*, 26 (1): 5–18.
55 E.E. Slutsky, 'Sushchnost' kooperatsii i eya formy', *Spravochnyi kalendar' zemledel'tsa na 1913* (Kiev, 1913) pp. 192–4.
56 Ibid, pp. 195–6.
57 Ibid, pp. 197–8.
58 Ibid, pp. 199–206.

5 Economic theory in late Tsarism, 1890–1913

1 V.K. Dmitriev, *Economic Essays on Value, Competition and Utility* (Cambridge: CUP, 1974) p. 188.
2 Ibid, p. 189.
3 Ibid, pp. 208–9.
4 Ibid, pp. 147–8.
5 RGAE, f. 7733, op. 18, del. 9743, p. 21.
6 Ibid, pp. 16–17.
7 *Ekonomicheskaya entsiklopediya politicheskaya ekonomiya* (Moscow: AN SSSR, 1980), vol. 4, p. 415.
8 A.A. Belykh (1991) 'O rabotakh N.N. Shaposhnikova', *Ekonomika i matematicheskie metody*, 27 (6): 1032.
9 Ibid, p. 1031.
10 N.N. Shaposhnikov, *Pervyi russkii ekonomist-mathematik Vladimir Karpovich Dmitriev* (Moscow, 1914) p. 3.
11 Ibid, p. 4.
12 Ibid, p. 5.
13 N.S. Chetverikov (1959) 'Zhizn' i nauchnaya deyatel'nost' E.E. Slutskogo', *Uchenye zapiski po statistike*, 5: 258.
14 A.A. Kaufman, *Statisticheskaya nauka v Rossii* (Moscow: TsSU, 1922) pp. 216–18.
15 P.P. Migulin, *Russkii gosudarstvennyi kredit, 1769–1899*, (Kharkov: Pechatnoe delo, 1899) vol. 1, pp. 25–6.
16 P.P. Migulin, 'V sashchitu Russkikh finansov', in *Vozrozhdenie Rossii* (Karkhov: Pechatnik, 1910) p. 269.
17 P.P. Migulin, 'Neobkhodimaya reforma gosudarstvennago banka', in *Vozrozhdenie Rossii* (Karkhov: Pechatnik, 1910) pp. 72–86.
18 A.I. Pashkov (ed.), *Istoriya Russkoi ekonomicheskoi mysli* (Moscow: SotsEkon, 1966), vol. 3, part 1, p. 236.
19 I.Kh. Ozerov, *Podokhodnyi nalog v Anglii* (Moscow: Levenson, 1898) p. 413.
20 Ibid, p. 415.
21 I.Kh. Ozerov, *Osnovy finansovoi nauki* (Moscow: Sytin, 1910), part 1, pp. 73–4.
22 V.I. Lenin, 'On the So-Called Market Question', in *Collected Works* (London: L&W, 1960) vol. 1, p. 99.
23 *The New Palgrave: A Dictionary of Economics* (London: Macmillan, 1987) vol. 4, p. 932.
24 W.S. Woytinsky, *Market and Prices* (New York: Kelley, 1964) pp. 2–3.
25 Ibid, pp. 183–93.
26 Ibid, pp. 46–8.
27 Ibid, pp. 204–19.
28 Ibid, p. 242.
29 Ibid, pp. 132–3.

6 Interregnum: the Russian economic mind at war, 1914–1917

1 P. Migulin, 'The State Bank and the Currency', *The Times Russian Supplement*, 26 April 1915, p. 5.
2 An expanded version of this account of Russian war finance can be found in Vincent Barnett (2001) 'Calling up the reserves: Keynes, Tugan-Baranovsky and Russian war finance', *Europe-Asia Studies*, 53(1): 151–69.
3 Keynes Papers, King's College, Cambridge, T/9/24. Unpublished writings of J.M. Keynes copyright: the Provost and Scholars of King's College, Cambridge 2005.

4 P.L. Bark (1924) 'Finansovye soveshchaniya soyuznikov vo vremya voiny', *Krasnyi arkhiv*, 5: 52.
5 Keith Neilson, *Strategy and Supply* (London: Allen and Unwin, 1984) p. 55.
6 Paul Apostol, 'Credit Operations', in *Russian Public Finance During the War* (New Haven: Yale University Press, 1928) p. 308.
7 Bark, 'Finansovye soveshchaniya soyuznikov vo vremya voiny', p. 51.
8 A.L Sidorov, *Finansovoe polozhenie Rossii v gody pervoi mirovoe voiny* (Moscow: AN SSSR, 1960) p. 551.
9 William Clarke, *The Lost Fortune of the Tsars* (London: Weidenfield and Nicolson, 1994) p. 179.
10 P.L. Bark (1924) 'O finansovykh soglasheniyakh, zaklyuchennykh c Angliiskim i Frantsuzskim ministrami finansov i s upravlyayushchim Angliiskim bankom', *Krasnyi arkhiv*, 5: 66.
11 Sidorov, *Finansovoe polozhenie Rossii v gody pervoi mirovoe voiny*, p. 170.
12 Apostol, 'Credit Operations', in *Russian Public Finance During the War*, p. 303.
13 P.L. Bark (1924) 'O peregovorakh ministra finansov v Parizhe i Londone v iyune i iyule 1916 goda', *Krasnyi arkhiv*, 5: 76.
14 Sidorov, *Finansovoe polozhenie Rossii v gody pervoi mirovoe voiny*, p. 166. Sidorov suggested that the transfer of gold overseas was intended as a measure to actually support the exchange rate of the ruble, as it facilitated the granting of foreign credit. If so it was not very successful, as the ruble had declined to around half its prewar level in relation to foreign currency by spring 1917, falling to 28% of its prewar level by October 1917 (pp. 167–8).
15 M.I. Tugan-Baranovsky, 'Vliyanie voiny na narodnoe khozyaistvo Rossii, Anglii i Germanii', in *Voprosy mirovoi voiny* (Petrograd: Pravo, 1915) p. 270.
16 M.I. Tugan-Baranovsky, 'Bumazhnyya den'gi i voina', *Rech'*, no.16, 17 (30) January 1915, p. 2.
17 M.I. Tugan-Baranovsky, 'Voina i narodnoe khozyaistvo', in *Chego zhdet" Rossiya ot" voiny* (Petrograd: Prometei, 1915) pp. 7–8.
18 Tugan-Baranovsky, 'Voina i narodnoe khozyaistvo' p. 9.
19 In 1917 Tugan-Baranovsky was also designing a system of economic planning for socialism. See Vincent Barnett (2000) 'Tugan-Baranovskii's vision of an international socialist economy', *European Journal of the History of Economic Thought*, 7(1): 115–36.
20 M.I. Tugan-Baranovsky, 'Voennye zaimy v teoreticheskom osveshchenii', in *Voennye zaimy: sbornik statei* (Petrograd: Pravda, 1917) p. 5.
21 Tugan-Baranovsky, 'Voennye zaimy v teoreticheskom osveshchenii' p. 25.
22 M.I. Tugan-Baranovsky, *Bumazhnyya den'gi i metall"* (Petrograd: Pravda, 1917) p. 158.
23 M.I. Tugan-Baranovsky, *Sotsial'nye osnovy kooperatsii* (Moscow: Ekonomika, 1989) pp. 46–7.
24 Ibid, pp. 68–72.
25 Ibid, p. 94.
26 N.N. Shaposhnikov, *Protektsionizm' i svoboda torgovli* (Petrograd, 1915) p. i.
27 Ibid, p. 1.
28 Ibid, pp. 4–8.
29 Ibid, p. 22–23.
30 Ibid, pp. 57–63.
31 Ibid, pp. 70–1.
32 Ibid, pp. 80–90.
33 V.I. Lenin, 'Imperialism as the Highest Stage of Capitalism', in *Selected Works* (Moscow: Progress, 1977) p. 232.
34 Mark Blaug, *Economic Theory in Retrospect* (Cambridge: CUP, 1985) pp. 260–1.

7 The Russian economic mind under Bolshevism, 1917–1929

1 V.I. Lenin, 'State and Revolution', in *Selected Works* (Moscow: Progress, 1977) p. 324.
2 Ibid, p. 309.
3 V.I. Lenin, 'Can the Bolsheviks Retain State Power?', in *Selected Works*, p. 372.
4 Ibid, p. 376.
5 Leon Trotsky, 'Planned Economy', in *The Challenge of the Left Opposition, 1923–25* (New York: Pathfinder, 1975) p. 119.
6 A more extensive exposition of Yurovsky's economics is provided in Vincent Barnett (1994) 'The Economic Thought of L.N. Yurovskii', *Coexistence*, 31 (1): 63–77.
7 PRO, T1/12303/13588 p. 2.
8 PRO, T1/12261/35246, p. 3.
9 PRO, T1/12261/35246, pp. 4–5.
10 J.M. Keynes, *The Economic Consequences of the Peace* (London: Macmillan, 1971) p. 9.
11 Ibid p. 183.
12 Nikolai Bukharin, *The Economics of the Transition Period* (London: RKP, 1979) pp. 134–56.
13 E.A. Preobrazhensky, *Finansy v epokhu diktatury proletariata* (Moscow: NKFin, 1921) p. 40.
14 Ibid p. 43.
15 Leon Trotsky, 'Planned Economy', in *The Challenge of the Left Opposition, 1923–25* (New York: Pathfinder, 1975) pp. 114–18.
16 Leon Trotsky, 'Amendments to Rykov's Resolution', in *The Challenge of the Left Opposition, 1926–27* (New York: Pathfinder, 1980) pp. 54–5.
17 Leon Trotsky, 'Platform of the Opposition', in *The Challenge of the Left Opposition, 1926–27* (New York: Pathfinder, 1980) p. 333.
18 Ibid p. 335.
19 J.M. Keynes, *A Short View of Russia* (London: Hogarth, 1925) p. 24.
20 For a more detailed account of Kondratiev's contribution to agricultural economics see Vincent Barnett, *Kondratiev and the Dynamics of Economic Development: Long Cycles and Industrial Growth in Historical Context* (London: Macmillan, 1998) pp. 21–85.
21 L.N. Litoshenko, *Evolyutsiya i progress krest'yanskogo khozyaistva* (Moscow: Sergiev, 1923) pp. 17–22.
22 A.A. Chuprov, 'Predislovie, in A.I. Chuprov, *Melkoe zemledelie i ego osnovnyya nuzdy* (Slovo, 1921) pp. v–xi.
23 A more thorough account of Kondratiev's planning efforts is provided in Barnett, *Kondratiev and the Dynamics of Economic Development*, pp. 143–68.
24 Naum Jasny, *Soviet Economists of the Twenties* (Cambridge: CUP, 1972) pp. 142–4.
25 W. Leontief, 'The Balance of the Economy of the USSR', N. Spulber (ed.), *Foundations of Soviet Strategy for Economic Growth* (Bloomington: Indiana University Press, 1964) pp. 92–3.
26 A. Bogdanov, *Essays in Tektology* (California: Intersystems, 1984) p. 2.
27 Ibid, pp. 49–50.
28 Ibid, p. 285.
29 In Fourier analysis a waveform is analysed to discover the sine wave frequencies that it contains. Through harmonic analysis it can be shown that periodic non-sinusoidal waveforms are composed of combinations of pure sine waves.
30 E.E. Slutsky (1937) 'The summation of random causes as the source of cyclical processes', *Econometrica*, 5: 121–2.

31 Slutsky's model series were taken from NKFin data used in drawing the numbers of a Soviet government lottery loan.
32 Slutsky, 'The Summation of Random Causes', p. 105.
33 Ibid, p. 126.
34 For a longer account of Pervushin's work see Vincent Barnett, 'Trading cycles for change: S.A. Pervushin as an economist of the business cycle', *Europe-Asia Studies*, 48 (6): 1007–25.
35 Thorstein Veblen, 'Some Neglected Points in the Theory of Socialism', in *The Place of Science in Modern Civilisation* (London: Routledge, 1994) p. 397.
36 Thorstein Veblen (1906) 'The socialist economics of Karl Marx and his followers: the later Marxism', a lecture given at Harvard University in April 1906, *Quarterly Journal of Economics* 20.
37 Thorstein Veblen, *The Engineers and the Price System* (New York: Viking, 1921), p. 95.
38 J.R. Commons, *The Economics of Collective Action* (Wisconsin: Wisconsin University, 1970) p. 31.
39 R. Tilman (ed.), *A Veblen Treasury* (New York: Sharpe, 1993) p. 389.
40 J.A. Hobson, *Veblen* (London: Chapman, 1936) p. 20.

8 The Russian economic mind under Stalinism, 1929–1940

1 Joseph Schumpeter, *History of Economic Analysis* (London: Allen and Unwin, 1954) p. 1158.
2 A.L. Vainshtein (1925) 'Novaya teoriya ekonomicheskikh tsiklov', *Voprosy kon"yunktury*, 1: 165.
3 Ibid, p. 179.
4 C.G. Abbot (1922) 'On periodicity in solar variation', *Annals of the Astrophysics Observatory of the Smithsonian Institute*, 4: 367.
5 Ibid, p. 372.
6 Ibid, p. 374.
7 E.E. Slutsky, 'K voprosu o solnechnoi postoyanoi', in *Izbrannye trudy* (Moscow, 1960), pp. 194–5.
8 Ibid, pp. 196–7.
9 Ibid, pp. 199–200.
10 P. Moore and G. Hunt, *Atlas of the Solar System* (London: Royal Astronomical Society, 1983) p. 33.
11 Abbot, 'On Periodicity in Solar Variation', p. 369.
12 E.E. Slutsky, 'Ob odinatsatiletnei periodichnosti solnechnykh pyaten', in *Izbrannye trudy* (Moscow: ANSSR, 1960) p. 204.
13 E.E. Slutsky, 'K voprosu ob ekstrapolyatsii v svyazi c problemoi prognoza', *Zhurnal geofiziki*, 5 (3): 274–5.
14 A.I. Malkis (ed.), *Predmet i metod ekonomiki Sovetski torgovli* (Moscow-Leningrad, 1932) p. 15.
15 Ibid, p. 17 and p. 23.
16 Ibid, p. 73.
17 G.Ya. Neiman, *Vnutrennyaya torgovlya SSSR* (Moscow, 1935) p. 30.
18 J. Stalin, 'The Right Deviation in the CPSU', in *Problems of Leninism* (Moscow, 1953) p. 351.
19 Stalin, 'The Tasks of Business Executives', in *Problems of Leninism*, p. 451.
20 Stalin, 'The Results of the First Five-Year Plan', in *Problems of Leninism*, p. 541.
21 L.V. Kantorovich, 'Mathematical Methods of Production Planning and Organisation', in V.S. Nemchinov, *The Use of Mathematics in Economics* (Edinburgh: O & B, 1964) p. 228.

22 L.V. Kantorovich, *The Best Use of Economic Resources* (Oxford: Pergamon, 1965) pp. 2–3.
23 Ibid, pp. xxiii–xxiv.
24 Ibid, pp. 45 and 122.
25 Ibid, pp. 184–8.
26 Schumpeter, *History of Economic Analysis*, p. 1158.
27 J. Frankel (ed.), *Vladimir Akimov on the Dilemmas of Russian Marxism* (Cambridge: CUP, 1969), p. 34.
28 *Byulletin' ekonomicheskogo kabineta prof. S.N. Prokopovicha*, June–July 1936 no. 129, pp. 57–9.
29 S.N. Prokopovich, *The Economic Condition of Soviet Russia* (London: King and Son, 1924) p. 61.
30 Richard Pipes, *Struve: Liberal on the Right* (Cambridge, MA: Harvard, 1980) pp. 406–8.
31 W.W. Leontief, *The Structure of American Economy* (New York: OUP, 1951) p. 3.
32 Ibid, pp. 35–6.
33 A.C. Pigou, *Economic Journal*, vol. XLVI 1936, p. 96.
34 E.F.M. Durbin (1936), 'Economic calculus in a planned economy', *Economic Journal*, XLVI: 678.
35 M. Polanyi, *The Contempt of Freedom* (London: Watts, 1940) pp. 29–30.
36 Ibid, pp. 35–9.

10 Epilogue: the Russian economic mind after 1940

1 Mark Harrison, *Soviet Planning in Peace and War, 1938–45* (Cambridge: CUP, 1985) pp. 20–1.
2 Janos Kornai, *Anti-Equilibrium* (Amsterdam: North Holland, 1971).
3 See M.E. Sharpe (ed.), *The Liberman Discussion* (IASP: New York, 1966).
4 Michael Ellman, *Planning Problems in the USSR* (Cambridge: CUP, 1973) pp. 57–8.
5 W.S. and E.S. Woytinsky, *World Commerce and Governments* (New York: 20th Century Fund, 1955) p. 14.
6 Abel Aganbegyan, *The Challenge: Economics of Perestroika* (London: Hutchinson, 1988) p. 127.

Select bibliography

Archive sources

Columbia University Special Manuscripts Collection (CUSMC), New York.
Keynes Papers, King's College, Cambridge.
Public Records Office (PRO), Kew, London.
Russian State Archive of the Economy (RGAE), Moscow.

Russian language sources – history

Blyumin, I.G. (1940) *Ocherki ekonomicheskoi mysli v Rossii v pervoi polovine XIX veka* (Moscow-Leningrad: AN SSSR).

Kovan'ko, P. (1901) *Glavneishiya reformy provedennyya N.Kh. Bunge* (Kiev).

Ministerstvo finansov 1802–1902 (St Petersburg: GosBumag).

Pashkov, A.I. (1966) *Istoriya Russkoi ekonomicheskoi mysli* (Moscow: SotsEkon).

Plekhanov, G.V. (1923) *Sochineniya* (Moscow: GosIzdat).

Rumyantsev, A.M. (1972) *Ekonomicheskaya entsiklopediya politicheskaya ekonomiya* (Moscow: AN SSSR).

Sidorov, A.L. (1960) *Finansovoe polozhenie Rossii v gody pervoi mirovoe voiny* (Moscow: AN SSSR).

Yakovtsa, Yu.V. (2003) *Rossiiskie ekonomicheskie shkoly* (Moscow: MFK).

Zlupko, S. (2000) *Ekonomichna dumka Ukraini* (Lviv: Lviv University).

Russian language sources – economics

Babst, I.K. (1872) *Izlozhenie nachal' narodnago khozyaistva* (Moscow: Shilovoi).

Bark, P.L. (1924) 'Finansovye soveshchaniya soyuznikov vo vremya voiny', *Krasnyi arkhiv*, vol. 5.

Bark, P.L. (1924) 'O finansovykh soglasheniyakh, zaklyuchennykh c Angliiskim i Frantsuzskim ministrami finansov i s upravlyayushchim Angliiskim bankom', *Krasnyi arkhiv*, vol. 5.

Bark, P.L. (1924) 'O peregovorakh ministra finansov v Parizhe i Londone v iyune i iyule 1916 goda', *Krasnyi arkhiv*, vol. 5.

Bulgakov, S.N. (1900) *Kapitalizm i zemledelie* (St Petersburg).

Bulgakov, S.N. (1913) *Istoriya sotsial'nykh uchenii v XIX veke* (Moscow).

Bulgakov, S.N. (1913) *Ocherki po istorii ekonomicheskikh uchenii* (Moscow).

Bunge, N. (1870) *Osnovaniya politicheskoi ekonomii* (Kiev).

Chernyshevsky, N.G. (1948) *Izbrannye ekonomicheskie proizvedeniya* (Ogiz).

Chuprov, A.I. (1909) *Rechi i stati* (Moscow: Sabashnikov).

Chuprov, A.I. (1924) *Istoriya politicheskoi ekonomii* (Riga: Gliksman).

Fal'kner, S.A. (1925) *Proiskhozhdenie zheleznogo zakona zarabotnoi platy* (Moscow: Truda).

Litoshenko, L.N. (1923) *Evolyutsiya i progress krest'yanskogo khozyaistva* (Moscow: Sergiev).

Malkis, A.I. (1932) *Predmet i metod ekonomiki Sovetski torgovli* (Moscow-Leningrad).

Mendeleev, D.I. (1950) 'Tolkovyi tarif, ili issledovanie o razvitii promyshlennosti Rossii v svyazi c eya obshchim tamozhennym tarifom 1891 goda', in *Sochineniya* (Moscow: AN SSSR).

Mendeleev, D.I. (1960) 'Opravdanie protektsionizma', in *Problemy ekonomicheskogo razvitiya Rossii* (Moscow: Sots-Ekon).

Migulin, P.P. (1899) *Russkii gosudarstvennyi kredit, 1769–1899*, (Kharkov: Pechatnoe delo).

Migulin, P.P. (1910) *Vozrozhdenie Rossii* (Karkhov: Pechatnik).

Neiman, G.Ya. (1935) *Vnutrennyaya torgovlya SSSR* (Moscow).

Ozerov, I.Kh. (1898) *Podokhodnyi nalog v Anglii* (Moscow: Levenson).

Ozerov, I.Kh. (1910) *Osnovy finansovoi nauki* (Moscow: Sytin).

Pervushin, S.A. (1914) *Teoriya krizisov M.I. Tugan-Baranovskago* (Moscow).

Preobrazhensky, E.A. (1921) *Finansy v epokhu diktatury proletariata* (Moscow: NKFin).

Shaposhnikov, N.N. (1914) *Pervyi russkii ekonomist-mathematik Vladimir Karpovich Dmitriev* (Moscow).

Shaposhnikov, N.N. (1915) *Protektsionizm' i svoboda torgovli* (Petrograd).

Slutsky, E.E. (1913) 'Sushchnost' kooperatsii i eya formy', *Spravochnyi kalendar' zemledel'tsa na 1913* (Kiev).

Slutsky, E.E. (1935) 'K voprosu ob ekstrapolyatsii v svyazi c problemoi prognoza', *Zhurnal geofiziki*, 5(3).

Slutsky, E.E. (1960) 'K voprosu o solnechnoi postoyanoi', in *Izbrannye trudy* (Moscow).

Slutsky, E.E. (1960) 'Ob odinatsatiletnei periodichnosti solnechnykh pyaten', in *Izbrannye trudy* (Moscow).

Struve, P.B. (1970) 'Khozyaistvo i tsena', in R. Pipes (ed.) *Collected Works* (Ann Arbor).

Tugan-Baranovsky, M.I. (1908) 'Metodologiya politicheskoi ekonomii', *Obrazovanie* no.12.

Tugan-Baranovsky, M.I. (1915) 'Bumazhnyya den'gi i voina', *Rech'*, 16, 17 (30).

Tugan-Baranovsky, M.I. (1915) 'Voina i narodnoe khozyaistvo', in *Chego zhdet" Rossiya ot" voiny* (Petrograd: Prometei).

Tugan-Baranovsky, M.I. (1915) 'Vliyanie voiny na narodnoe khozyaistvo Rossii, Anglii i Germanii', in *Voprosy mirovoi voiny* (Petrograd: Pravo).

Tugan-Baranovsky, M.I. (1916) 'Znachenie birzhi v sovremennom khozyaistvennom stroe', in *Bankovaya entsiklopediya* (Kiev).

Tugan-Baranovsky, M.I. (1917) 'Voennye zaimy v teoreticheskom osveshchenii', in *Voennye zaimy: sbornik statei* (Petrograd: Pravda).

Tugan-Baranovsky, M.I. (1923) *Periodicheskie promyshlennye krizisy* (Petrograd-Moscow).

Tugan-Baranovsky, M.I. (1989) *Sotsial'nye osnovy kooperatsii* (Moscow: Ekonomika).

Tugan-Baranovsky, M.I. (1996) 'Kant i Marks', in *K luchshemu budushchemu* (Moscow: Rosspen).

Tugan-Baranovsky, M.I. (1997) *Izbrannoe: Periodicheskie promyshlennye krizisy* (Moscow: Nauka).

Vainshtein, A.L. (1925) 'Novaya teoriya ekonomicheskikh tsiklov', *Voprosy kon" yunktury*, no. 1.

English language sources – Russian studies

Bogdanov, A. (1984) *Essays in Tektology* (California: Intersystems).

Clarke, W. (1994) *The Lost Fortune of the Tsars* (London: Weidenfield and Nicolson).

Frankel, J. (1969), *Vladimir Akimov on the Dilemmas of Russian Marxism* (Cambridge: CUP).

Gerasimov, I. (1976) *A Short History of Geographical Science in the Soviet Union* (Moscow: Progress).

Gordin, M. (2004) *A Well-Ordered Thing: Dmitrii Mendeleev and the Shadow of the Periodic Table* (New York: Basic Books).

Harrison, M. (1985) *Soviet Planning in Peace and War, 1938–45* (Cambridge: CUP).

Hecker, J.F. (1934) *Russian Sociology* (London: Chapman and Hall).

von Haxthausen, A. (1972) *Studies on the Interior of Russia* (Chicago: University of Chicago Press).

Jasny, N. (1972) *Soviet Economists of the Twenties* (Cambridge: CUP).

Kindersley, R. (1962) *The First Russian Revisionists* (Oxford: Clarendon Press).

Prince Kropotkin (1912) *Fields, Factories and Workshops* (London: Nelson).

Lenin, V.I. (1977) *Selected Works* (Moscow: Progress).

Lenin, V.I. (1987) *Materialism and Empirio-Criticism* (Moscow: Progress).

Letiche J.M. (1964), *A History of Russian Economic Thought* (Berkeley: University of California).

Mackenzie Wallace, D. (1877) *Russia* (London: Cassell).

Mavor, J. (1925) *An Economic History of Russia* (London: Dent and Son).

Neilson, K. (1984) *Strategy and Supply* (London: Allen and Unwin).

Pipes, R. (1980) *Struve: Liberal on the Right* (Cambridge, MA: Harvard).

Plekhanov, G.V. (1961) *Selected Philosophical Works* (London: Lawrence and Wishart).

Polanyi, M. (1940) *The Contempt of Freedom* (London: Watts).

Sharpe, M.E. (1966) *The Liberman Discussion* (New York: IASP).

Stalin, J. (1953) *Problems of Leninism* (Moscow: Foreign Languages Publishing House).

Tegoborski, M.L. (1855) *Commentaries on the Productive Forces of Russia* (London: Longman).

Trotsky, L. (1975) *The Challenge of the Left Opposition, 1923–25* (New York: Pathfinder).

Walecki, A. (1980) *A History of Russian Thought* (Oxford: Clarendon).

'The years 1881–94 in Russia: a memorandum found in the papers of N.Kh. Bunge', *Transactions of the American Philosophical Society*, 71(6).

English language sources – economics

Barnett, V. (1992) 'Recent Soviet writings on economic theory and policy from NEP', *Coexistence*, 29 (3): 257–75.

Barnett, V. (1992) 'Conceptions of the market among Russian economists: a survey', *Soviet Studies*, 44 (6): 1087–98.

Barnett, V. (1993) 'Exchange rate policy and the purchasing power of the *chervonets* in the USSR during NEP', *Coexistence*, 30 (2): 125–44.

Barnett, V. (1994) 'The economic thought of L.N. Yurovskii', *Coexistence*, 31 (1): 63–77.

Barnett, V. (1994) 'As good as gold? A note on the *chervonets*', *Europe-Asia Studies*, 46 (4): 663–9.

Barnett, V. (1994) 'Trotsky, Kondrat'ev, and long waves', *Journal of Trotsky Studies*, 2: 1–16.

Barnett, V. (1995) 'A long wave goodbye: Kondrat'ev and the Conjuncture Institute, 1920–28', *Europe-Asia Studies*, 47 (3): 413–41.

Barnett, V. (1995) 'Soviet commodity markets during NEP', *Economic History Review*, XLVIII (2): 329–52.

Barnett, V. (1996) 'Trading cycles for change: S.A. Pervushin as an economist of the business cycle', *Europe-Asia Studies*, 48 (6): 1007–25.

Barnett, V. (1997) 'The People's Commissariat of Supply and the People's Commissariat of Internal Trade', in E.A. Rees (ed.), *Decision-Making in the Stalinist Command Economy, 1932–37* (London: Macmillan).

Barnett, V. (1998) *Kondratiev and the Dynamics of Economic Development: Long Cycles and Industrial Growth in Historical Context* (London: Macmillan).

Barnett, V. (1999) 'Soviet economists in opposition and overseas', in *Regime and Society in 20th Century Russia* (London: Macmillan).

Barnett, V. (2000) 'Tugan-Baranovskii's vision of an international socialist economy', *European Journal of the History of Economic Thought*, 7 (1): 115–35.

Barnett, V. (2001) 'Calling up the reserves: Keynes, Tugan-Baranovsky and Russian war finance', *Europe-Asia Studies*, 53 (1): 151–69.

Barnett, V. (2001) 'Marx, Karl Heinrich', in R.J. Barry Jones (ed.), *Routledge Encyclopedia of International Political Economy* (London: Routledge), vol. (2), 987–95.

Barnett, V. (2001)'Tugan-Baranovsky as a pioneer of trade cycle analysis', *Journal of the History of Economic Thought*, 23 (4): 443–66.

Barnett, V. (2002) 'Mr Smith goes to Moscow: Russian editions of *The Wealth of Nations*', *Research in the History of Economic Thought and Methodology*, 20(A): 35–42.

Barnett, V. (2002) 'Which was the "real" Kondratiev: 1925 or 1928?', *Journal of the History of Economic Thought*, 24 (4): 475–8.

Barnett, V. (2004) *The Revolutionary Russian Economy, 1890–1940: Ideas, Debates and Alternatives* (London: Routledge).

Barnett, V. (2004) 'Catalysing growth? Mendeleev and the 1891 tariff', *Research in the History of Economic Thought and Methodology*, 22(A): 123–44.

Barnett, V. (2004) 'E.E. Slutsky: mathematical statistician, economist, and political economist?', *Journal of the History of Economic Thought*, 26 (1): 5–18.

Barnett, V. (2004) 'Tugan-Baranovsky, the methodology of political economy, and the "Russian historical school" ', *History of Political Economy*, 36 (1): 79–101.

Barnett, V. (2004) 'Historical political economy in Russia, 1870–1913', *European Journal of the History of Economic Thought*, 11 (2): 231–53.
Blaug, M. (1985) *Economic Theory in Retrospect* (Cambridge: CUP).
von Bohm-Bawerk, E. (1973) *Karl Marx and the Close of His System* (New Jersey: Kelley).
Bucolo, P. (1980) *The Other Pareto* (London: Scolar).
Bukharin, N. (1979) *The Economics of the Transition Period* (London: RKP).
Bulgakov, S. (2000) *Philosophy of Economy* (New Haven: Yale University Press).
Commons, J.R. (1970) *The Economics of Collective Action* (Wisconsin: Wisconsin University).
Commons, J.R. (1974) *Legal Foundations of Capitalism* (New Jersey: Kelley).
Dmitriev, V.K. (1974) *Economic Essays on Value, Competition and Utility* (Cambridge: CUP).
Durbin, E.F.M. (1936) 'Economic Calculus in a Planned Economy', *Economic Journal*, vol. XLVI.
Galbraith, J.K. (1987) *A History of Economics* (London: Hamish Hamilton).
Heckscher, E.F. (1994) *Mercantilism* (London: Routledge).
Hobson, J.A. (1936) *Veblen* (London: Chapman).
Hodgson, G. (2001) *How Economics Forgot History* (London: Routledge).
Howard, M.C. and King, J. E. (1989) *A History of Marxian Economics, 1883–1929* (Princeton: Princeton University Press).
Hutchison, T.W. (1953) *A Review of Economic Doctrines, 1870–1929* (Oxford: Clarendon).
Ingram, J.K. (1967) *A History of Political Economy* (New York: Kelley).
Kantorovich, L.V. (1965) *The Best Use of Economic Resources* (Oxford: Pergamon).
Keynes, J.M. (1925) *A Short View of Russia* (London: Hogarth).
Klein, J. (1997) *Statistical Visions in Time* (Cambridge: CUP).
Leontief, W.W. (1951) *The Structure of American Economy* (New York: OUP).
Malthus, T.R. (1986) *An Essay on the Principle of Population* (New Jersey: Kelley).
Marshall, A. (1919) *Industry and Trade* (London: Macmillan).
Marx, K. (1958) *Theories of Surplus Value*, part 1 (Moscow: Foreign Languages).
Marx, K. (1968) *Theories of Surplus Value*, part 2 (Moscow: Progress).
Marx, K. (1981) *Capital* vol. 3 (London: Penguin).
Mendeleeff, D. I. (1893) 'Introduction: Review of the Manufactures and Trade of Russia', in J.M. Crawford (ed.), *The Industries of Russia, Manufactures and Trade* (St Petersburg).
Migulin, P. (1915) 'The State Bank and the currency', *The Times Russian Supplement*, 26th April.
Nemchinov, V.S. (1964) *The Use of Mathematics in Economics* (Edinburgh: Oliver and Boyd).
Normano, J.F. (1945) *The Spirit of Russian Economics* (New York: Day).
Prokopovich, S.N. (1924) *The Economic Condition of Soviet Russia* (London: King and Son).
Ropke, W. (1936) *Crises and Cycles* (London: Hodge).
Rostow, W.W. (1990) *Theorists of Economic Growth from David Hume to the Present* (New York: OUP).
Sieber, N.I. (2001) 'Marx's Theory of Value and Money', in P. Zarembka (ed.), *Research in Political Economy*, vol. 19.

Slutsky, E.E. (1937) 'The summation of random causes as the source of cyclical processes', *Econometrica*, 5.

Veblen, T. (1921) *The Engineers and the Price System* (New York: Viking).

Weber, M. (1975) *Roscher and Knies: The Logical Problems of Historical Economics* (New York: Macmillan).

Woytinsky, W.S. and E.S. (1955) *World Commerce and Governments* (New York: 20th Century Fund).

Woytinsky, W.S. (1964) *Market and Prices* (New York: Kelley).

Author index

Subject index